ACTA UNIVERSITATIS UPSALIENSIS
Studia Historica Upsaliensia

247

Utgivna av

Historiska institutionen vid Uppsala universitet
genom Torkel Jansson, Jan Lindegren och Maria Ågren

Cover photo: Wellwood farm, Graaff-Reinet (by author).

Cover layout: Camilla Eriksson

Fredrik Lilja

The Golden Fleece of the Cape

Capitalist expansion and labour relations in the periphery of transnational wool production c. 1860 – 1950

UPPSALA
UNIVERSITET

Dissertation presented at Uppsala University to be publicly examined in Universitetshuset sal IX, Uppsala, Friday, March 15, 2013 at 10:15 for the degree of Doctor of Philosophy. The examination will be conducted in English.

Abstract

Lilja, F. 2013. The Golden Fleece of the Cape: Capitalist expansion and labour relations in the periphery of transnational wool production, c. 1860–1950. Acta Universitatis Upsaliensis. *Studia historica Upsaliensia* 247. 225 pp. Uppsala. ISBN 978-91-554-8588-7.

This thesis is about the organisation, character and change of labour relations in expanding capitalist wool farming in the Cape between 1860 and 1950. It is an attempt to analyse labour in wool farming within a transnational framework, based on an expansion of capital from core to periphery of the capitalist world-economy.

Wool farming in peripheries like the Cape was part of capitalist production through the link to primarily the British textile industry. This relationship enabled wool farmers to invest in their farms in sheep, fences and windmills. They thereby became agents of capital expansion in the world-economy, which was a prerequisite for a capitalist expansion. Although wool production in the Cape was initially an imperial division of labour, that relation changed during the twentieth century as Britain's leading role as textile producer was challenged by other capitalist core countries. Capitalism as a transnational production system, based on commodity chains from periphery to core, became the most crucial structure for wool farmers in the Cape, who could increase their exports.

The thesis also shows that the pre-capitalist generational division of labour among black peasants, through which farmers acquired labour, especially shepherds, was both discarded and intensified. Shepherding was intensified along with fencing during the late nineteenth and early twentieth century due to threat from jackals and lack of sufficient water supplies. Those farmers who invested in technology in the form of jackal-proof fences and windmills managed to change production from herding to rotational grazing in camps, which meant that shepherds were replaced by camp walkers, who controlled fences instead of sheep. Those farmers who did not invest were forced to exploit the pre-capitalist relations more intensively and hire shepherds in order to be able to produce and sell wool to textile manufacturers in capitalist core areas. As the young adult males disappeared from farms to the mines, the role of children and youths as shepherds became increasingly important. By the 1940s almost all the shepherds were children or youths, but they were about to be made redundant, as the number of shepherds decreased during the 1930s and 1940s.

Keywords: capitalist expansion, transnational production, commodity chains, accumulation of capital, labour relations, shepherds, wool farming, fencing, environment, generational division of labour, gendered division of labour, imperialism, capitalism, British Empire, Rosa Luxemburg, South Africa, the Cape, eastern Cape.

Fredrik Lilja, Uppsala University, Department of History, Box 628, SE-751 26 Uppsala, Sweden.

ISSN 0081-6531
ISBN 978-91-554-8588-7
urn:nbn:se:uu:diva-193053 (http://urn.kb.se/resolve?urn=urn:nbn:se:uu:diva-193053)

Printed by Elanders Sverige AB, 2013
Distributor: Uppsala University Library, Box 510, SE-751 20 Uppsala, Sweden
www.uu.se, acta@ub.uu.se

Contents

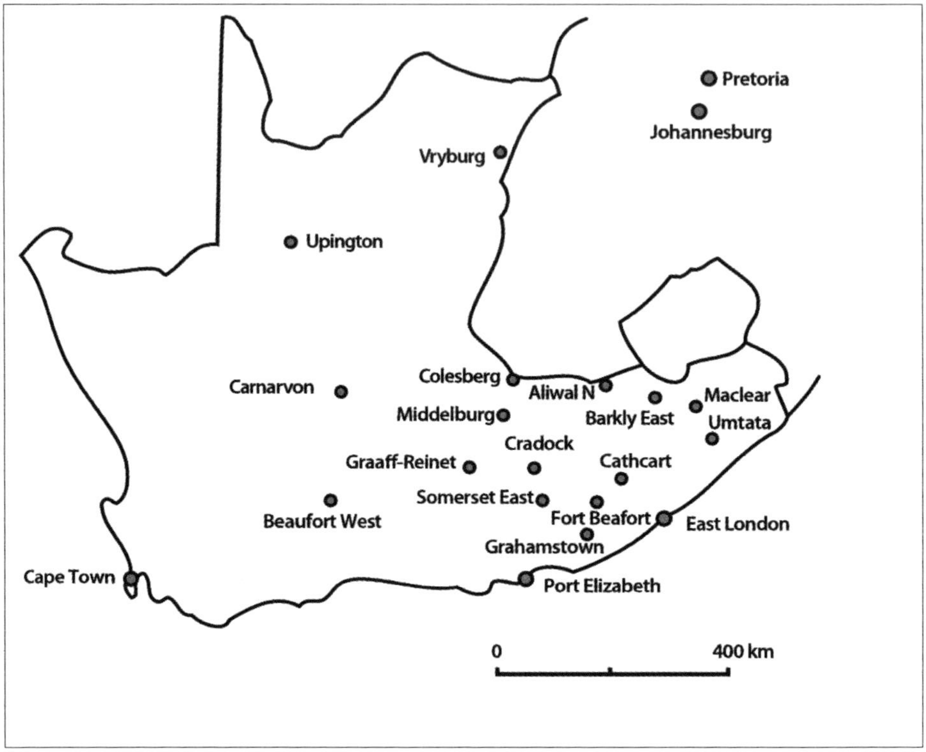

Map 1. Place names in the Cape. (No claim of representing authentic geographic relations.)

Preface

This book is about people who have lived and laboured on farms in the Cape in South Africa. I am fortunate to have learned about them and their land. I hope this book will contribute to making their history more well-known in South Africa and elsewhere.

My supervisors, Jan Lindegren and Lars Olsson, have always been enthusiastic and supportive in all matters. They have taught me to go, ascend if you will, from the abstract to the concrete. I am happy to have been able to learn from two such eminent historians and I have enjoyed our discussions. I sincerely thank them for believing in my work. Tekeste Negash has read early versions of the manuscript and Maria Ågren has read the whole manuscript. They have both contributed with constructive comments, which have improved the thesis. There are additional people, who must also be thanked. Jonas Sjölander has read and contributed with expertise in South African labour history and helped with collecting source material. Tomas Högberg and Pontus Rudberg have read selected parts of the thesis. Pontus has also helped with collecting source material. Susan Levine in Cape Town has been helpful with practical concerns and discussions about labour, wool farming and sources. Thanks to the Rubidge family in Graaff-Reinet for their hospitality, the staff at the National Library and the Western Cape Archives in Cape Town, Sally and others at Cory Library in Grahamstown and the staff at the Nordic Africa Institute in Uppsala.

The research travels to South Africa have been funded by Anna-Maria Lundin's Stipendiefond (Smålands nation), the Nordic Africa Institute travel scholarship, Helge Ax:son Johnsons Stiftelse, Stiftelsen till Ernst Wigforss Minne.

I also want to thank the people I have met in South Africa, Andrew, Bernard and others who have made research travels more fun. Most of all I want to thank my parents, Anders and Eva, and Sheila Mulenga.

Uppsala February 2013
Fredrik Lilja

CHAPTER 1

Cape Wool in the World-Economy

The Golden Fleece

Wool farming has been a central feature of the Cape Colony, later the Cape Province of South Africa, since the early nineteenth century. The merino sheep that grazed on the dry veld of the Karroo in the eastern and northern parts has been the backbone of the rural economy since commercial wool farming began in the early nineteenth century. Wool farming in the Cape started as a response to the British textile industry. Almost all the wool was exported to the UK during the nineteenth century. The introduction of merino sheep in the Cape was a crucial step in the incorporation of southern Africa into the capitalist world-economy. The white farmers and the black and coloured labouring people who constituted the largest share of the labour force and herded the sheep, became involved in a global network of production, transport and further production, which started in the Cape and ended in the wool textile centre Bradford in England. The two places were far apart geographically, but were bound together by the strong twine of the golden fleece.

As a consequence of the dominance of wool farming, it has largely shaped the social organization of the Eastern Cape, wherein labour practices have been of fundamental importance. Young and old, men and women, have all been exposed to, and asserted some influence on, the global and colonial production of wool. We will in the following examine the relationships in wool production more closely from the viewpoint of labour practices and production methods in the Cape. The people involved have all played a central role, either as individuals or as members of classes, and sometimes both. An analysis of the farmers and labourers of the Karroo and the greater part of the Eastern Cape can broaden and deepen our understanding of expanding capitalism during the nineteenth and twentieth centuries.

William Beinart argues that an analysis of pastoralism in general, which has been so important for the Cape and South Africa in economic terms, will contribute with perspectives on the development of capitalism in rural areas. After the 1870s gold overtook the position as the foremost bearer of revenue to

South Africa, but wool continued to have an important economic role for the Cape and South Africa. In fact, it was second only to gold as export product between 1910 and 1950.[1] Wool farming was incorporated into the capitalist world-economy to a much greater extent than other rural sectors. Therefore, an analysis of wool farming contributes with perspectives on capitalism itself that transcends national borders. Wool farming was part of transnational capitalist production.

International division of labour and transnational production processes

In all essential I agree with Eric J. Hobsbawm who argued the relevance of writing the history of societies. According to him, social and societal aspects cannot be separated from politics, economics or from the materialistic surrounding from which people make their living, which thus means a more comprehensive view on history than what was implied in the term social history.[2] Much research has been done in that tradition, including labour history, but it has most often been conducted within the nation state. Marcel van der Linden has instead argued that labour history should be global, or rather transnational, in scope. As he mentions, there are historic processes, which can only be understood if our definition of society is not limited by geography.[3] Further, he argues that the traditional view on labourers and the working class, which has largely focused on industrial labour in Europe, does not reflect the role of the working class worldwide. The majority of the world's working people have not been involved in "free" wage labour as proletarians. Labour has been commodified in different ways; tenants, share-croppers and indentured servants should also be regarded as labourers.[4] This has most notably been the case in colonial areas where expanding capitalism has incorporated peasants into capitalist production, often for international markets.[5] Wool farming in the Cape is an example of such expanding capitalist production, which must be regarded as transnational as it involved actors in several nation states at a level that was separate from the international one. Settler farmers were agents of capitalist expansion through their establishment as a capital owning class in the periphery who sold wool to the British textile industry. The farmers in turn hired labourers on their farms, and these two

[1] Beinart, W 2008, pp. 4-5, 10-17.

[2] Hobsbawm, E. 1971, pp. 21-32.

[3] Van der Linden, M 2004, p. 141.

[4] See for example van der Linden, M 2008, pp. 1-2, 6, 18-19; 2004, pp. 136-56.

[5] See for example Wallerstein, I 1979, pp. 14-19.

constituted the principal classes in the periphery of transnational wool production. In this thesis we will analyse more exactly how the expansion occurred and how it affected labour relations.

In South Africa the transition to capitalism in rural areas received attention from historians during the 1970s and 1980s. It was a significant contribution to our understanding of capitalism and its expansion. There were at least two problems with that research, however. Firstly, it left out wool, although for example Robert Ross acknowledged that relations in the Cape were capitalist at an earlier stage than the rest of the country, much because of wool.[6] Secondly, and which must be seen as related, capitalism was defined nationally, not as a system based on an international division of labour. The period after the discovery of gold, and especially the interwar period, was focused as the crucial one to changes in farming.[7] An analysis of labour in wool farming cannot exclude such factors, and must largely cover the same period, but it must also contextualize wool farming within the capitalist world-economy, which turned farmers and labourers in the Cape into producers of raw material for textile manufacturers in primarily Britain. Philip McMichael argues that Australian wool production was a "product of a particular phase of world-capitalist development [namely] metropolitan industrial capitalism and its growing world market [...]".[8] The Cape was a smaller producer of wool than Australia, but relations with Britain were not different. Through the relationship with Britain, wool farmers and labourers in the Cape became involved in a transnational production process. The two places were tied together by a commodity chain, which aimed at producing a finished commodity.[9] According to van der Linden, historians should give much more attention to these relations and view labour as part of a larger entity, capitalism on a world scale.[10] This thesis will reach further in that direction.

An attempt to write labour history based on transnational production must start with the commodity. As Karl Marx noted, the commodity, which can be sold and fulfil a need or demand in society, is the fundamental part of capitalist production.[11] The nature of the need or demand does not matter. It can be social, economic, biological, cultural etc. As few things, except certain types of food, can fulfil human needs without having been processed and refined, it is safe to assume that most finished commodities have been through at least one, and most often several, labour processes. That is, stages in the production of a finished commodity from raw material to finished product that can be sold and

---

[6] Ross, R 1986, pp. 56, 65, 87.

[7] For example Morris, M 1976 focused the interwar period.

[8] McMichael, P 1984, p. 1.

[9] See Hopkins, T and Wallerstein, I 1994, p. 17.

[10] Van der Linden, M 2008, p. 363, 372-74.

[11] Marx, K 1990, p. 125.

fulfil a need. During the past five hundred years, and especially the last two hundred and fifty of those, that is, after the industrial revolution in England started, an increasing amount of that production has taken place in industrial factories, most often located in the North Atlantic region. This area has come to constitute the *core* of capitalist production. At the same time, however, an increasing amount of the raw material for that production has been produced in other areas than the core. These areas, where an increasing production of raw material has taken place, can be called *peripheral.* They have thereby contributed to capitalist production, but without producing the finished commodities.[12] But that does not mean that they have been outside capitalist production, on the contrary, they have been integral and essential parts of it. People working in these peripheral areas have thus been involved in capitalist production, but in a setting that is usually not described as capitalist.

The specific peripheral setting where raw material has been produced is therefore an important object for analysis of capitalism. While production of wool in the Cape was based on a relation to the core, and especially to capital in Britain, it was also conducted in a specific geographical and political area in southern Africa. Issues of labour supply, legislation and the environment were consequently of great importance for wool farming. By including both transnational and local perspectives, it will be possible to analyse farmers and labourers in relation to structures at two levels, which were involved in a dialectical relationship. Hobsbawm has argued that the main difference between the activities of a wool producing peasant in England during the thirteenth century and a wool producing settler farmer in New Zealand during the nineteenth century is the spread of capitalism. There would have been no wool farmer at all in New Zealand without the capitalist world-economy.[13] For the Cape we can say: there would have been sheep and shepherds even without capitalism, but the shepherds would certainly not have herded merino sheep on farms producing wool for textile industries in Britain. By focusing on production of the commodity, in this case wool, which was intended for further production in core areas of the world-economy, we can reach further in explaining the capitalist transformation in rural areas in southern Africa.

Thus, *the purpose* of this thesis is to analyse the labour relations in expanding capitalist wool farming in the Cape between c. 1860 and 1950. By labour relations we mean relations between farmers on the one hand and the hired labour force on the other. This will be done by *firstly* contextualizing Cape wool production within the expanding capitalist world-economy. *Thereafter* the labour practices will be analysed both locally and regionally, on one farm in particular, but also for the Cape as a whole. *Finally,* but simultaneously, the

[12] See Hopkins, T & Wallerstein, I 1982; Hobsbawm E 1975; 1987; Also Luxemburg, R 2003.

[13] Hobsbawm, E. J. 1980, p. 3-4; See also Olsson, L 2005 for the same argument.

labour practices will be analysed in relation to both the transnational character of wool production and the regional and local conditions for wool farming and capital accumulation in the Cape. The development and implementation of productive forces, and their relation to the farmers and labourers involved in production, will constitute the central analytical frame.

The rest of the thesis will be arranged as follows. Initially, the literature on labour relations in wool farming and adjoining sectors will be discussed. This will lead to a framing of the problem, where divisions of labour and the Cape's position within the capitalist world-economy are focused. The ways towards a solution of the problem, that is, the methodology and material, will then be discussed.

Thereafter, the Cape wool production will be contextualized within the expanding capitalist world-economy. The expansion of capital from core to periphery and the prerequisites for wool farming and capital accumulation in the Cape will be of primary interest, but also the relations between settlers and indigenous African groups.

Subsequently, the labour relations in Cape wool farming will be analysed. The production process, that is, where farmers and labourers meet, will be the focus of analysis, but seen in relation to the transnational character of wool production within the British Empire and globally. The time period covered ranges from the 1860s to c. 1950. After the labour relations on Cape wool farms during the 1860s and 1870s have been established, the changes in production, and how they affected labour relations, will be analysed. The relations with the imperial power Britain will be especially important during the period between c. 1870 to 1910. Thereafter the impact of mining and legislation will be discussed, but also how the Depression and the environment affected accumulation of capital and labour relations. The concluding chapter discusses the changes in production and labour relations in the context of capital expansion and capital accumulation in the Cape.

Farm labour

Farm labour has characterized rural Cape for as long as there have been farms. In essence, the farmers have been white, and although they have been forced to work themselves, a hired black and coloured labour force has been vital since farms were established. Farming has been intended to be large scale.

Those who have analysed farm labour in South Africa during the nineteenth and twentieth centuries have outlined a capitalist development, which mainly occurred after the discovery of gold, and especially after about 1920. Still, a general feature of labour relations has been various forms of tenancy along with cash wage labour. As Francis Wilson shows, tenants consisted of families who were allowed to live on the land of a farmer in exchange for either labour or money. However, during the period between the 1860s and 1960s, farming went through great changes. For example, the role of tenancy diminished, and cash wage labour became dominant instead of land and grazing rights.[14] But the role of women as farm labourers also increased. Other things, such as the personal relations between farmers and labourers remained or became even more unequal. Further, he suggests that cash wages for farm labourers in the Eastern Cape, in monetary terms, were at a constantly low level.[15]

The labour tenancy system is further elaborated on by Mike Morris, who studies the transition to capitalism on the Highveld. Unlike Wilson he focuses the class struggle. He suggests that by the 1920s production was clearly capitalist in that region as the labour tenants worked with the means of production owned by the farmers. The male tenants relied on being able to offer the labour of family members to farmers. The farmers, on the other hand, desired labour tenancy as they could not pay much cash wages.[16] Morris also notes that as a response to decreasing grazing rights after 1920, many labour tenants withdrew their labour from farmers, and moved to other farms, especially to those in pastoral areas to find better conditions.[17] But Morris does not further analyse the difference between agriculture and pastoralism, and therefore cannot say if the practice of grazing rights differed between various forms of farming. Timothy Keegan also notes that labour tenants were often preferred by farmers, especially the poorer ones. But he argues that the dispossession of South African peasants on the Highveld and subsequent proletarianization was not a one-way process. Many of the tenants gained from increased commercialization of agriculture and could accumulate, but during a relatively short time.[18] Labour tenancy was not widespread in the Cape wool farming regions, but it is clear that we must analyse both parties of the class struggle in order to decide how labour relations in wool farming were formed.

However, Wilson, Morris and Keegan emphasize the importance of mining and industrialization, for example the issue of labour shortage, and remedies to it, as pivotal factors of change in farming, not the production process itself.[19] Mining was undoubtedly important, but the focus on the Highveld region and the absence of analysis of the actual production process on farms, has meant that crucial aspects of the capitalist development in rural South Africa has been overlooked. Wilson and Morris do distinguish between various forms of farming, but they do not analyse them separately. In other words, they do not

---

[14] Wilson, F 1971, pp. 117, 155.

[15] Wilson, F 1971, pp. 154-55, 157, 160-61.

[16] Morris, M 1976, pp. 306, 294, 327, 330

[17] Morris, M 1976, pp. 323-24.

[18] Keegan, T 1987, pp. 203-05.

[19] Wilson, F pp. 113, 121, 125-32, 164; Morris, M 1976, p. 293; Keegan, T 1987, p. 202.

analyse production of the commodity. Morris, more than any other scholar in the field, focuses the role of the class struggle in the transition to capitalism. However, he asserts that capitalism was brought on from "above", by large landowners and the state.[20] While that is a valid point for the Highveld region, we must remember that labour relations in wool farming in many areas of the Cape were largely capitalist already during the first half of the nineteenth century, at least according to Clifton Crais, who argues that the labourers were proletarians. Crais even suggests that "capital accumulated in the countryside helped fuel the early mineral revolution.[21] The role of the state and mining must thus be revised in favour of explanations that focus the actual farming.

Crais claims that "[w]age labour was pervasive on the wealthier farms" in wool farming areas around the mid-nineteenth century. The labourers had grazing rights, but "depended on their wages to purchase food" and were therefore proletarians according to him.[22] The labourers were, however, not completely proletarianized. A striking feature of labour in wool farming has been the combination of remunerative practices. Kenneth Smith and Saul Dubow have both studied one of the most successful wool farming districts, Graaff-Reinet, during the mid and late nineteenth century. They both identified that wages in cash and in kind along with grazing rights dominated.[23] Beinart's study of soil conservation in South Africa includes the farm Wellwood in Graaff-Reinet. Although he does not analyse labour relations, Beinart mentions that there was never any labour tenancy on the farm, but a combination of grazing rights, which were decreasing after the 1930s, and wages.[24] He does not estimate the relation between grazing rights, cash wages and rations, though, so we do not know to what extent remuneration changed.

Richard Bouch has studied another successful wool farming district, Cathcart, during the early twentieth century. He more or less confirms what Smith, Dubow and Beinart found in Graaff-Reinet, that is, a combination of remunerative practices. Bouch suggests that labour practices and production methods were set in the late nineteenth century and remained stable through the interwar period.[25] He may very well be correct, but does not offer statistics regarding the number of labourers or exemplify how these relations were manifested. Furthermore, since Bouch focuses on one of the more successful districts, it is highly likely that relations were different there than in other districts or in the Cape as a whole.

---

20 Morris, M 1976, p. 310.

21 Crais, C 1992, p. 154.

22 Crais, C 1992, p. 154.

23 Smith, K 1976, p. 212-13; Dubow, S 1982, pp. 46-50.

24 Beinart, W 2008, p. 309, 316.

25 Bouch, R 1997, p. 99, 104.

Grazing rights are in some ways different from tenancy, which implied allowing cultivation on a portion of the farm to the tenant. But both practices meant allowing use of land in exchange for labour and were based on the fact that farmers could not pay enough cash wages, but also that many labourers were not completely proletarianized and still owned means of production in the form of animals. In that regard grazing rights also had a disciplinary effect. Dubow states that allowing shepherds and labourers to have some stock on the farm increased their interest in its success. But if they had too many stock, they were regarded as a problem by the farmers, since the labourers became too independent and their stock a burden.[26]

The decreasing importance of grazing rights indicated by Beinart, Morris and others should not be disputed, but the process behind it has not been thoroughly explained. Analysing the process in detail will enable us to see how the production itself affected labour relations. As grazing rights were an intricate part of the organization of production, its changes must be seen in relation to technological changes in farming.

The relevant technological changes in wool farming have been fences and mechanical water supply. Together with labour, these have constituted the main productive forces. Both Sean Archer and Lance van Sittert have shown how fences and windmills for water were implemented in the Cape beginning in the late nineteenth century and throughout the first half of the twentieth century. By subdividing farms into camps, farmers desired to replace human labour power in the form of shepherds with fences and windmills and improve the health of sheep, increase the number of stock on farms and improve the veld on farms.[27] Van Sittert claims that fencing increased farmers' "span of control" over farming activities and the environment, which aided them in the search for profits. Production yield also increased after fencing started.[28] Also Beinart, underlines that fencing was done to prevent soil erosion and the spread of livestock disease, and that it would increase the wool yield.[29] But since the soil and the animals were the basis for wool farming, it is important to emphasize that all those reasons were directly related to farmers' desires for increased profits. This thesis will shed light on how farmers' long-term interests in improving their farms through investments, which constituted a spatial expansion of capital, and subsequent accumulation of capital, affected labour relations.

The enclosures clearly had an impact in rural areas, but no conclusive study of the effects on labour relations has been conducted. As van Sittert shows,

---

[26] Dubow, S 1982, p. 50.

[27] Archer, S 2000, pp. 675, 681, 686, calls it "artificial" water supply; Van Sittert, L 2002, pp. 98-99, 101-07

[28] Van Sittert, L 2002, p. 117.

[29] Beinart, W 2008, p. 140.

enclosures, both private and public, both "hastened" the process wherein peasants were turned to labour migrants,[30] thus the proletarianization process, and increased the number of people convicted of trespassing and vagrancy. Thereby it had a disciplinary function regarding "respect for private property" among the "colonial underclass".[31] Labourers definitely belonged to this class, and were surely affected by fencing, but van Sittert does not specify how. We must thus be more specific and define labourers not as an "underclass", but as a class, which sold labour in exchange for money, rations and grazing rights. They were in opposition to the class of capital owners, that is, farmers, who wanted to accumulate capital by implementing technology in the form of fences and windmills.

Archer claims that, according to "every historical account", fencing and subdivision into camps and mechanical water supplies made shepherding redundant by the end of the 1920s in "most areas" of the Karoo.[32] But he does not offer any statistics or specify which historical accounts. Colin Bundy similarly states that capitalization of farming reduced the white farmers' demand for shepherding.[33] Archer and Bundy do not study labour in wool farming, and do not discuss the number of shepherds, nor do they mention anything further about them. To some extent they thus have a deterministic interpretation of the relationship between human labour power and technology. Their conclusions may be accurate, but Reggie Africa has demonstrated that mechanization in South African agriculture actually increased the demand for manual labour. Farmers did thus not replace humans with machines. New technology resulted in increased production, which required manual labour.[34] The nature of farming operations decided how the relationship between humans and machines was formed. The low wages paid to labourers definitely made it easier for farmers to invest in machinery while also hiring more labour. But without actually analysing the labour process on wool farms, we will not know how human labourers and farmers interacted with fences and windmills.

Introduction of new technology is not the only decisive factor of how labour relations changed, though. The specific peripheral setting must be acknowledged. Recurring droughts were a problem to farmers in the dry areas of the Cape. The droughts caused loss of sheep, lowered the quality of the wool and contributed to soil erosion. Beinart mentions that droughts contributed to a continuation of trekking of sheep from dry to more fertile areas. However, the impact this, and other environmental factors, had on labour relations is unknown.

---

[30] Van Sittert, L 2002, p. 112.

[31] Van Sittert, L 2002, p

[32] Archer, S 2000, p. 675.

[33] Bundy, C 1979, p. 116.

[34] Quoted in Wilson et al. 1977, p.27.

Further, the organization of production must be seen in relation to the labour force. The role played by the family members of the male labourer, that is, his wife, children and perhaps brothers and sisters, were highly important in wool farming. Wilson, for example, points out the importance of family relations and that the role of women as farm labourers increased during the twentieth century, but does not analyse if or how labouring families changed and how generational relations were affected. Morris has shown that younger sons of labour tenants left farms in order to find work in mining or urban industries as their chances to accumulate stock, find grazing and establish contracts of their own with farmers were diminished during the interwar period. The 1932 *Native Service Contract Act*, which allowed farmers to evict tenant families if any member of the family deserted service, was designed to halt this development, but appears to have been unsuccessful.[35] There is no reason to assume that relations in wool farming differed significantly from other forms of farming in that regard. But shepherding, which was often done by children, was a crucial work operation in wool farming. An analysis of the actual production will therefore be able to nuance and further elaborate on how children and youths were involved in production and how they acted. We will therefore turn to children and families.

Children, families and the generational division of labour

Shepherding was the work for young boys in pre-colonial and pre-capitalist societies in southern Africa. The boys started with this work around the age of seven. When they were older they moved on to herd cattle. The young girls accompanied their mothers in agricultural production and household work. The pre-colonial and pre-capitalist family relations within societies in southern Africa were thus based on a generational and gendered division of labour. According to Jeff Guy the object of production was the "continuous acquisition, creation, control and appropriation of labour power".[36] This was accomplished through the bridewealth system, *lobola*, wherein a man exchanged a certain amount of cattle for the labour power of the woman he married. By exchanging cattle for a woman's labour, her father was compensated for loss of labour. In essence, the control over women's labour was transferred from her father to her husband. Her children were then considered as children until they

[35] Morris, M 1976, pp. 327-28.

[36] Guy, J 1987, p. 22.

could establish homesteads of their own. Until then they were dependants of their father, and thereby they constituted his labour power.[37]

These structures were utilized by capitalist farmers. Charles van Onselen's study of the Highveld sharecropper Kas Maine testifies to the importance of pre-capitalist relations for both farmers and labouring male head of families. The sons of Kas Maine were usually given herding duties, and the daughters worked in the household of farmers, which demonstrates the gendered division of labour on farms in South Africa.[38] Also Beinart demonstrates how white farmers made agreements with their male labourers and tenants to engage their children as shepherds.[39] The existence of this form of arrangement is confirmed by other scholars, but we do not know to what extent or if changes occurred. In fact, little is known about the shepherds, despite their importance for wool farming and their frequent occurrence in the Cape. This goes especially for the young shepherds. They have been doubly subordinated; both as members of a labouring class, and as young labourers dependent on their fathers. This thesis will attempt to lift both the young and adult shepherds from the depth of rural labour history and contextualize their labour within the expanding capitalist farming. For we know that family relations among the labourers have been important for farm labour in southern Africa.

For example, Susan Levine notes that children have always been crucial as labourers on farms in South Africa. Furthermore, farmers have actively tried to gain access to their labour, for example through apprenticeship.[40] Wiseman Chijere Chirwa accounts for the prevalence of children and youths in especially tobacco and tea farming in Malawi between the 1920s and the 1950s. Farmers mainly gained access to the labour of children through the families who were hired as labour tenants.[41] Children and youths were also important in colonial Zimbabwe. Beverly Grier shows that children and youths were employed in farming, mining and as domestics.[42] For white farmers the family relations among tenants were an important way to access the labour of children, but many children and youths also hired out on their own account for wages.[43] Grier argues that children and youths constituted a group, which both parents and white settlers wanted access to, and wage labour became a part of African childhood. According to Grier, children ran away to cities as a form of resistance to increased exploitation, especially after the First World War. Their leaving upset white farmers, who wanted labour, and caused "juvenile

[37] Guy, J 1987, pp. 21- 22, 24.

[38] Van Onselen, C 1997, pp. 257, 271, 147

[39] Beinart, W 1991, pp. 54-55.

[40] Levine, S 2009, pp. 302-03.

[41] Chirwa, W. C. 1993, pp. 670-72.

[42] Grier, B 2006, pp. 69-70, 79-87; see also Grier, B 1994.

[43] Grier, B 2006, pp. 88-93, 95.

delinquency" in urban areas as children had to steal to survive.[44] The children and youths who ran away were, however, not so much resisting the system, which implies trying to change it according to their role in it, as they tried to avoid exploitation. In order to avoid it they had to endure some exploitation and earn enough money to survive, or turn to stealing as many did.

While Grier is occupied with the active role played by children and youths, and how the state tried to turn them into labourers, she does not analyse the production where children were involved. She gives an example of tea farmers who attracted labour by promising education for those children who laboured. The children constituted a source of cheap labour, which increased profits.[45] But there were other ways of increasing profits, for example mechanization of production, which she does not discuss. Research on industrial child labour in Europe has shown that the work operations of children were the first ones to be mechanized. Capitalists implemented machines when it was profitable, which made children redundant.[46] Grier does not analyse production, though, so we do not know if or how the labour of children changed. It is even likely that some children ran away as there was less work for them in rural areas. This will be of importance in a study of wool farming, where children and youths had their primary role in shepherding, a crucial work operation.

Levine points out that child labour should not be seen as an anomaly in capitalist production, but rather as an intricate part of it.[47] That is correct, but the concept child labour cannot be applied without contextualizing it historically and geographically. As we have seen, the generational and gendered division of labour was used to gain access to the labour of children. In pre-colonial societies that was a foundation for production. All family members were expected to contribute, as has usually been the case in peasant societies. Instead, child labour is a construction of industrial capitalist society, where children of the working class no longer have a given place in production. Surely, as Marx and Engels showed, both children and women – those who diverted from the norm of male labourers – were used in factories to increase profits.[48] But children were ousted from production as machinery was introduced. At the same time the role of young people became more important in peripheral areas of capitalism as peasant families were drawn into capitalist farming. It is thus important to acknowledge that expanding capitalism has meant that children have been used in different ways in capitalist production depending on time and place.

---

[44] Grier, B 2006, pp. 93-94, 103-105, 112-115

[45] Grier, B 2006, pp. 174-77

[46] Olsson, L 1980, pp. 145-46, 162-63; Rahikainen, M 2004, pp. 106-08, 118-19, opens up for a similar interpretation of decreasing child labour in for example British agriculture.

[47] Levine, S 2009, p. 305.

[48] Marx, K 1990 pp. 353-58, 367-74, 595-605; Engels, F 2009, pp. 164-73.

The labour of children in peripheral areas was still performed as a part of family labour. But we cannot, like Morris, say that the family was still the producing and consuming unit.[49] The family was still the consuming unit, as they lived in a household. But as the family members had to sell their labour to white farmers the productive unit was outside the family. The children continued with their activities, that is, shepherding etc., but their labour was performed in the capitalist world-economy and it benefitted most of all those outside the family. The principal class struggle in rural areas was thus between farmers and labouring families, not between individuals. That struggle was linked to production of finished commodities in capitalist core areas, which was made cheaper by imports of raw material from colonial areas. The labour of families on Cape farms therefore contributed to capital accumulation in both the Cape and in core areas of the world-economy. None of the studies referenced here has explored how children and families became involved in the capitalist world-economy. Labour in wool, tea and tobacco farming had at least one thing in common. It was production which arose as a response to a demand in core areas of capitalism. We will therefore also analyse how the role of families changed by being involved in expanding capitalist farming.

To summarize, labour in wool farming included both adults and children. Their labour was performed in the capitalist world-economy. The place where labourers and farmers met was in the production process on Cape farms. Since we know very little about how the relations between farmers, human labour power and technology changed, they will be central to the analysis.

Framing the problem

From the literature three central points of interest can be discerned, which will frame the analysis and make the overall aim of the thesis concrete. They are all interrelated, but can be phrased separately in the following way.

Firstly, how did Cape wool farmers change the organization of production between c. 1860 and 1950 and how did a changed production affect labour relations?

Secondly, how was the generational and gendered division of labour within labouring families affected by, and what influence did it have on, labour relations in wool farming?

Thirdly, in which ways were the relations between wool farmers in the Cape and textile manufacturers in primarily Great Britain manifested and how did these relate to labour supply, legislation and the environment in the Cape?

---

[49] Morris, M 1976, p. 327.

While the first two questions are directly related to developments in the Cape, that is, the geographical area of the Cape, the third question transcends national or colonial boundaries. However, as wool farmers and labourers in the Cape were intricately a part of the British imperial wool industry, the relationship with Britain, but also with other international actors, must constitute a part of the analysis. Wool farming in the Cape was production aimed at core areas of the world-economy, not the domestic market. Thus, it can hardly be understood if seen as separate from Britain. To include Britain thus forms a more comprehensive analysis of the Cape political economy.

A process of change – notes on methods and material

In order to explain how and why labour relations changed, the factors deciding how they were formed must be identified. This requires a theoretical assumption, but one which is solidly empirical and will enable an ascent from the abstract to the concrete;[50] the relations of production are first and foremost decided by the access to means of production. Therefore, viewing means of production as central, we must start there.

In wool farming the means of production are primarily land and sheep. Ownership of these is consequently a central issue to determine. It should be mentioned that throughout the thesis the term *farmer* refers to white people, and *peasant* refers to black people, unless otherwise indicated. Ownership of land was increasingly in the hands of whites, both due to political and economic factors. But there are other factors, which affect labour relations, primarily the development and implementation of productive forces. The main productive forces in wool farming consisted of labour and technology intended to improve pastoral and agricultural production in general, and wool farming in particular, such as fences and mechanical water supply. Means of production and productive forces can, however, not be seen as isolated phenomena, but must be contextualized, in our case within the capitalist world-economy.

The process of capital expansion can be measured, firstly by analysing the extent of capital implements, their origin and destination, and secondly their implementation rate. Once those factors are decided, their impact can be determined through an analysis of the production process itself and how a changed production process brought about *quantitative* and *qualitative* changes in labour relations. As the primary interest of this thesis is to analyse labour relations in the Cape, we must give attention to the prerequisites for farming and capital accumulation, i.e. the political economy, there.

---

[50] Cf. Lindegren, J 1987, p. 87.

A central feature of the political economy was the development of a market for labour. The impact of the mining industry was important in that regard. But also legislation and the basis for farming – the land and the environment – will be given attention. Legislation aimed at limiting the options for peasants surely affected the supply of labour to capitalist farming. Environmental aspects such as water supplies, droughts and possibilities to find grazing must also be included in an analysis of wool production and labour relations. But the political economy exceeded the geographical borders of the Cape. Britain, and its textile industry, was a central actor for Cape wool farmers.

The export of wool from the Cape was thus important, but this is not an analysis of an "export-oriented industry". Such a definition disregards the transnational character of wool production. It also presupposes the nation state or similar entities instead of viewing them as results of historic processes. Export from one area to another is in fact a sign of a relation in regards to the overall production system. The term commodity chain on the other hand identifies that both sender and recipient are involved in the same production process, but have different roles.[51] This thesis is thus an analysis of the production process in peripheral wool farming, which is contextualized within the capitalist world-economy. Therefore we must acknowledge the relations between core and periphery. Following Hopkins and Wallerstein, that relationship is based on unequal exchange,[52] but we can certainly not view it as static. Farmers in the periphery and manufacturers in the core were both aiming at increasing their share of the overall profits made from finished commodities.

The study is limited to the Cape Colony/Province as it was the primary region for wool farming. From the literature it is apparent that wool farming started to change in the 1870s with fencing. To begin the analysis in the 1860s is thus justified as it covers any changes caused by fencing. By 1950 labour relations in farming in general were definitely capitalist, meaning that any significant changes in wool farming had occurred by then. The late 1940s marked the start of a new phase of South African society of industrial capitalism, as manufacturers in Europe relocated entire textile factories to South Africa. The late 1940s were therefore the closing years of peripheral wool production in the Cape.

The material used in this thesis is made up of farm diaries, census material, Select Committee reports, journals, contemporary farming literature and magistrates' records of court cases make up the bulk of the material.

The *farm diaries*, primarily from the Rubidge's farm Wellwood in Graaff-Reinet, cover the entire period analysed. Other diaries are more fragmentary, and only cover shorter periods of time. The Rubidge diaries are also generally

[51] See Hopkins, T & Wallerstein, I 1982, pp. 58-62, for a discussion on commodity chains and international trade.

[52] Hopkins, T & Wallerstein, I 1982, pp. 47-48.

richer in information on various aspects of farming and life on the farms than the others. Diaries from other farms, however, complement and are used as examples of the developments made in wool farming. Farm diaries offer possibilities to analyse how production and labour could be organized, the number of labourers involved and what they did. The diaries will be discussed in detail in the section on Wellwood.

The first *census* used is from 1865. Subsequent to that censuses for the Cape were taken in 1875, 1891 and 1904. For the Union of South Africa censuses including occupations of the entire population were taken in 1911, 1936 (not provincial level) and 1946. These censuses contain information on occupation, but some of them also include livestock numbers and farming implements. The first agricultural census was taken in 1918. Thereafter agricultural censuses with information on production, livestock numbers, farming implements, the labour force etc. were taken at regular intervals.

We should be aware that certain categories in the censuses were not always enumerated, and were sometimes included in different categories. There can also have been some discrepancies regarding the number of labourers and livestock, especially for the early censuses.[53] In some censuses the term "workers on farms" is used. This category is always larger than the category farm labourer/servant and most likely includes also the farmers and their family.[54] It has therefore not been used to quantify farm labour as the thesis focuses on the hired labour force. The fact that categories such as shepherd and farm labourer were included in the censuses reveals that they were important at the time to officials and presumably to others as well. The enumerating process is more difficult to assess. Examples from the diaries on the farm Wellwood show that there were some discrepancies in the number of shepherds reported to the census in 1875, and the actual number of people performing the work of a shepherd that year.[55] This indicates that there were actually more people working as shepherds than the number enumerated in the census. By enumerating the labouring classes they disclose categories of people and occupations, which have largely been hidden in other official material.

Reports from *Select Committees* and *Commissions* contain testimonies from primarily white farmers, politicians and officials, but to some extent also representatives of black people. These testimonies offer insights into farming life, and descriptions of farming practices. Furthermore, the reports often tried to cover large parts of the Cape, meaning that testimonies were taken from several districts. These reports offered opportunities for farmers to influence officials and politicians, indicating that some testimonies may have been

[53] See, for example, Cape of Good Hope Census 1891, pp. cx, cxiii.

[54] See, for example, Cape of Good Hope Census 1891, pp. cxiii, 446-47; Cape of Good Hope Census 1904, pp. 496-97.

[55] Rubidge diaries 1875. Preparation for census.

exaggerated in order to enhance the seriousness of for example labour or fencing issues. When farmers gave testimonies on their own farming practices, there is less reason to assume inaccuracies, although it may have occurred.

The journals, the *Agricultural Journal of the Cape of Good Hope*, first printed in 1889, *Farmers' Weekly* in print since 1911, and *Die Wolboer*, first printed in 1947, together cover the greater part of the period analysed. Articles from all these journals are used to provide examples of various aspects of farming. The distribution of the journals and their influence on farmers has been debated,[56] but for this thesis the journals will not be used to measure their impact on farmers; the purpose of using them is to gain access to debates and trends in farming, primarily from the viewpoint of labour practices and the influence of capital expansion.

Court cases from the districts of Graaff-Reinet and Carnarvon have been used, covering the period from 1870 to 1940. Unfortunately the court cases are incomplete from the year 1900 onwards, which makes them unfit for quantitative analysis. But they are instrumental as a source of qualitative analysis demonstrating life in the wool farming regions. Furthermore, they describe labour relations as they were perceived by those involved, especially regarding children and young persons, who may not have been enumerated as labourers in censuses if they were dependents of the father. The cases from Carnarvon have been especially rich in descriptions of conditions on farms, which is why sections regarding life on farms primarily focus on that region. The cases chosen for analysis have all concerned labourers and/or farmers. A majority of the cases concern thefts or losses of stock, usually with labourers as the accused. This does not mean that most labourers were thieves, and the thefts themselves are not central to the analysis; instead the underlying relations are of main concern, although in some instances the actual thefts illuminate relations in farming areas.

To include material from other parts of the world, for instance Britain, would have been excessive to the aims of this thesis, which is to analyse labour relations in the Cape. However, for example export figures, as presented in the *Statistical Register* and the *Annual Statement on Trade and Shipping*, indicate where the Cape wool was sent, and various material imply wherefrom ideas, capital and implements came. It is thus the aim that makes the analysis transnational, not the material used.

[56] See Van Sittert, L 2004; Beinart, W 2005.

Wellwood

The farm Wellwood in Graaff-Reinet will be used continuously throughout this thesis as a point of reference and as an example of how production *could* be organized in Cape wool farming. Using Wellwood as an example does not mean that it represents an average farm in the Cape at any point during the time period analysed here. Quite the contrary, Wellwood has always been a forerunner in terms of new technology and farming methods. Since the nineteenth century the farm has been a leading merino stud farm and served as an inspiration to others.[57] The fact that it has been a model farm makes it an interesting object of closer analysis. Any important changes made in Cape wool farming regarding labour practices and capital expansion would have been seen on Wellwood, probably some time before it had an impact on the regional level.

Wellwood has been owned by the Rubidge family since 1838. During that period of time a farm diary has been kept on almost a daily basis. This is a unique source of everyday rural Cape life in general, and of Cape wool farming in particular. By using the diary throughout the period analysed in this thesis, it will be possible to closely examine changes in farming methods and labour practices with accuracy. There is, of course, a risk in doing so. It may lead to over-interpretations of small details specific to Wellwood, but when used together with complementing material, such inaccuracies will be avoided.

During the period from 1860 to 1950, three generations of Rubidges farmed at Wellwood. Charles Rubidge was in charge until 1887, thereafter his son Richard Rubidge took over as owner. Richard was succeeded by his son Sidney Rubidge in 1913, although Sidney seems to have written most of the diaries already since 1905. All of them were renowned for their progressive nature and will to improve the merino sheep on Wellwood.

As the diary was written by the farmer, it reveals the viewpoint of the farmer. Farming practices were important in that regard. For example, if sheep were herded, and where on the farm it took place, indicates the number of shepherds and the practice of shepherding. Capital investments into the farm such as fences, windmills and machinery were frequently noted, as were some of the people involved in those activities. References to the farm labour force are scarcer, but occur in situations related to farming practices, when labourers arrive to and leave the farm, and in some enumerations for censuses. Wages are referenced occasionally, but more specified between 1920 and 1950. Much of the labour on the farm is, however, hidden. Especially the reproductive labour conducted by women and children is largely outside the written sources. While that labour was important in labour relations, we must remember that the focus

[57] Beinart, W 2008, p. 305; See Van Sittert, L 2004, 2005 and Beinart, W 2005 for further discussion on the "representativeness" of Wellwood.

of the thesis is on production of wool and the immediate labour in relation to it.

The size of the farm has shifted somewhat throughout the period covered here. In 1872 it was reduced to about 6,700 morgen or 5,700 hectares.[58] By 1930 the farm had been reduced to 6,000 morgen, but in 1935 it was 6,400 morgen.[59] As Beinart notes, it was by no means one of the largest farms in extent of morgen, but not among the smaller ones either.[60] Some farms ranged up to 15,000 morgen or even more, while others did not exceed 2,000 morgen. Wellwood was, however, quite unique as there is no running water on the farm, unlike most other successful farms, which may have been a reason for the progressive nature of the farmers there; they have been forced to improve the farm constantly in order to be able to farm there. On the other hand, the lack of water is also evidence to the successful nature of the farm: the Rubidges have been able to create a model farm without access to running water.

The number of sheep and livestock on Wellwood has not been possible to conclude for all years, but a general overview of certain periods can be done. During most years the number of sheep did not exceed 3,000, and was usually somewhere around 2,000. Other livestock such as goats usually numbered between 100 and 500, cattle between 50 and 100, but sometimes more. As Wellwood was a merino stud farm, income was generated from breeding and sale of animals as well. Between the 1920s and 1950 the sale of stock generated more income than the sale of wool, which could have been the case also before 1920, although this income was also related to the wool industry. Those farmers who did not have merino studs had to rely more on wool. But they could probably receive income from ostriches, goats or oranges, which was done on Wellwood. Ostriches became an important feature of the farm, and many other farms, during the late nineteenth and early twentieth centuries. At the most there were more than one hundred ostriches on the farm. The Rubidges also produced oranges for sale. Such income was important when the wool price was low. The focus of Wellwood has, however, always been the merino sheep, which is why the farm is of vital importance to this study.

[58] Beinart, W 2008, p. 311. 1 morgen equals 0.85 hectares.

[59] Rubidge diaries, Sept. 12, 1930; Sept. 12, 1935.

[60] Beinart, W 2008, p. 305.

CHAPTER 2

The Establishment of Cape Wool Farming – Core-Periphery Relations, Imperialism and Accumulation of Capital

The Cape, Australia and Britain

Cape wool farming on a commercial basis dates back to the late eighteenth century. In 1789 the military commander at the Cape, Colonel Robert Gordon, received six merino sheep from the Dutch royal family. The sheep were originally a gift from the King of Spain to the House of Orange. Gordon kept the sheep near Cape Town and found that they did well in the climate. Two years later the Dutch wanted their sheep back, but Gordon only sent back the original number, six, and kept the offspring. Some of the sheep were sold to Australia, which meant the start of the wool industry in that colony. Several farmers such as the van Reenen brothers, J. F. Reitz and Michiel Breda, farmed successfully with merinos in the western parts of the Cape during the early nineteenth century.[61] But the future of the wool industry was in the eastern parts, which had been recently colonized by the British.

In 1815 the Governor-General to the Cape, Lord Charles Somerset, imported additional merino sheep to the Colony. Somerset bought 10 rams and 25 ewes from King George III's Kew Gardens, making the wool industry an imperial affair. Somerset put the sheep on the Governmental farm Groote Pos and kept them for breeding purposes. Cape farmers could thereafter come to the farm and buy the merino lambs, thereby enhancing their own flocks.[62] The most important of the wool farmers belonged to the 1820-settlers, who emigrated to the Cape from Britain with a promise of ownership of 100 acres of land. They experimented with sheep already in the 1820s. Richard Daniell and T. C. White were two early successful wool farmers among the 1820-settlers. Another one was Miles Bowker, who seems to have purchased his first merino

---

[61] Hanekom, A. J. 1960, p. 24-26.

[62] Hanekom. A. J. 1960, p. 33.

sheep from Groote Pos in 1823, which was the foundation of his wool farming ventures.[63] Wool farming in the Cape was thus partly the result of Government initiatives where leading officials introduced sheep in order to help the farmers accumulate capital, and subsequently improve the economy of the colony. The eastern parts of the Colony, especially the Karroo, were dry and not suited for agricultural pursuits except for the coastal areas. Pastoral farming offered the best opportunities and especially sheep that could produce wool for exports was lucrative for those who settled in these areas. Already during Somerset's time in office there were several Cape farmers who imported sheep on their own behalf.[64] But also joint efforts were made by Cape farmers in sheep imports; in 1834 the *Eastern Province Joint Stock Sheep Association* was founded in Grahamstown. The main shareholders were members of the 1820-settler families; Maynard, Carlisle, Philipps, Griffiths, Norden and Godlonton. The Association purchased merinos from both Britain and Germany, which were auctioned in Grahamstown.[65] These farmers definitely belonged to those with foresight and capital, and a belief that the expensive investments would be profitable.

In Australia the wool industry advanced rapidly.[66] The Cape farmers consequently turned to their fellow colonial subjects in Australia, whose flocks were reputedly of good quality, in order to further enhance their flocks. In 1827 merinos were bought from Australia, thereby completing the circle of inter-colonial sheep sales. The ships brought fairly large numbers of sheep to the Cape. In 1836 about 300 merinos were landed in Port Elizabeth, where farmers from all over the Eastern Province gathered to purchase the sheep.[67] In 1855 the sheep had increased fourfold from the beginning of the century, to 6.5 million, of which 75 per cent were woolled.[68] The Cape wool production, although comparatively small internationally, simultaneously became increasingly important to the colonial economy in the first half of the nineteenth century. By 1851 wool constituted 59 per cent of all exports from the Cape.[69] The export figures for the period 1838 to 1865 clarify the rapid advance of the industry:

---

[63] Keegan, T 1996, pp. 63, 72; Collett, J 1990, p. 38.

[64] Hanekom, A. J. 1960, p. 33

[65] Keegan, T 1996, p. 72.

[66] McMichael, P 1984, p. 55.

[67] Collett, J 1990, p. 38; Hanekom, A. J. 1960, p. 33.

[68] Beinart, W 2008, p. 53.

[69] Kirk, T 1980, p. 230.

Table 1. Wool exports from the Cape Colony 1838 - 1865.

Year	Lbs	£
1838	490,754	26,627
1840	911,118	45,986
1845	3,219,769	176,741
1850	5,912,927	285,610
1855	12,106,415	634,130
1860	23,172,785	1,446,510
1864	36,296,698	1,865,703
1865	32,767,679	1,680,826

Source: Statistical Register of the Colony of Cape of Good Hope, 1886, p. vii.

The advancements made by the Cape farmers, and even more so by their Australian counterparts, must, however, be seen in the light of increased textile production in the imperial homeland Britain. After all, the wool produced in colonial areas was not turned into finished commodities in the colonies, but in Britain, where technological inventions revolutionized the production in textile mills.

Creation of a core and its periphery

As noted by Friedrich Engels, the British wool production was greatly enhanced by the introduction of certain machinery. The gin and the loom were the two most notable inventions increasing the production of textiles. Furthermore, "all this machinery was made doubly important by James Watt's steam engine, invented in 1764, and used for supplying motive power for spinning since 1785".[70] The introduction of the steam engine coincided with the import of the first merinos at the Cape and, although it was a coincidence, it represented the start of a new phase in the global and the British wool industry.

During the first half of the nineteenth century the production of woollen textiles increased rapidly in Britain, but at the same time the domestic production of wool did not keep up, according to Engels; instead the wool was bought from Ireland and other colonial areas and from other countries in Europe. In 1801, 101 million lbs. of wool was worked up, of which 7 million, or roughly seven per cent, were imported. Three decades later, in 1835, the production of wool had almost doubled as 180 million lbs. of wool was worked up, and the imports had increased six times; 42 million lbs., or 23 per cent,

[70] Engels, F 2009, p. 54.

were imported.[71] So, the English woollen textile industry was increasingly relying on imports of wool, and the capitalist production of wool undoubtedly became transnational during the first decades of the nineteenth century.

The process of finding new supplies of wool constituted a crucial feature of capitalist production: expansion. As new areas became involved in wool production the capitalist sphere started to expand globally. Previously this had been restricted to Scotland and Ireland, but the new colonial areas in the southern hemisphere brought new possibilities for the capitalist class in England. They no longer had to rely on a domestic supply of wool for their factories, although British sheep farmers contributed with the majority of the wool during the first half of the nineteenth century.[72] Instead the colonial areas in Australia and southern Africa became the new producers of raw material.

Rosa Luxemburg has asserted that expansion into new geographical areas and economic sectors is an essential feature of capitalism. According to her, not all profits could be invested into production in, for example, Britain. As capital must be reinvested into production in order to continue its transfer from money to capital to more money, capitalism requires new land and sectors, which can be incorporated into production and into which investments can be made. According to Luxemburg, investments in railways and international loans were typical features of this expansion.[73] But this expansion was not only carried out by capitalists who invested in colonial areas. In Cape wool farming it was the farmers who invested, although most of their capital came from Britain. Unexploited land, which could be incorporated into capitalist production, was plentiful in the Cape at the time of the British conquest in 1807. Most importantly, it was land suited for sheep. When farmers realized that the sheep thrived in the dry climate of the Karroo and other parts of the Colony, their interest increased, as did the interest of the colonial Government, which is why officials like Lord Somerset imported sheep and sold to farmers. The farmers subsequently turned land and sheep into capital, which could be productive and generate profits for the capital owning classes in both the Cape and Britain through the export of wool. Thereby the farmers were agents of capitalist expansion. Without capital there can be no capitalist production.

The establishment of Cape wool farming was thus an expansion of capital. The number of sheep bought during the early years testifies to the humble beginnings of Cape wool farming compared to its importance in the 1850s. But the farmers were successful and bought more sheep and sold wool to Britain. The farmers of British origin were among the most successful, but also

[71] Engels, F 2009, p. 56

[72] Engels, F 2009 p. 56; Jenkins & Ponting 1982, p. 93.

[73] Luxemburg, R 2003, pp. 13, 79-91, 104-110.

Afrikaners ventured into wool farming.[74] As wool farming expanded, farmers found themselves in a position which can be described as peripheral in relation to the core in Britain. Core-periphery relations were thus the result of actions taken in both places. We can even say that it was in the interest of Cape farmers to establish themselves as peripheral farmers in a relationship with the core. This enabled them to find an outlet for their wool. Consequently, they could profit and accumulate capital in the periphery. The power relations between the two were, however, not equal. Without the textile production in Britain, the Cape farmers could hardly have managed to farm with sheep at all. But the position as peripheral farmer was for many a more attractive option than being proletarianized in Britain. A major reason for the emigration to the Cape and other parts of the British Empire was the capitalist transformation in Britain.[75] Emigration became a way to maintain class position as farmer, and to some it even meant an opportunity for advancement. A new class of capital owners thereby established themselves in the Cape, largely as a reaction to the British textile industry.

The expansion of capital was clearly an expansion of the capitalist sphere. It was also an expansion of capitalism, but the relations in the periphery were not capitalist in the sense that proletarian cash wage labour dominated. By viewing capitalism as a global system, where the modes of labour control differ between core and periphery, we avoid the issue.[76] But doing so discloses as much as it reveals. Bernard Magubane has used the term "colonial capitalism" to describe the mode of production in colonial areas, and Donald Denoon has used the term "settler capitalism" to differentiate settler societies from others.[77] But those terms imply that capitalism in colonial or settler areas was somehow different from capitalism elsewhere and will not be used here. Instead, it is more productive to regard the expansion of capital as a process where the capitalist sphere expanded, which gradually affected relations of production in the Cape as classes of capitalist farmers and labourers emerged in the periphery.

A crucial measure in the process of establishing new relations of production was the privatization of land. The land itself became a commodity, which could be bought and sold and produce another commodity, wool.[78] During the Dutch reign at the Cape a loan farm system had been established in the pastoral regions. There was no individual title to the land and the farms could not be subdivided between children of farmers. But in 1813 the loan farms were replaced by freehold land tenure under a system of perpetual quitrent. The

---

[74] Many of these Afrikaners were intermarried with families of British origin. See Beinart, W 2008, p. 61.

[75] Crais, C 1992, p. 88; Olsson, L 2005, pp. 71-78.

[76] See for example Hopkins, T and Wallerstein, I 1982, pp. 73-74.

[77] Magubane, B 1985; Denoon, D 1983.

[78] Crais, C 1992, p. 109.

reasons were twofold. Firstly, the British did not want to extend the borders of the Colony at that time, meaning that no new farms would be established on untouched land. Private property which could be subdivided between sons of farmers was therefore required. Secondly, the British colonial authorities thought that private ownership of land would generate more investments into farming land and further the development of production through more progressive methods. However, it was not until after 1820 that the system of freehold was carried out to any greater extent.[79]

These measures were not exclusive to the Cape. As Hobsbawm argues, the establishment of private property was a central feature in the expansion of capitalism throughout the British Empire. Land that was owned communally could not be bought and sold, and not generate accumulation of capital.[80] The loan farms were a form of private ownership of land, but were based on an endless supply of land and extensive farming and extended settlement. As the land allocated for farming became limited, production would have to be more intensive and the settlements closer. This, of course, meant that not all whites could be sustained through farming. Instead, the whites in the Cape who became landless would be turned into skilled labourers.[81] Capitalist expansion implied stratification among farmers and expropriation for some of them. However, those who remained on the farms became an integral part of British imperial wool production.

According to Hobsbawm, there was specialization and even monoculture in those peripheral areas where pastoral production dominated.[82] Farmers in the Cape had options to farm with other things, but sheep, and also goats and ostriches, offered the best possibilities. Cultivation of agricultural crops took place where this was possible, but sheep and their wool became the dominant commodity as there was a demand from Britain, and because the soil was not suited for other things. As McMichael clarifies regarding Australia, British expansion largely decided possibilities for settler production in colonies.[83] But as long as there was a demand for their wool, the farmers had no reason to be dissatisfied with the arrangement. As Marx notes, in capitalist society the commodity is a way to enhance accumulation of capital, not important in itself.[84]

Although the power relations between the core and the periphery were in the favour of the core, it became clear by the mid-nineteenth century that the British textile industry was also dependent on a supply of foreign wool. And,

---

[79] Keegan, T 1996, p. 57.

[80] Hobsbawm, E. J. 1980, pp. 8-11.

[81] Keegan, T 1996, p. 57.

[82] Hobsbawm, E 1975, p. 177.

[83] McMichael, P 1984, p. 1.

[84] Marx, K 1990, p. 293.

equally important, it was clear to the colonial farmers in southern Africa. In 1864 the *Natal Almanac and Yearly Register* reported that "[w]ool, required in the manufacturing districts of England, [...] is an article of very increasing demand and value, [...]". Furthermore, in 1862 about 110 million lbs. of 160 million lbs. of British wool imports came from the colonial areas.[85] The British import of wool had thus more or less quadrupled between 1835 and 1862, and about 68 per cent came from the colonial areas. By mid-century the core-periphery relations were well established. Governor Wodehouse, the British Commissioner General to the Cape, even stated in 1867 that "[f]or what do we now hold this country but for wool? Take away wool [...] and, commercially speaking, what is left?"[86]

Wool farming areas were connected with the core initially through Cape Town, which during the 1830s and 1840s was "the link in the chain of dependence between the metropolitan and peripheral economies".[87] But due to the wool production's location in the eastern parts of the Colony, new cities such as Port Elizabeth and East London soon became new centres for the colonial wool trade. Already in 1844 Port Elizabeth had overtaken Cape Town as the leading wool exporting port in the Cape.[88] The relations in transnational wool production between Britain and the Cape did thus not only rely on existing trade centres such as Cape Town, it also created new ones, which were based on the wool trade.

The distance between core and periphery in the Empire were still vast, though, which meant that it could take a year or more for farmers to realize the profits from the wool.[89] When railways were built in the 1870s, the distance decreased. Alan Mabin has argued that the railways were crucial for the expansion of capitalism in South Africa. These were mainly meant for the mineral deposits, but also wool farmers gained from them. Mabin suggests that wool farming capital fuelled the initial diamond boom, but that wool was disadvantaged by the discovery of minerals.[90] While the railway was crucial in bringing the Empire closer together, and thus expanding the capitalist sphere, we must remember that the railway was only the means to an end. Wool farmers could not gain from the railway without a commodity to send on it. And capital expanded before railways were constructed, although at a slower

---

[85] *Natal Almanac and Yearly Register*, in Houghton & Dagut 1972, pp. 139-40.

[86] Gov. Wodehouse, Commissioner General to the Cape, 1867, quoted in Dubow, S, 1982, p. 13.

[87] Keegan, T 1996, p. 162.

[88] Smith, K 1976, p. 58.

[89] McMichael, P 1984, pp. 102, 108-09. For Australia.

[90] Mabin, A 1984, pp. 122-26, 320. For spatial expansion of capitalism, see also Harvey, D 2006.

rate. Instead, the crucial intermediaries of capital expansion were the agents with money: the merchants.[91]

Wine was the first real export commodity of the Cape, but its share declined in the 1820s and merchants thereafter became more interested in wool, which became the dominant export product in the 1830s and 1840s. Many firms, such as the Mosenthal Brothers, established branches throughout the wool farming districts in the 1840s. The merchants constituted the link between the producers of raw material in the Cape and the producers of finished commodities in Britain. As Keegan notes, "Western Cape merchants became the chief financiers of the first eastern Cape wool boom [...]".[92] The initial wool farming was thus dependent on existing trade routes and the backing of capital from Britain. But this, in turn, relied on future sale of wool from the Cape to Britain.

Merchants gave extended credit to farmers. Farmers brought the wool to storekeepers, who forwarded it to traders in for example Port Elizabeth. In exchange for the wool, the farmers received food and other means of livelihood. And if he was in debt, his credit was extended.[93] Many of the early wool farmers were thus involved in barter rather than cash exchange for products. But there were also those farmers who received cash for their wool, and merchants invested into wool farming. The role of merchants as intermediaries of capital expansion can thus not be underestimated. But the wool boom created a situation of severe competition among the merchants, who all wanted to profit. As they all wanted to keep their customers they gave long-term credit to farmers, who "bought beyond their means". When the debts could not be collected, an economic depression started in wool farming in the 1860s.[94] The eagerness among merchants to profit similarly meant that they did not differentiate enough between various qualities of wool. As Dubow argues, merchant capital is outside the sphere of production and could not affect farming practices to any great extent. Farmers therefore had few incentives to change their practices. This gave the Cape wool a reputation on the London wool market of being dirty, unsorted and generally too short, as many farmers shore twice a year instead of once. This generated wool of poor quality, which suffered most severely in times of lowered demand and depression.[95]

Despite bringing depression to the Cape, merchants were still crucial to expansion of capital through the commodity chain of wool. Their intermediary role enabled farmers to sell their wool on the international market.

---

[91] McMichael, P 1984, pp. 102, 108-09.

[92] Keegan, T 1996, p. 162.

[93] Dubow, S 1982, p. 23.

[94] Dubow, S 1982, pp. 24-26.

[95] Dubow, S 1982, pp. 21-22, 26-28.

The settlers – expansion, accumulation and stratification

While sale of wool was important, there were other ways for settlers to accumulate capital, especially during the early years. Many of the settlers started as traders and merchants and profits from those ventures were later invested into farming.[96] Crais even calls this the time and place of primitive accumulation in the Cape, which is accurate to some extent. Those settlers who had little money could surely acquire it through trade. However, there were also those who came with much capital, like the Bowkers. Furthermore, following the argument that merchants were intermediaries, we see that the primitive accumulation had already been made in Britain. Traders and merchants were thus not so much involved in primitive accumulation as in expansion of capital.

One of the settlers, James Collett, who came to the Cape as an indentured servant in General Campbell's party in 1821, bought a farm already in 1826, but traded on the frontier and also had a shop in Grahamstown.[97] The money from trading was invested into farming. The initial farming ventures were mainly fruits. Prospects were not as good, though, and his interest soon turned to merino sheep, which he farmed on Leeuwfontein. But the area south of Grahamstown was not suited for wool farming, as the grass was sour. After having accumulated more capital, he moved further north, where the grass was more suitable for merinos. In 1834 he bought the farm Elephant Fountain south-west of Fort Beaufort. He was by then established as a merino farmer.[98]

Similar migrations were done by many other settlers, for example Robert Henry Rubidge. Initially, he settled close to Grahamstown in the Albany district, but the prospects in wool farming drove him north. In 1838 he bought "extensive farming land" in the Graaff-Reinet district together with two other families, the Southeys and the Powells. The suitability for wool farming and subsequent sale of wool to Britain were primary reasons for his decision to relocate. The three families purchased land from an Afrikaner, who later moved to the north-eastern Cape. The land was subsequently subdivided between the families, and Robert's son Charles Rubidge became the owner of Wellwood.[99] The northward expansion into the dry interior of the Cape was thus largely caused by the relationship with British textile capital. The dry areas were not suited for cultivation, but the merinos thrived, and the settlers followed.

---

[96] Crais, C 1992, p. 116

[97] Collett, J 1990, pp. 8, 28, 33, 36.

[98] Collett, J 1990, p. 38.

[99] Beinart, W 2008, p. 56.

The endeavours of British settlers were not without problems, but they were usually equipped with more capital than their Afrikaner[100] counterparts, had the support of the colonial Government and had access to the British wool market. The success of the British settlers was partly at the expense of the Afrikaner farmers. Less than two decades after the arrival of British settlers, Afrikaners moved out of the Colony in large numbers in the Great Trek. Some of the trekking Afrikaners sold their farms cheaply or sometimes even for "a wagon or a span of oxen".[101] For example, in 1841 R. Southey bought a farm called Knoffelhoek for £50 from a trek-boer. Ten years later he sold it for £900.[102] The great progress made by wool farmers quickly enhanced the value of farms. And it increased the land prices. Smith notes a survey in the Graaff-Reinet district, where the value of 49 farms increased six times between 1843 and 1857, from about £30,000 to more than £192,000.[103]

While the abolition of slavery and general antipathy against British rule in southern Africa were surely important factors behind the Trek, there were also other explanations. With the arrival of the British there was competition over land. The success of wool farming increased prices on land. Keegan suggests that in the 1830s most Afrikaners were not landowners and those who did not own land had problems finding grazing land for their stock.[104] In other words, the Cape Colony ran out of land for expanding rural capitalism. Most Afrikaners stayed in the Colony, though; in the 1860s as many as two thirds of them lived in the Cape and they constituted 75 per cent of the white population there.[105] One alternative to trekking was to become a "bywoner", a tenant, on another man's farm. These constituted a large part of the group of "poor whites", which started to appear in the Cape in the 1860s, although the term was not used at that time.[106] The arrival of British settlers, and expanding wool farming for British textile industries, subsequently stratified the farmers.

During the first half of the 1860s, wool farmers experienced problems. There were droughts, the wool price fell and the British demand for wool declined until 1863. The end of the American Civil War disrupted wool prices and the establishment of imperial banks caused excessive speculation and credits. As a result Cape wool farming went into depression and quite a few farmers went bankrupt.[107] The dependence on the imperial wool textile market made Cape

---

[100] The term Afrikaner (Afrikaander) was first used in 1707, but took on its present day meaning during the early twentieth century. See Gilliomee, H 2003, pp. 22-23, 356.

[101] Noble, J 1875, p. 149.

[102] Dubow, S 1982, p. 17.

[103] Smith, K 1976, p. 59.

[104] Keegan, T 1996, pp. 186-87.

[105] Giliomee, H 2003, p. 201.

[106] See Bundy, C 1986.

[107] Smith, K 1976, p. 74.

wool farming vulnerable. At the beginning of the 1870s conditions stabilized, however. The British demand on wool returned to previous levels and the price reached its peak in the first half of the 1870s.[108]

The crisis of the 1860s and the recovery thereafter, however, also intensified stratifications in the rural areas. The wealthier and progressive farmers, who had invested in their farms, managed the crisis much better than the poorer group of farmers. Similarly, the wealthy farmers were the first ones to benefit when the crisis was over. In Graaff-Reinet the conditions of the 1860s created an opportunity for farmers to buy crown lands at a cheap price, which affected the ability of black and white peasant farmers who grazed there to produce wool.[109]

International division of labour, proletarianization and capitalist farming

As the international division of labour increased, new classes emerged in both the periphery and the core. We know that in core areas an urban proletariat arose along with capitalist factory production, but labour relations changed also in the periphery. The spatial expansion of capital cannot be regarded as separate from expansion into new economic sectors or strata of society. Space in itself, in our case land, is not productive for capital until it is exploited. Thus, new land must be inserted into production and meet labour. Only then can it generate accumulation of capital.

In the Cape, a labouring class emerged along with the establishment of farms. The settlers desired to be large-scale farmers, which required labourers. They generally identified themselves according to race and not class, and thus thought that whites should not be engaged in manual labour where blacks did so.[110] After the end of slavery in 1838 the British and Afrikaner farmers had to find other ways of acquiring labour. As most of the farmers had little cash, they relied on being able to offer land and grazing rights in exchange for labour. The abolition of slavery did not change the relations between farmers and labourers to any great extent, though. Legislation was passed to "stabilise the new labour system that had emerged after 1838".[111] These relations were established through the *Masters' and Servants' Ordinance* of 1841 and the *Masters' and Servants' Act* of 1856. The 1841 Ordinance "bound workers with severe criminal sanctions for breach of contract, including such subjectively determined 'crimes' as disobedience, defiance and resistance". As a result,

[108] Beinart, W 2008, p. 20.

[109] Dubow, S 1982, p. 30.

[110] Crais, C 1992, pp. 89-92.

[111] Keegan, T 1996, p. 126.

labourers were largely defenceless as farmers had the law on their side.[112] Servants were also required to carry passes when leaving the farms of their masters, which limited the mobility of the labour force.[113] The 1856 Act, which was not abolished until 1974, also functioned as a vagrancy act. Furthermore, it made it possible for farmers to "detain children against their and their parents' will [...]" as long as they could demonstrate to the magistrate that it was in the interest of the child.[114]

The abolition of slavery thus paved the way for capitalist relations, which "was to be the fundamental force driving imperial expansion and black dispossession for decades to come [...]".[115] But the capitalist relations were to be "based on the ever more rigid assertion of racial hegemony".[116] The new relations of production thus centred around white farmers with more or less access to capital, and black and coloured labourers with little or no access to capital. Thereby a class conflict became visible in the colonial setting. It was even more visible than in most other places since it was formed along racial lines. This division was the foundation for racial oppression, which aimed at controlling and acquiring labour.

The racial class conflict in the Cape was, however, only one of many which were formed along the commodity chain of wool. These class conflicts reveal further divisions of labour in the wool industry.

Each link in the commodity chain of wool represents a stage of production and is made up by the actors involved in production, that is, owners of capital and labour, and raw material and means of production. The *first* stage then contains two principal actors, one raw material and one means of production: the farmer, the land, the sheep and the shepherd. Within this link the fundamental relations of production of wool is found. The farmer owns the sheep and the land, and buys the labour of the shepherd to make sure the sheep is in its best possible condition when it is time for shearing. The *second* stage thus includes the farmer, the sheep and the shearer. The shearer is paid by the farmer to take off the wool in a manner which gives the best possible quantity and quality. A *third* stage includes the sorting and packing of wool, which was done on the farm after shearing. The farmer or a foreman generally supervised this work operation, but it was done by the farm labourers. The *fourth* stage comprises the transport of the wool from the farm to the market. In some cases this transport was done by farmers themselves, but also by transport companies which hired labourers. Especially railways contributed substantially to an efficient transport of wool from farming regions in the interior to port cities

---

[112] Keegan, T 1996, p. 126.

[113] See for example Crais, C 1992, p. 157, 194; Ross, R 1999, p. 38.

[114] Crais, C 1992, p. 194.

[115] Keegan, T 1996, p. 127.

[116] Keegan, T 1996, p. 127.

such as Port Elizabeth. The colonial state was a main actor in this regard, and contributed to accumulation of capital. The *fifth* stage comprises dock workers employed by transport companies, but also farmers' cooperative movements, who stored and loaded the wool awaiting shipping in port cities.

The *sixth* stage includes the transport of wool overseas, from the Cape to Britain. This stage is perhaps the most obvious example of transnational production as it includes the crossing of borders and transport from one part of the world to the other, from periphery to core where sailors hired by shipping companies constituted truly transnational labourers. The *seventh* stage is constituted by the offloading of wool in Britain by dock workers employed by transport companies. The *eighth* stage includes the transport from harbour to factory. Railway companies and engine drivers constitute the principal actors on the British side of the commodity chain. The *ninth* stage contains the cleaning process in a factory by wool washers. Washing (or scouring) the wool was, however, not done in the English factories initially, but seems to have been relocated there from the Cape during the end of the nineteenth century. Wool washing was also done on some farms, but is not mentioned in sources such as the Rubidge diaries. The *tenth* and *eleventh* stages include the spinning and weaving of the wool, which was done by spinners and weavers in factories owned by industrial capitalists.

More stages could be added depending on the final product, and for work operations among the eleven stages. But let us settle with these eleven stages in the commodity chain of wool during the nineteenth and early twentieth centuries. The labourers in all the stages of the commodity chain have all been involved in the final wool textile product. Similar divisions of labour is apparent in many production processes, for example in the one from grain to bread, and applies equally well to processes within nation states. However, the international division of labour has separated the shepherd, the sailor and the factory worker from each other. They have all sold their labour to others, but at different stages of the chain. It is a geographical alienation, which further separates the primary producer from the product. It is likely that shepherds did not know what the sailors or the factory workers did and vice versa, although in at least one case black peasants in the Eastern Cape collected £46 to support suffering labourers in English textile factories.[117] Nonetheless, the international division of labour has created very distinct lines between the different stages of production and thereby contributed to a division between those in colonial areas and those in colonizing areas, the periphery and the core.

In this thesis we will mainly deal with the first three stages. However, none of them should be regarded as static categories. No farmer hires a shepherd if there is no demand for it just as no manufacturer hires a labourer if a machine is more profitable. The stages were results of historic processes of capital

[117] Bundy, C 1979, p. 60

accumulation, or if you will, capitalist production on a world scale. This commodity chain was thus a structure in a certain historical time and place, thus itself a process, which was formed by the actors involved. But Cape wool farmers and labourers were also involved in a local process of dispossession and proletarianization, in which farm labour must be regarded.

Labour in wool farming in the periphery meant capitalist production. As in the core, the commodification of labour followed. Crais suggests that the labour force on wool farms was largely proletarianized in the 1840s. While that may have been the case in some regions we must remember that there were many who resisted proletarianization. And labour relations were formed from this struggle.

The dispossession of black peasants aimed at proletarianization, but race was not the only decisive factor in the nineteenth century. In fact, the Cape had the most liberal constitution in the world. Every male could vote – if he was rich enough, that is.[118] Some black peasants also prospered for quite a while during the late nineteenth century, as Bundy has shown. Due to the "appreciation by peasants of wool as a cash crop",[119] many of them started to farm with wool. The high wool price was the main reason for this. But they also farmed with barley, wheat and oats for which the implementation of the ox-drawn plough was crucial. The peasant activities were often combined with transport riding. There were even peasants who hired labour, and thus wanted to advance to the class of farmer. The relative success of peasants meant that they could find other ways of making a living than becoming labourers on farms.[120] Many of the peasants were tenants, living on land belonging to white farmers. Some of them offered labour to farmers during parts of the year, but others were cash rent tenants.[121] The success of the peasantry threatened white farmers, who wanted their labour.

White farmers unified against the peasantry, and were supported by the state. During the late nineteenth century, and even more so during the twentieth century, measures to prevent black peasants from being independent from white farmers were taken by the state. For example, several location acts, aimed at limiting cash tenancy in favour of labour tenancy and cash wage labour, were passed in parliament, but their impact was rather limited. The 1913 *Natives Land Act* and the 1936 *Native Trust and Land Act* limited the amount of land available for black people to 14 per cent of the country. But they also fortified capitalist relations of production in the countryside as they aimed at abolishing tenancy relations in favour of cash wage labour and labour tenancy.[122]

---

[118] Ross, R 1999, p. 48.

[119] Bundy, C 1979, p. 76.

[120] Bundy, C 1979, pp. 77, 79.

[121] Bundy, C 1979, p. 79.

[122] Bundy, C 1979, p. 134-37 .

Luxemburg described the process of capital expansion and its effects on the black peasantry and the Afrikaner farmers. She asserted that the Afrikaners had replaced the natural economy with simple commodity production, which was replaced by capitalism. She argued that capitalism relies on other modes of production for labour and raw material. At the same time, however, capitalism consumes other modes of production and becomes dominant. Wool farming definitely benefitted from other modes of production, both for labour and reproduction. But Luxemburg clearly did not analyse wool farming. Instead, she argued that until the 1860s the Cape was a peasant economy and emphasized the importance of the mining industry, which created a larger interest among British and other international capital, as the driving force behind the capitalist transition.[123] Wool farming was never a peasant activity in the Cape. However, the mining industry accelerated both the dispossession of the peasantry as labour demands increased, and the capitalist transformation in general. This affected farming insofar as there was competition over labour and the cash economy increased. Morris argues for the Highveld that the "development of capitalist production relations elsewhere, mainly in mining [...], and the consequent creation of a larger home market [...]" started to change relations in farming.[124] Although most of the labourers were labour tenants, these worked with the means of production owned by the farmer. And the "surplus labour was extracted [...]" from the labour tenant "through the appropriation of the surplus value embodied in the agricultural commodities he produced".[125] These relations were visible in Cape wool farming already during the mid-nineteenth century. We should therefore at least try to find out if there were other factors involved in the transformation of labour relations.

The position in the capitalist world-economy, wherein wool was important and maize was not on a global scale, must surely have had an impact. Production and sale of wool can, however, not alone account for accumulation of capital, and capital alone did not transform labour relations. The nature of farming operations and the prerequisites in the Cape for wool farming and capital accumulation must therefore be given a central role in an analysis of labour relations. Luxemburg, Morris and others have pointed out several important aspects of the capitalist transformation in South Africa, but largely disregarded the actual production process, which is the central arena for class struggle. They have thereby overlooked the most profound part of capitalist production: the commodity. By analysing the production of the commodity we will be able to explain how labour relations changed in a way that visualizes the actors and their relationship to the structures that both helped and hampered them.

---

[123] Luxemburg, R 2003, pp. 348-50, 392-97.

[124] Morris, M 1976, p. 293.

[125] Morris, M 1976, p. 305 (304-06).

CHAPTER 3

Wool Farming and Labour – an Overview

Statistical material from censuses constitutes an important part of the empirical material for this thesis. Initially, an overview of the central statistical material is in place. The relevant categories are shepherds, sheep and livestock, farmers, farm labourers and wool exports.

Table 2. Shepherds, sheep and pastoral farmers in the Cape, 1875 to 1946.

Year	Shepherds	Sheep (mil)	Sheep/shepherd	Farmers	Shepherd/farmer
1875	17,233	10.9	633	8,524	2.0
1891	38,869	16.7	430	15,846	2.5
1904	34,093	11.8	346	17,178	2.0
1911	42,582	17.1	402	18,664	2.3
1946	24,210	20.7	855		

Source: Cape of Good Hope Census 1875, pp. 185, xiii ; Cape of Good Hope Census 1891, pp. 304-05, 438; Cape of Good Hope Census 1904, pp. 344-45, 478; South Africa Census 1911, pp. 564-65, 1208-09; South Africa Census 1946, vol V; Agricultural census 1945-46, pp. 102-03, 110.

It is clear that the number of shepherds was not only related to the number of sheep; the number of sheep per shepherd fluctuated significantly during this period. The figures for 1875 are uncertain; the census only mentions "pastoral servants" and not shepherds or herds. Pastoral servants may have included the entire labour force on pastoral farms, which means that the number of shepherds was considerably lower. Ultimately, the trend during the first half of the twentieth century was that fewer shepherds were hired, and that each shepherd was responsible for more sheep. One main concern of the analysis will therefore be to explain changes in the ratio between sheep and shepherds.

While the number of sheep per shepherd indicates the relationship between labourer and means of production, that is, how much each shepherd could produce through herding, the number of shepherd per farmer indicates how farmers organized production. During the 1870s and 1880s farmers managed to increase the shepherding labour force, but could not keep it around the turn of the century. However, as the number of shepherds per farmer increased again in 1911, farmers could find shepherds.

The censuses mention shepherds and herds in the same category. The two have not been enumerated separately. We must therefore consider if changes in the number of shepherds were caused by other livestock, some of which were herded, such as goats and to some extent cattle.

Table 3. Livestock (cattle and goats) and shepherds or herds in the Cape 1875 to 1946.

Year	Cattle	Goats	Total livestock	(Shep)herds	Livestock/herd
1875	1,111,713	3,065,202	4,176,915	17,233	242
1891	2,210,834	6,628,037	8,838,871	38,869	227
1904	1,954,390	7,162,463	9,116,853	34,093	267
1911	2,715,330	7,953,414	10,668,744	42,582	251
1946	4,008,981	3,380,426	7,389,407	23,624	313

Source: Cape of Good Hope Census 1875, p xiii; Cape of Good Hope Census 1891, p 438-39; Cape of Good Hope Census 1904, p. 478-79; South Africa Census 1911, pp. 564-65, 1208-09; South Africa Census 1946; 1945-46, p. 94-95, 113; Agricultural census 1945-46, pp. 94-95, 111.

Cattle and goats certainly contributed to an increased demand for herds during the late nineteenth century as the total number doubled between 1875 and 1891 and also increased further during the twentieth century. But the number of livestock per herdsman did not change considerably; it fluctuated between 227 and 267 per herdsman between 1875 and 1911, but during the first half of the twentieth century each herdsman became responsible for considerably more livestock. The fluctuations were, however, similar to those of sheep per shepherd. Altogether, cattle and goats cannot explain to any great extent increasing and decreasing numbers of shepherds or herds.

A large share of the labour force on Cape farms were mainly recruited from the black and coloured peasantry. Therefore, those two categories will be compared in order to analyse the proletarianization process in the Cape. As the category farm labourer included also those who worked in agriculture, not only in pastoralism, their number does not indicate the development in wool farming exclusively. However, many of the farms in the Cape were pastoral, and particularly focused on wool. It is therefore relevant to include also the farm labour force.

Table 4. Farm labourers and peasants in the Cape and their share of the total population in the Cape 1891 to 1946.

	Farm labourers		Peasants		Population
Year	No	% of pop	No	% of pop	No
1891	57,825	3.8	489,037	32.0	1,527,224
1904	85,854	3.5	757,066	31.4	2,409,804
1911	89,195	3.5	749,589	29.2	2,564,965
1946	242,967	6.0	491,462	12.1	4,053,848

Source: Cape of Good Hope Census 1891, pp. 18-19, 304-05; Cape of Good Hope Census 1904, pp. 344-45; South Africa Census 1911, pp. 8, 564-65; 1946, Vol I, V.

It is obvious that the farm labourers increased most drastically during the first half of the twentieth century, as much as 83 per cent between 1911 and 1946 compared to a 58 per cent increase in the total population during those years. But there was a steady increase also between 1891 and 1904, which more or less corresponds to the increase of the total population, indicating that farmers could find labour. As the number of peasants decreased drastically after 1911, while the farm labour force increased, we should assume that the transformation from peasant to labourer mainly took place during the twentieth century. Interestingly, there was no significant change in the ratio between farm labourers and peasants between 1891 and 1911.The proletarianization process was thus slow around the turn of the century, which will be analysed in relation to stock ownership and the generational and gendered division of labour.

As almost all Cape wool was exported until the 1940s, we must also view the export figures in order to understand the development of the industry.

Table 5. Cape and South African wool exports 1860 to 1950.

Cape			SA		
Year	*Lbs.*	*£*	*Year*	*Lbs.*	*£*
1860	23,172,785	1,446,510	1910	121,668,932	3,830,830
1865	32,767,679	1,680,826	1915	170,009,886	5,380,281
1870	37,283,291	1,669,518	1920	119,504,747	15,988,103
1875	40,339,674	2,855,899	1925	208,615,868	15,095,446
1880	42,468,662	2,429,371	1930	275,024,421	8,644,490
1885	34,432,562	1,426,108	1935	259,791,037	9,515,832
1890	65,655,917	2,196,040	1939	187,329,957	7,256,301
1895	65,632,613	1,695,920	1940*		
1900	27,671,036	837,809	1945	154,071,706	10,693,943
1905	63,473,934	1,887,459	1950	187,158,354	61,105,223
1909	101,007,893	2,820,716			

Source: *Statistical Register* 1886-1909; *Annual Statement on Trade and Shipping* 1910-50. * Not available.

The success of wool farming continued also after the 1860s and the price for wool reached a peak in 1875. But thereafter the wool price fell and never returned to previous levels. Clearly, such a development implied that not all farmers could accumulate capital, which meant they were forced to other solutions for their livelihood. However, the amount of wool exported continued to increase, reaching more than 100 million lbs in 1909, which brought in nearly £3 million to the Cape farmers, merchants and the state. After the creation of the Union of South Africa in 1910, wool exports and the wool price fluctuated due to wars and depression. The first half of the 1920s meant an increase of exports by 75 per cent, but the price was more or less unchanged. In 1930 the exports were higher than any previous year, but the price was only little more than half compared to 1925. The marks of the Depression were even more visible in 1932 when a record was reached in wool exports; more than 300 million lbs. was exported, also then at a low price. But the amount of wool exported was still enough to make wool the most important agricultural export product, and in the 1950s it was second only to gold as export product.

CHAPTER 4

Wool Farming, the 1860 and 1870s

Kraaling and trekking

Before we can analyse labour relations in wool farming we have to establish the condition of farming operations. Some descriptions of wool farming are available. For example, J. Noble's *Descriptive Handbook of the Cape Colony*, published in 1875, offers several insights. According to Noble the sheep farms were "of various sizes. The general average is somewhere above 3,000 morgen [...]. There are some, however, that are four or five times this extent [...]."[126] The size of the farm did not necessarily indicate success. Thus a smaller farm with green pastures could have been better than a large one with dry veld. In the dry areas of the Karroo, a large farm was necessary. For example in dry districts one sheep required two morgen for grazing, while in other areas the ratio was the reversed.

Nor did the size of the farm affect how farming was conducted. Noble stated that on both the larger and smaller farms "there are out-stations, or divisions of both flocks and farm, and under the care of separate herds. The old and still most common practice of farming is to graze the flocks by day, under the care of a herd, who guides their depasturing over the part of the farm allotted to the special flock under his charge, and at evening time drives them home to the kraal, where they are kept all night."[127] The practice of using shepherds was seemingly the overall most common way of wool farming in the 1870s, just as it had been the previous decades. The number of outstations, of course, varied according to the size of the farm and the number of sheep on it. Large farms, with several thousand head of sheep, thus had more outstations and more shepherds than a small farm with few sheep.

The outstation was also called a Veepost, and was the place where shepherds lived. Some had their families along, and some lived alone. But there were also many shepherds who stayed close to the homestead and herded the sheep from

126 Noble, J 1875, p. 258.

127 Noble, J 1875, pp. 258-59.

there. They lived where there was a kraal for the sheep they were herding. This proximity to the animals was necessary for their duties as the guardians of the sheep. A shepherd was expected to protect the sheep both night and day, from animals and stock thieves, and to watch the condition of the sheep. This could not be done without staying close to the sheep all day and all night.

During the night the sheep were placed in a *kraal*. The kraal originally referred to a rounded, sheltered place, where people and animals lived. It was thus common that the dwelling place of black people was called a kraal; both people and animals lived there. In this case, however, it refers to the place where sheep spent the night. Noble described the appearance of the kraal in the following way: "The kraal, or fold, is made of various materials, the commonest fences being a high, thick hedge of thorny bushes, or an enclosure built with blocks cut out of the accumulated dung and *debris* of the old kraal."[128] The kraals were thus mostly made of natural material found nearby on the farm. But stone walls became more frequent "in many places where stones are handy". Furthermore, "where the farmer has the enterprise and ability, the stone walls are converted into sheds".[129] It appears that some farmers, i.e. those with enterprise, were not satisfied with the shelter provided by the open kraal, and made investments into sheds that could protect the sheep better from the various threats in the Karroo.

Somewhat romantically, Noble thought that "[t]he coming home of flocks at night is a pretty sight". Surely, he must have referred to the simultaneous movement of a large number of animals, or to the fact that the sheep represented a large part of the wealth of the Cape Colony. Aestheticism aside, bringing the sheep home to the kraal every night was not only a way of protecting the sheep, it also provided farmers with control over the farming operations. It "gives the full opportunity to the owners to count them, look to their health, and other matters of management, as well as to check depredation both human and brute".[130] Shepherds were relied upon and provided necessary skills, but were not automatically trusted. The human depredation, meaning the condition of the shepherds, was therefore controlled when the sheep were brought home. As the shepherds were in charge of the sheep, they could potentially damage the capital of the farm if they did not perform their work properly.

While kraaling provided a solution to farmers' requirements regarding protection of sheep at night, it also implied that they would have to be moved, trekked, to the grazing pasture the next morning. The trekking of sheep sometimes required shepherds to take the sheep on several hours' walk every day, which caused numerous problems in the long run for farmers. As Noble

[128] Noble, J 1875, p. 259.

[129] Noble, J 1875, p. 259.

[130] Noble, J 1875, p. 259.

pointed out, "this kraaling has no doubt an injurious effect both on the farm and the flocks, injures the wool and the health of the sheep, [...], and wearing out the pasture by constant treading of the ever-moving animals."[131] The long-used way of farming with kraaling and trekking may have been the easiest solution, but it would ultimately lead to the demise of the entire industry in the colony. Already in the first half-century after the establishment of a commercial wool industry in the Cape it was evident that the expansion of capital and subsequent exploitation of the land had made a severe impact on the soil to the extent that it could not continue. The exploitation of the thereto relatively untouched pastures of the Karroo quickly made a mark, and started to deteriorate the foundation of any farming industry, the land.

Noble was not the only observer who noticed that the practices in wool farming destroyed the veld. Several other veterinarians, wool experts and politicians demanded changes to be made. There was, however, controversy regarding the extent of damage made by trekking of sheep across farms. Some farmers did not regard it as damaging, and saw no reason to change matters. The M. L. A[132] for Graaff-Reinet, Mr. Ziervogel, for example, suggested to the *Select Committee on Fencing Bill* in 1872 that it made no difference to the pasture if the stock was kraaled or not. He agreed that driving the sheep across the farm could cause great damage, but insisted that it "depends very much upon the management of the sheep, and upon the way in which they are driven", but he had not had any personal experience of destruction of veld due to kraaling.[133]

The advocates of new methods of farming did seem to gain the upper hand though, and some farmers seemed to be set on reversing the marks left by kraaling and trekking. Noble pointed out that "[a]rrangements are being made by some of the eastern and western farmers by which the sheep can run night and day, and rest in their leisure in the open veldt, and many miles of fences for this purpose have already been put up".[134] The solution to the problems caused by constant trekking of sheep over the farms was to subdivide the farm and create enclosed camps, in which the sheep could graze during the day and sleep during the night. For this purpose farmers required fences.

---

131 Noble, J 1875, p. 259

132 Member of the Legislative Assembly.

133 Select Committee on Fences Bill, 1872. Evidence of Mr. Ziervogel, M. L. A. Graaff-Reinet, pp. 14, 9.

134 Noble, J 1875, pp. 259.

Fencing the veld

A proof of the importance given to fencing was the introduction of a Fencing Bill in 1872. The Select Committee appointed to investigate the matter took evidence from a number of farmers and representatives of local communities around the Cape. Most of the witnesses agreed that fencing was necessary to prevent the spread of erosion, which became visible in the formation of sluits and gulleys, i.e. deep furrows, in the tracks of sheep and cattle across the Karroo. Several witnesses testified to the value of having enclosed farms. For example, P. Watermeyer, the M. L. A. for Richmond, stated that according to his own experience "land fenced in is trebled and quadrupled in value".[135] His viewpoint was shared by several others, who stated that the value of the farm would increase substantially if enclosed. But this did not mean that the bill should be implemented. On the contrary, many suggested that it was not possible to implement the bill at that stage, primarily as it was unfair to the poorer farmers, and that many of them would not afford to enclose their farms. J. van der Byl in Caledon reported that his brother had a farm with enclosures, which he paid £300 for. Evidently the price was £75 per mile for fencing and one shilling the running yard for stone walls (about £80 per mile).[136] A farm of 3,000 morgen would thus cost £1,000 to enclose, a substantial investment for most farmers. Therefore, it was better to wait, according to some witnesses. The Bill did not become implemented for another decade, and then in a slightly different version, which did not make it applicable if it was not supported by a majority of the farmers in the district.

Despite the controversies over the Fencing Bill, fencing was undertaken in a number of districts, as stated by Noble and several of the witnesses to the Select Committee. The reasons for this was evidently related to the damaging effects of kraaling and trekking on the pastures of the farms, but this practice also damaged the other valuable asset for farmers, the sheep and their wool.

Trekking and kraaling affected sheep in four different ways. Firstly, the long walks to and from pastures every day made them tired, which affected their overall condition and thereby the quality of the wool. Secondly, during the walks the sheep came close to bushes, and sticks, which got stuck in the wool, thereby reducing its quality. Thirdly, when the sheep were kraaled they were forced to spend the night huddled up closely together and sleep in dung and debris, which got stuck in the wool. Fourthly, spending the night in the kraal facilitated the spread of diseases among the sheep.[137] J. van der Byl in Caledon thought that "it is very evident that the less cattle and stock are driven about,

---

[135] Select Committee on Fences Bill, 1872, Evidence of Mr. P. Watermeyer, M. L. A., Richmond, p. 33.

[136] Select Committee on Fences Bill, 1872. Evidence of J. van der Byl, Caledon, p. 17.

[137] McKee, W. M. 1913, pp. 330-33; Archer, S 2000, p. 686.

the more advantageous it is to them; and the driving about is, of course, avoided when they are left to feed at their own discretion."[138] Similarly, John Ogilvie in Fort Beaufort believed that fencing would make the sheep free from scab, and it would also increase the weight of the wool. Furthermore, it would double the number of sheep on farms.[139] H. W. Breda, M. L. A. for Caledon, agreed with Ogilvie and concluded that with enclosed farms the stock "would be in better condition, and consequently their produce would be more valuable. It would certainly give a heavier fleece of wool, and the fibre of the wool would obtain higher prices in the market."[140] While improvements of the veld would be a long-term investment, which would pay off in the future, the improvement of the wool, which was the foundation of farmers' income, would be profitable already in the short run. Farming with enclosed camps was thus undoubtedly a better option than relying on trekking and kraaling. Although other actors than the Cape farmers affected the price of wool, it was clear that they could greatly enhance their income if these measures were taken. In this case, the fellow sheep producing colony in Australia was referred to.[141]

Better sheep, better wool

The debate about enclosing of lands obviously became public in the 1870s, but it was not the start of enclosures in the Cape. Farmers had started building enclosures already in the 1850s. At that point there were no fences available, and instead stones were used to create enclosures. The Rubidges in Graaff-Reinet were probabaly among the first to implement these stone walls. Charles Rubidge built a "stone wall enclosure of 5 acres [...]" in 1853.[142] This enclosure was supposedly for sheep, although it is not stated in the diary. The early enclosing of lands is nonetheless important as it demonstrates that this activity was not merely a result of threats of soil erosion voiced by lobbyists or experts. Farmers built enclosures because they would be profitable. Surely, the soil erosion was a factor that Charles Rubidge may have been aware of, but at that point it had not yet become a matter of public debate and there were no demands on farmers to enclose their farms. This demonstrates that the arguments by both Beinart and van Sittert must be revised. Van Sittert claims that there were five different reasons for fencing. Firstly that it improved the

---

138 Select Committee on Fences Bill, 1872. Evidence of J. van der Byl, M. L. C., Caledon, p. 18.

139 Select Committee on Fences Bill, 1872. Evidence of John Ogilvie, Fort Beaufort, p. 24.

140 Select Committee on Fences Bill, 1872. Evidence of H. W. Breda, M.L.A., Caledon, p. 26.

141 Select Committee on Fences Bill, 1872. For example, Evidence of E. J. Dunn, pp. 2-8.

142 CL MS 6189, Old Extracts from Old Wellwood, 1853.

veld, secondly that it improved the health of the stock and quality of the wool, thirdly that it enabled farmers to manage increasing stock numbers, fourthly that it kept jackals out and fifthly that it kept stock thieves out.[143] All of these reasons were no doubt important to farmers, but they clearly started enclosing for mainly one reason. As seen in the case of the Rubidges it was a way to improve the farm and thereby produce better sheep and wool. Saving the farm from erosion and producing better wool did not constitute two opposites, they coincided to a great extent; improving the veld would improve also the wool as it provided sheep with better grazing. The low frequency of fencing in the western parts of the Cape, which was not stock-farming, around the turn of the century also shows that improvement of farms and production was a primary reason for fencing.[144] Wine and fruit farming in the western parts of the Cape was not immediately aided by fences, for example.

Another advantage with enclosures was that it would save the expense of herds, at least according to the witnesses to the Select Committee. Once the farm was divided into camps the shepherds would more or less be made redundant. Mr. H. W. Breda from Caledon even thought that fencing would mean a "great saving in the expense of herds".[145] Several other witnesses, for example T. King of Victoria East and J. Miller of Port Elizabeth, agreed with him. P. Watermeyer also believed this would be the case, but he was not only concerned with the costs of having shepherds, but also the cost of them losing sheep. He had experience with several bad shepherds, who, according to him, lost sheep several times a week.[146] This view was not voiced by other witnesses, but it may have been shared by many farmers throughout the Cape. However, the allegedly poor skills of shepherds were a main reason for erecting fences. Not all farmers were convinced that the fences would replace the shepherds. J. van der Byl argued that the farmer "would still require for his flocks an equal number of herds". He meant that the sheep would go through wire fences and walk onto the land of neighbours, which meant that a farmer "would require to bring home his flocks of an evening, just as he does now." A wire fence would thus not be enough as the sheep could slip through. Van der Byl agreed, however, that subdividing the farm into camps would be another matter. It would save the expense of shepherds "to a great extent". However, according to

143 Van Sittert, L 2002, p. 98.

144 See Cape of Good Hope Census 1891, pp. 456-57; Cape of Good Hope Census 1904, pp. 506-07; South Africa Census 1911, pp. 1254-59; Van Sittert, L 2002, p. 102-06, shows how fences were initially spread in the eastern parts.

145 Select Committee on Fences Bill, 1872. Evidence of Mr. H. W. Breda, M. L. A., Caledon, p. 26.

146 Select Committee on Fences Bill, 1872. Evidence of T. King, M. L. A., Victoria East, p. 29; J. Miller, Port Elizabeth, p 45; P. Watermeyer, M. L. A., Richmond, pp. 35-36.

him the farmer would still require a few herds to protect the crops and the garden.[147] Thus, they could not be dispensed with all together.

Reducing labour costs in the form of shepherds did not seem to be the most important issue for the Cape wool farmers, at least not those who testified to the Select Committee. A reason for this may have been that they all belonged to the more successful farmers, most of them also politicians, which meant they were men of substantial financial assets. However, the difference between farming with shepherds and with fences was quite significant. The Select Committee provided a calculation of the costs involved. According to the calculation an enclosed farm of 7,000 acres with 6,000 sheep would require four shepherds at £36 each, which meant £144 in total per year. Without fences the same farm would require twelve shepherds at £18 each, which meant an annual cost of £216 in total.[148] Fencing would thus reduce labour costs to the farmer by £72 per year, a saving most farmers would have been attracted by.

The wage figures are, however, misleading. Few shepherds earned £18 per year, most probably earned around £10 or less.[149] The saving may therefore have been substantially less to the average farmer. Erecting fences may, however, have been important to farmers in other ways. John Ogilvie in Fort Beaufort argued that enclosing farms would "make something of the nigger. Finding that we can be perfectly independent of them if it does not make them good, there is a chance of their becoming better servants."[150] Unenclosed farms automatically created a situation where the farmers to a great extent became dependent on the shepherds, who therefore had an advantage against the farmers. The fences would show them that they were not necessary for farming operations and consequently, according to Ogilvie, have a disciplinary effect. Ogilvie's argument is quite illuminating of labour relations in the Cape. While many farmers, seemingly, could not afford fencing, they simultaneously had problems controlling the labour force. It is possible, and even likely, that the ones who could not afford fencing were the same ones who had problems with the labourers. Lack of money and capital meant that they relied on wages in kind, and also various forms of tenancy. Both these factors contributed to the labourers' ability to gain some independence from farmers, which was perceived by farmers as lack of discipline. Being dependent on the labourers was not what farmers wished for. But as long as shepherds were required for farming, they would stay on the farms and have a degree of relative independence.

---

[147] Select Committee on Fences Bill, 1872. Evidence of Mr. van der Byl, M. L. C., Caledon, pp. 19-20.

[148] Select Committee on Fences Bill, 1872. Appendix, p. 48.

[149] Based on accounts from Rubidge diaries and Commission on Native Affairs 1865.

[150] Select Committee on Fences Bill, 1872. Evidence of Mr. John Ogilvie, Fort Beaufort, p. 24.

Boundary and internal fencing

A general argument for enclosing farms, and other sorts of property, is that it was a way of marking private property and demonstrating power relations in the rural areas. This is, of course, true. It definitely demonstrated that those who owned farms could decide who was allowed to enter the property. However, fencing in the Cape was not merely a way of demonstrating power relations or a symbol of the colonial intrusion. It was done for practical reasons, whereof the wish for better wool production, and thereby more profit, was the main one. There is one crucial point that illuminates the issue: the difference between boundary fencing and internal fencing. Whereas boundary fencing definitely demarcated private property and established clear and definite boundaries between farms, the purpose of internal fencing was merely to create camps for sheep and livestock in general. In the Cape it was definitely obvious that internal fences were being erected at a much greater speed than those enclosing the boundary.

The reasons for the faster rate of internal fencing were rooted in practicality and purposefulness. Firstly, creating camps required less fences than the boundary, so it could be done gradually and was therefore quicker. Secondly, as boundary fencing was a long-term process, it was to a great extent useless until the whole farm was enclosed. Having a stretch of the farm fenced may have hindered intrusion in that particular part of the farm, but it did nothing for the rest. Furthermore, as far as sheep management was concerned internal fencing was far more important than having the boundary enclosed. Enclosed boundaries simply demarcated the boundary, and prevented sheep to exit the farm to some extent, but did not change the way of farming with shepherds and long treks and kraaling; the two elements that destroyed the wool and the veld.

One of the sources that best describes this process, and the challenges posed to farmers, are the Rubidge diaries. It is unclear when fencing started on Wellwood. Archer mentions that the first wire fence was erected in 1877.[151] However, already in 1862 Charles Rubidge "bought wire (No. 1) and standards as samples [...]", they were one of "the first in E. Province" to do so.[152] In 1874 it is mentioned that work with preparing for fencing was conducted and in 1875 the Rubidges "[c]arried on fencing for the big kraal".[153] This seems to have been wire fences. At that point they had already erected some enclosures on the farm. Some examples of these are the "lower enclosure" and the "ostrich enclosure" (1875).[154] As mentioned previously some of them were made of

151 Archer, S 2000, p. 681.

152 CL MS 6189, Old Extracts from Old Wellwood, 1862.

153 Rubidge diaries, July 30, 1874; June 17, 1875.

154 Rubidge diaries, July 14, Aug. 9, 1875.

stones and bushes, but some wire fences also seems to have been used.[155] These enclosures were in use at the time. There were thus at least three enclosed camps in use by 1875 and in 1880 there appears to have been six camps, as one of the labourers "washed dam in camp No 6".[156] In 1880, the extent of boundary fencing was about 7,000 yards, but possibly more. The entire boundary appears to have been about 32,000 yards. The Rubidges had thus only fenced a little more than a quarter of the boundary at that time while there were six camps. One of the camps that were completed in 1880 was called "new camp".[157] It bordered one of the old camps, the lower camp, which indicates the development of fencing; a new camp was established next to an older one. This method may seem simple, but saved a lot of energy and money. Assuming that each camp had four sides, one side of the camp was already finished, meaning that there were only three sides to fence. Furthermore, this method added to the boundary fence each time a new camp was created along the boundary line.

Although there was awareness on Wellwood to practice rotational grazing, the old system of kraaling and trekking was still used. In fact, new kraals were built or repaired during the late 1870s. For example, in March 1877 the Rubidges completed "new kraal with dung on walls".[158] The following year in November they "[m]ade new kraal" and in December "[t]wo men commenced work at kraal".[159] The practice of kraaling was thus not at all to an end. Quite the contrary, completing the fencing of the farm and implementation of a rotational system of grazing was a long-term project and in the meantime the sheep would have to be protected. The kraals therefore constituted a vital part of sheep farming also on those farms that could be called progressive. The technique used in making kraals, where stones were piled on each other, could also be used for making larger enclosures. In several cases during the late 1870s the enclosures used on Wellwood were made of stone.[160] Investments were thus not just made in new technology, that is, fences, but also in old technology. The ratio between investments in old and new technology was definitely in favour of the latter, but withholding investments in kraals was equally bad for business as a lack of investment in fences.

Some of the camps were, however, not used for sheep exclusively. On Wellwood there were both barley and lucerne fields, which were enclosed. The barley was used for rations and for the household, the lucerne was used for drought feeding. As the witness to the Select Committee pointed out, farmers

155 CL MS 6189, Old Extracts from Old Wellwood.

156 Rubidge diaries, Dec. 7, 1880.

157 Rubidge diaries, Sept. 10, 1880.

158 Rubidge diaries, March 15, 1877.

159 Rubidge diaries, Nov. 4, Dec. 12, 1878.

160 Rubidge diaries, June 1, 1876; March 28, 1877.

still required shepherds to protect their crops and gardens. The enclosures were also often limited. P. Watermeyer in Richmond stated that except for occasional enclosures for animals "[f]encing in our part of the country is limited to small plots of agricultural land; [...]. But those enclosures, as a rule, are close to the homestead, which is generally situated somewhere about the centre of the farm."[161] This was exactly the case with Charles Rubidge's barley field. The barley had to be shielded from the animals in a way that would ensure the best management of both. The fence kept animals and people from entering the field, and on the other side of the fence the animals could graze and sleep for themselves both day and night.

In a setting like the Karroo, with large tracts of land that could not be supervised, it seems likely that farmers wanted fences in order to keep people off the farms, prevent thefts and trespassing etc. This was certainly the case with many of the farmers, but it was actually not the most important reason for fencing. For the Rubidges it was definitely more important to create camps than to fence the boundary. Had they thought boundary fencing was more important, they would have invested more heavily in it in order to complete the boundary fence more quickly. From this we can conclude that trespassing, theft etc. was not considered a large enough problem by the farmers to create a rush for boundary fencing, especially not in the Graaff-Reinet district. Creating enclosed farms in order to demonstrate ownership was perhaps important to some, but people who lived in the area knew the farm boundaries quite well, or could guess their location. Trespassing was therefore mostly a conscious act, without necessarily including intentional theft. More often it seems that trespassing was conducted in order to graze on the neighbouring farm, or by people on trek who sought temporary grazing for their stock.

Early fencing in the Cape must, however, also include a discussion of ostriches. Ostriches became popular among farmers in the Cape in the 1860s and 1870s. European ladies of the bourgeoisie started to wear hats decorated with ostrich feathers, which created a wool boom that lasted until 1913. Farmers in the Cape profited from this.[162]

On Wellwood there had been attempts to farm with ostriches already in the 1860s, but there were only a handful of birds on the farm until the mid-1870s when "Henry's ostrich hen laid the first egg".[163] The following decades the number grew and made up a considerable and increasing share of the farm's income; in 1911 there were almost 200 farmed ostriches on Wellwood.[164] Throughout the Colony ostriches increased ten times between 1875 and 1911

---

161 Select Committee on Fences Bill, 1872. Evidence of Mr. P. Watermeyer, M. L. A., Richmond, p. 32.

162 Smith, K 1976, p. 87; Beinart, W 2001, p. 41.

163 Rubidge diaries, Oct. 19, 1875. Rubidge accounts, 1875.

164 Beinart, W 2008, p. 316.

and must be considered as a tremendously good complement to most farmers. Ostrich farming contributed to both cultivation of lucerne, which was required as fodder for the ostriches, and fencing. It is usually stated that ostriches, unlike sheep, could not be herded. However, the Rubidges paid wages to an "ostrich herd (2 months) 10/-" in 1907.[165] The relatively low wage indicates that a child or young person was responsible for herding the birds. Generally, the references to ostrich herds are few, however. Enclosing them was therefore the most widespread method for successful ostrich farming. The Rubidge diaries mention a farmer called Booysen, who seems to have been among the first to farm with ostriches in the 1860s. But at that time "fencing [was] unknown. Booysen had built large stone wall enclosure. C. Rubidge copied and built against mountain [...]".[166] The stone walls, later seen on many places on Wellwood, thus functioned well as enclosures for the ostriches. The first camps for the birds were therefore made up of stone walls, and were later combined with wire fences, but also other fences.

Although ostrich farming was not widespread until the 1870s we should assume that many of the first enclosures in the Cape were used for this purpose. Some of the camps on Wellwood were, for example, called "the ostrich enclosure(s)". There appears to have been at least four in the 1880s, the "2 upper ostrich camps" and the "2 lower ostrich camps".[167] These camps seemingly made up the largest share of camps on Wellwood at the time. In the middle of the 1880s there were probably six camps altogether on the farm, but possibly more. But the ostrich camps also benefitted wool farming. There is no doubt that sheep could graze in the same camps as the ostriches.[168] The fenced camps were used to combine the two. Wool farmers who had ostriches were consequently forced to fence their farms at a quicker rate than those who only had sheep and goats, which could be herded. This does not mean that all fencing was caused by ostriches, but their impact cannot be disregarded. The income from ostrich feathers definitely contributed to improvement of farms both regarding cultivation of lucerne and fencing. The fences were expensive, but generated income from both sheep and ostriches as they were combined.

Controlling nature for intensification of wool farming

One of the worst threats to sheep and farmers were droughts. Droughts were not unusual in the Karroo, quite the contrary; they were recurring at almost regular intervals. One especially severe drought occurred in 1873. Charles

---

165 Rubidge Accounts, Dec., 1907.

166 CL MS 6189, Old Extracts from Old Wellwood, 1866.

167 Rubidge diaries, May 29, 30, 1885.

168 Rubidge diaries, Jan. 8, 1886; April 17, 1895.

Rubidge reported in December that "[a]ll the sheep were sent away on account of the drought".[169] Some of the sheep stayed off the farm throughout January, thus having been away for more than a month. These flocks were spread out on at least three different farms and appear to have scattered during their time there; at the end of January 1874 Richard "went to Botha, Dippeinaar's & Du Toits [sic] to look for sheep and goats."[170] Du Toit's farm Dasjiefontein was neighbouring Wellwood, which suggests that the surrounding farms were primarily used when sending sheep away during droughts. There is no indication of a grazing fee being paid; perhaps neighbours helped each other out when necessary. However, sending the sheep off the farm could not be done every time a drought occurred. A better solution was required.

The best defence against droughts was, of course, a steady water supply. As Wellwood had no natural spring water, or a river, the issue was even more important. The search for water on the farm was conducted almost continuously, but it was seldom found. A second way to combat the effects of droughts was to make sure the veld was in its best possible condition. This could only be done through extended rotational grazing, which required subdivision of the farm into fenced camps.

During the drought of 1873 there was at least one dam on Wellwood, but it is uncertain how big it was. During the following year construction of a new dam, called the "Groote Dam" or Big Dam, began. Before the work was completed another dam, the "Willow dam" was being built. When the Groote Dam was completed in the beginning of 1875 Richard "put pump in the 'Bigdam'".[171] The Rubidges were thus progressive also when it came to water supply, and invested in a pump that would transport water from the dam to the veld. Later in 1875 two more dams were constructed. One of them, called the "long dam" was finished in October.[172] Dam building had been conducted for over two years by then. The long dam was the fourth dam to be built in the mid-1870s on the farm.

Despite lack of running water, Wellwood could demonstrate at least four dams, which could be used to enhance grazing pastures and expand cultivation of mealies, barley, lucerne and oranges. The dam with the pump further enabled the Rubidges to control the farm and utilize its resources, which must be seen as a vital part of reshaping the land in order to create a profitable wool industry. Trekking sheep to water might still have been necessary, but these investments made the farm better prepared for the next drought.

The lucerne was used for drought feeding, and it was of course important considering the climate in the Karroo. Having a supply of lucerne could be the

---

[169] Rubidge diaries, Dec. 7, 1873.

[170] Rubidge diaries, Jan. 30, 1874.

[171] Rubidge diaries, Jan. 20, 1875.

[172] Rubidge diaries, Oct. 19, Nov. 20, 1875.

difference between having to trek off the farm with the sheep and staying on it through a drought. To some extent it was thus more important to fence in the lucerne than to fence in the sheep. The lucerne had to be protected from animals trampling in it or eating it. Not just sheep, but also horses, mules, cattle and wild animals were threats to lucerne and other cultivations. Establishing a secure place to cultivate on was therefore a priority. Although rotational grazing and fenced camps would improve the veld and the grazing pastures, it could not be relied upon if droughts struck. But having a supply of lucerne could counter the effects of the drought, which gave room for improving the veld later. Cultivation of lucerne was of course made possible by the supply of water from the dams. Securing the water resources was thus pivotal to all other farming endeavours.

After plantation lucerne did not require much labour, except occasional weeding. This was conducted by women,[173] but also men and their sons were given this duty: "[l]et Danster & Klein D to weed in upper partition of lucerne field".[174] The harvest required additional labour, but it was easily found among the families on the farm. We know that children took part also in the harvest, and that it could be dangerous work; one day in 1886 a "Hottentot child had finger cut off by lucerne cutter".[175]

Droughts and soil erosion could also be combated through plantation. Especially aloes and prickly pear was used for this purpose. Neither of them were natural to southern Africa, but were planted. The aloe grew thick and tall and therefore made a good fence. Already in 1869 a "2nd Aloe fence [was] planted parallel to 2 stone walls" on Wellwood. Further work was done with "line of aloe fence" in 1877.[176] The prickly pear was introduced on Wellwood in the 1860s, and continued to be planted in new camps when they were completed. After completing a camp in 1880 Charles Rubidge noted: "[p]lanted prickly pears between my lower camp and new camp".[177]

The Rubidges did thus consider these plants already during the 1860s, which was long before the aloe and prickly pear had spread out and become characteristic of the Karroo vegetation. At this time the steel fences were expensive, and although the Rubidges were fairly wealthy, they did not purchase any larger quantities of wire fences nor invest in the labour to any great extent. Stone walls and aloes were, however, cheaper, and could provide good protection from erosion and keep animals enclosed. Despite the lack of wire fences there were therefore still opportunities to improve the pastures and implement new systems of grazing and farming in general. Natural and man-

---

173 Rubidge diaries, Jan 11, 1879.

174 Rubidge diaries, Dec. 26, 1879.

175 Rubidge diaries, Dec. 3, 1886.

176 CL MS 6189, Old Extracts from Old Wellwood, 1869; Rubidge diaries, April 2, 1877.

177 Rubidge diaries, Sept. 10, 1880.

made fences were combined in order to produce better wool and drought fodder, and to combat soil erosion. For the most part, the 1870s was a time when kraaling and trekking still played a vital role in wool farming, but the dams, cultivation of lucerne, mealies and barley had started to change farming practices.

CHAPTER 5

Labour Relations

The labour force

In this chapter the labour relations during the 1860s and 1870s will be established. Firstly the Cape broadly speaking will be treated, thereafter one particular farm, Wellwood.

One invaluable source is the *Commission on Native Affairs* in 1865, which contained replies to a questionnaire to farmers on their labour force. Altogether 77 farmers have been analysed from that report. For all the districts together, the average number of labourers – that is, men, women and children – on a farm was twelve. We should remember that many of the farmers who gave witness belonged to the more successful ones and were not representative of the farmers as a whole. According to the 1865 census there were only about two "agricultural labourers" per "farmer", which is considerably less than twelve. But that account was most likely not accurate in regards to the number of people who actually worked on farms. Tenants and bywoners, for example, were not a part of that group. However, it could also have meant that a large majority of farmers did not have any labourers at all, but were peasants, as that category was not included in the census.[178] But due to differences between districts, and between the farmers themselves, it is crucial to view each district separately. These are the results from those replies according to district, except Bathurst and Colesberg.

[178] Cape of Good Hope Census, 1865, Part VII, Occupation, p. 133-35.

Table 6. Average number of farm labourers according to district in the Eastern Cape, 1865.

District	Labourers	N
Albany	16.0	9
Alexandria	14.8	7
Victoria East	7.0	9
Bedford	14.0	3
Stockenstrom	8.5	2
Queenstown	9.1	7
Peddie	7.6	5
Albert	7.0	3
Aliwal North	9.1	8
Graaff-Reinet	11.3	4
Murraysburg	23.1	14
Middelburg	10.2	6
Total	12.3	77

Source: Commission on Native Affairs, 1865, Appendix No. 2, pp. 4-71. N=number of responding farmers.

The compilation is somewhat askew as there were different numbers of farmers responding from various districts, but it provides a strong indication of the composition of the labour force in the various districts. The variation in number, from less than 7 to as many as 23 not only demonstrates the difference between districts, but between various farmers. The average number for all districts, twelve, thus seems to be rather accurate. On some farms there were more, on others less, depending on the size of the farm, the number of sheep on it, and the farmer's ability to attract labour. But in order to give a more detailed account of labour practices, we must view the statements from farmers more closely.

The testimonies to the Commission complicate the issue of labour. W. M. Bowker on Thorn Kloof stated that he had "67 blacks of all sorts upon my farms, consisting of 14 men, and 7 women, that are constantly employed: the others are women and children; some are occasionally employed and always paid when at work."[179] We do not know how many farms Bowker had, but there were 35 people who did not work regularly, which means that the actual labour force for the whole year was considerably larger than the 21 regulars. The family relations among labourers were thus frequently exploited. The family members were allowed to live on the farm in exchange for labour when required.

The labour force on the farm Bowker called "my farm", Thorn Kloof, was not dispossessed of stock, quite the contrary. According to Bowker the servants

[179] Commission on Native Affairs,1865. Appendix No.2. Mr. W. M. Bowker, Albany, p. 4.

had about 500 small livestock and 35 head of cattle and some horses, "all these are herded with my own, free of all charge." The grazing rights were clearly a central part of the remuneration, but Bowker also paid cash wages: "My men servants receive from £1 sterling, down to 7s. 6d.; women 6s. to 3s., per month [...]." In addition to this he also gave rations, which amounted to 1 lb meal or corn and 2 lbs meat during nine months per year.[180] Apparently, the rations did not make up part of the wages for three months of the year, meaning that labourers would have to find their own food during that period. It is unclear which months the rations were given. The rations were not the only source of food for the labourers; they were allowed to "cultivate as much land as they choose, [...]". Bowker was, however, not impressed by their efforts: "[...] they do not dig up one acre in a year; this is the best argument that can be brought forward to prove that they are perfect strangers to hunger".[181]

Most farmers did not have as large a labour force as Bowker. The Bowker family was among the wealthiest of the 1820-settlers, which was a main reason for their success compared to others. Other farmers in Albany employed considerably less people. Joseph Gush employed six men and six boys; C. Rippon had two families in his employ, "out of which four individuals are in service"; J. K. Wilmot had five black men, three women and one boy. The wages did not differ that much though. Gush paid men "7s. 6d. to 9s. per month; boys 2s. 6d. to 4s. 6d." and Rippon "always give to herds [...] ten shillings per month". Wilmot stated that "men receive 10s. a month and the women 5s. The men get 3lbs. of food per diem and the women 2lbs. as rations, with clothes." Besides that they were also allowed grazing rights and the right to cultivate.[182]

In Victoria East, the district with the lowest average number of labourers, the wages were similar to other places. Joseph Gadd had four black herds. One of them was paid 12 shillings per month and the others were paid 10 shillings per month. However, unlike in almost all other cases, the "families of my herds do not reside on the farm". G. W. Morris on Douglas Dale had five servants and paid between 8 and 12 shillings per month. N. Ely on Brakfontein had "7 men servants, 3 maid servants, and 1 child [...]". The men were paid one cow per year and the maid servants £3 per year.[183]

The reason for the larger labour force in Albany and Bedford may have been that these areas were not exclusively stock farming regions; some cultivation also took place there. But Graaff-Reinet, Middelburg and Murraysburg, where the

---

180 Commission on Native Affairs,1865. App. 2. Mr. W. M. Bowker, Albany, p. 4.

181 Commission on Native Affairs,1865. App. 2. Mr. W. M. Bowker, Albany, p. 4.

182 Commission on Native Affairs, 1865. App. 2. Mr. Joseph Gush; C. Rippon; J. K. Wilmot, Albany, pp. 5-7.

183 Commission on Native Affairs, 1865. App. 2. Joseph Gadd; G. W. Morris; N. Ely, Victoria East, pp. 18-21.

average number of labourers was more than ten, were sheep farming regions. It thus seems that other factors decided the size of the labour force. We should assume that the farmers' ability to pay wages was a crucial factor. But the wages were not higher in these areas. In Graaff-Reinet the wages ranged from five shillings paid to women and ten shillings for men. One farmer, James Parkes, presumably at the farm Wheatlands, had twenty labourers "on average" and paid slightly more: between nine and fifteen shillings per month. The grazing rights occurred also there, but Parkes only allowed "[a] limited number; when that is exceeded they are made to pay a rent, either by labour or money".[184]

In Murraysburg the wages ranged from seven shillings per month to as much as £1. All fourteen farmers in that district who replied to the Commission stated that they allowed grazing rights. Some, like W. T. Burger, "[a]llow them to keep stock only", while others, like T. J. van Heerden, allowed the labourers both grazing and cultivation.[185] In Middelburg the wages were more or less similar to those in Murraysburg, around 10 shillings per month and grazing rights, although Daniel Kruger and a Mr. Whitehead only paid wages in kind.[186] It was thus not higher wages or more liberal grazing rights that contributed to a larger labour force in those areas, but most likely the ability to pay more labourers. Graaff-Reinet especially, but also Middelburg to some extent, constituted the centre for wool farming, meaning that farmers there were more well-off than those in the Eastern districts such as Victoria East, Albert, Peddie and Aliwal North. But farmers in Albert actually produced more wool than those in Graaff-Reinet and Middelburg and there were more sheep there. And there was probably a stratification of farmers also in those areas. For example P. E. L. Smith in Aliwal North had eighteen "natives", thus twice the average number for the district, consisting of eight male adults, three female adults and seven children.[187]

The large average in Murraysburg was to some extent caused by T. L. V. Heerden and J. A. Burger who stated that they had 60 and 66 labourers respectively. This may have been due to a misunderstanding and referred to the total number of people on the farm. But also others in the district reported large numbers of labourers, between 20 and 30. Some did, however, only have as few as three.[188] While it is unlikely that Heerden and Burger employed 60 or

[184] Commission on Native Affairs, 1865. App. 2. J. P. Evans; W. T. Tweedie; S. Robertson; James Parkes, Graaff-Reinet, pp. 57-62

[185] Commission on Native Affairs, 1865. App. 2. W. T. Burger; T. J. van Heerden, Murraysburg, p. 65.

[186] Commission on Native Affairs, 1865. App. 2. J. Trollip; C. Schlimmer; H. C. Fisher; D. Kruger; R. Wilson; Mr. Whitehead. Middelburg, pp. 66-70.

[187] Commission on Native Affairs, 1865. App. 2. P. E. L. Smith, Aliwal North, p. 55.

[188] Commission on Native Affairs, 1865. App. 2. For example T. L. V. Heurden, 30; R. P. Piennaar, 20; W. T. Burger, 30; G. P. Roussouw, 3, H. P. van der Merwe, 3, Murraysburg, pp. 64-65.

more people each, there were large numbers of people on their farms, who were available for labour during some part of the year.

It is hard to estimate the value of rations and grazing rights, but in one case it was stated. R. Wilson in Middleburg paid 10 shillings per month to his servants, thus £6 per year, and rations for their families. The total "cost" per year for each servant was, according to him, £50. Rations, cultivation and grazing rights, but also wages to the family members and perhaps also costs related to the labour force such as lost or stolen animals, thus amounted to £44 per employee. We remember that the *Select Committee on Fences Bill* in 1872 estimated that a shepherd cost £18 per year. Assuming that their wage was £6, as it was on Wilson's farm, grazing rights and rations to them were worth £12 per year, thus two thirds of the remuneration. The remaining costs mentioned by Wilson were then wages and rations to the family members, but perhaps also other "costs" such as lost stock. As Wilson had 12 servants, the labour force cost him £528 per year excluding cash wages, which amounted to £72.[189] Such figures indicate that grazing rights were valued highly and that many family members were hired at least parts of the year.

Although cash wages occurred as remuneration, the wages were to a great extent paid in kind. G. F. Stephenson at Paarde Verlies in Aliwal North paid the male labourers "from £8 to £10 per year, generally paid in cattle [...]". The women were paid between £3 and £5. It does not seem like the women were paid in kind though. P. C. Myburgh, also in Aliwal North, did not seem to pay cash wages at all. According to him "the males receive as wages per year, one cow each and a calf; and the females two goats, the rations per day I think about from 3 to 4 lbs. of flesh and about 1 lb. of bread – and they also get milk and other things [...]".[190] H. C. Fischer in Middelburg paid 10 shillings per month "if money asked, otherwise, a riding horse, mare, or heifer per annum [...]". Daniel Kruger, also in Middelburg, paid the males a cow or a mare per year and the females three sheep per year.[191] Women could thus also receive animals as payment, but it was probably more common that the males were paid that way. In most cases there was probably a variation of remunerative practices even on the same farm. For example T. A. King at Botha's Kloof in Victoria East had five men and two women employed. In addition to rations and clothing he paid "one man, one mare per year; his wife and daughter 5s. per month; one man 7s. per month; one man, 7 goats per year; two boys 5s. per year [...]".[192]

---

[189] Commission on Native Affairs, 1865. App. 2. R. Wilson, Middleburg, p. 70.

[190] Commission on Native Affairs, 1865. App. 2. G. F. Stephanson; P. C. Myburgh, Aliwal North, pp. 50-51.

[191] Commission on Native Affairs, 1865. App. 2. H. C. Fischer; Daniel Kruger, Middelburg, pp. 68-69.

[192] Commission on Native Affairs, 1865. App. 2. T. A. King, Victoria East, p. 26.

Payment in kind was not only a fairly easy way for farmers without much capital or cash to pay labourers; it was also what the labourers wanted. The lobola system required men, who wanted to get married, ownership of a certain amount of stock, preferably cattle, to be paid to the father of the bride. Instead of saving money to buy cattle, the labourers preferred to take cattle as payment directly, thereby skipping the stage of sale and purchase. This signifies the simple commodity production described by Rosa Luxemburg.[193] The pre-capitalist economy based on non-monetary exchange thus certainly contributed to the system of payment in kind. But it was also prolonged in capitalist farming by the willingness of both buyer and seller of labour to enter agreements where wages were paid in kind.

Shepherds, children and squatters

Noble claimed that some of the largest sheep owners were found in Beaufort West. The Premier, Molteno, for example, had a farm with 35,000 sheep owned by him and partners. A Mr. de Villiers, who owned a neighbouring farm, had 20,000 sheep.[194] Based on the Select Committee on Fences Bill in 1872, which argued that each shepherd was responsible for about 500 sheep, Molteno and de Villiers had 70 and 40 shepherds respectively. Such figures should not be regarded as common. In some cases it has been possible to establish the number of shepherds on farms. John Slater in Alexandria stated that he had roughly thirty black people, "men, women and children", in his employ. "The men are chiefly herds." Joseph Gadd in Victoria East had four black herds, which constituted his entire labour force. J. Stirk in Peddie reported that he had "nine servants – sheep and cattle herds". The number of shepherds thus varied greatly, mainly depending on the number of sheep on the farm.

Large flocks of sheep could, however, be handled if the shepherd had assistants. W. Wynne in Victoria East mentioned that he had five black males employed: "They have wives and some children. One of them has three sons, big enough to be useful as herds, and are so employed."[195] As they were described as big, and probably old, enough, they appear to have been quite young. Possibly, they assisted their father with shepherding. In pre-colonial societies, boys started herding around the age of seven, sometimes assisting older brothers. This may have been the case also on Wynne's farm. But there were cases where young children worked on their own too. According to S. McCum in Queenstown "[t]he children of my servants, seven or eight years of

[193] Luxemburg, R 2003, pp. 348.

[194] Noble, J 1875, p. 134.

[195] Commission on Native Affairs, 1865. App. 2. W. Wynne, Victoria East, p. 22.

age, I employ at some light work – lamb herds, calf herds, or the like – for which they receive rations [...]".[196] Young children could thus be responsible for their own flocks, although it may not have been common. Wynne and McCum and probably most other farmers were, however, dependent on the exploitation of families and pre-colonial divisions of labour.

The children who worked as shepherds or did other work were usually a part of the father's labour power, which meant that the wages were paid to him. According to J.B. Evans in Graaff-Reinet, fathers controlled also older sons, which upset him. Thus, there were labourers and shepherds "having a family – some grown up, but who will not engage, as the father generally wants some of them to help him to take charge of his master's sheep [...]".[197] The father's control over the children subsequently meant that the sons did not work on other farms, but aided their father on the farm where he was hired, at least according to Evans. Fathers who had sons to help with shepherding could of course focus more on their own farming activities where this was possible. Evans stated that this gave the father "the pleasure of wallowing in his hut [...]",[198]instead of working for the farmer. Farmers generally viewed labourers as lazy, but such views say more about the labour relations than anything else. In this case the labour relations were largely based on pre-colonial family ties, where fathers could control the labour power of their family completely. We should assume that fathers could "wallow" as wives and daughters took care of subsistence farming while the sons were herding sheep for the farmer. The fathers could challenge farmers like Evans for control over the labour force, which gave them a position of power.

While describing the large sheep areas in Beaufort West, Noble mentioned that there were white shepherds as well, called superintendents. These seem to have been overseers and not involved in the actual labour. But they lived in the veld close to water reservoirs and controlled the health of the sheep.[199] It is unlikely that a majority of farmers employed white head shepherds to any great extent. Judging by the censuses there were very few whites working as shepherds. However, they may have been remunerated as managers or overseers. In 1875 there were 910 overseers, whereof 737 where white. In 1891 there were 2,720 managers or overseers, whereof 2,200 were white.[200] Having an overseer for every flock or kraal was expensive. The farmer A. van der Byl in Bredasdorp mentioned that he employed white shepherds, who "were once respectable farmers", but had become bywoners on his farm. He estimated that the land

[196] Commission on Native Affairs, 1865. App. 2. S. McCum, Queenstown, p. 42.

[197] Commission on Native Affairs, 1865. App. 2. J. B. Evans, Graaff-Reinet, p. 58.

[198] Commission on Native Affairs, 1865. App. 2. J. B. Evans, Graaff-Reinet, p. 58.

[199] Noble, J 1875, p. 134.

[200] Cape of Good Hope Census, 1875, p. 185; Cape of Good Hope Census 1891, pp. 304-05.

they were allowed to live on was the equivalent of £60 per year and in addition they earned cash wages.[201] This suggests that only the wealthiest farmers could afford a large number of head shepherds. The head shepherds or overseers were, according to Noble, "young men of good families", who could learn wool farming and after some years could "take the charge of other farms or lease lands on their own account".[202] There were thus two types of white shepherds; those who had been farmers and those who wanted to be farmers. Regardless of type they were landless.

Wages to black and coloured shepherds appear to have been somewhat lower than the wages for general labourers. McCum paid "[a]dult men (herds), £5; labourers, from £6 to £7 10s. per year, with food and rations, and the option of taking money or stock at the end of the contract". G. White in Albany similarly stated that the herds were paid 7 shillings and sixpence per month, while labourers were paid between 10 and 15 shillings per month. T. Leppan at Doorn Kloof in Bedford paid "the herds from 5s. upwards per month [...]. The men that work at home, wagon drivers, &c, I pay from 5s. to 15s. per month [...]."[203] The reasons for the lower wages paid to shepherds are unclear, but it could have been because they were younger than the general labourers. Another reason could have been that they received more rations than general labourers. This is, however, not stated. A third possibility could have been that it was easier to find people who were willing to work as shepherds than as general labourers. Noble mentioned that black and coloured people "make careful herds [...]", wagon drivers and even ploughmen, but there was "a very scanty supply of field labourers [...]".[204] General farm labour was definitely harder than shepherding, which may have required farmers to pay them slightly better wages, especially if they wanted males.

While the family labour system was dominating on the wool farms, and seems to have been vital to farmers, it also created problems. Primarily because it generated what was known as squatting. Squatting was in essence tenancy, but the tenant did not work for the farmer on whose land he lived. This was unacceptable to officials and many farmers. Still, a majority of the farmers who testified to the Commission on Native Affairs stated that they did not know of squatting in their area. It is likely that they did not want to admit to allowing squatters. W. C. Bouwer in Queenstown said that "several" farmers in his area allowed squatting "under pretence that the squatters are hired servants [...]".[205]

---

201 Select Committee on Supply of the Labour Market, 1879, Evidence of A. van der Byl, Bredasdorp, p. 16-17.

202 Noble, J 1875, p. 134.

203 Commission on Native Affairs, 1865. App. 2. S. McCum, Queenstown, p. 42; G. White, Albany, p. 10; T. Leppan, Bedford, p. 28.

204 Noble, J 1875, p. 292.

205 Commission on Native Affairs, 1865. App. 2. W. C. Bouwer, Queenstown, p. 41.

And it seems like a great deal of farmers relied on it. T. Leppan in Bedford stated that "we have a great number of so-called squatters [...]". When he was taking the census he found 90 on one farm, "who only pay the owner of the property £25 per annum". On two other farms he found one hundred and sixty three and two hundred and sixty three respectively. According to Leppan, squatting withheld labour from farmers, but it also increased thefts.[206] W. C. Stapelburg in Aliwal North had eight men employed, and in addition had two squatter families, and his neighbours had the same arrangement.[207] The squatters were not only black. In Graaff-Reinet J. B. Evans claimed that there were "ten squatters for every landed proprietor [...]". They were a "heterogenous conglomeration of the lowest order of white and black".[208] This caused thefts. S. J. Robertson and James Parkes confirmed that there were squatters in Graaff-Reinet, but did not say how many. W. T. Tweedie, on the other hand, said that there were no squatters there.[209]

W. M. Bowker similarly believed that squatting was bad, but his reflections show that it was an integral part of labour relations: "They [other farmers] allow the natives to live on the land, charging them so much a year for the privilege of grazing their stock, and requiring them to assist in shearing sheep and reaping the crops." Apparently, the number of people on farms could be as many as one hundred, according to Bowker. This caused stock thefts. Bowker himself had been offered £10 per month for renting out land, presumably to one family, but he had not had tenants since 1840 and denounced it strongly.[210] But not all farmers could afford to say no to the rent, especially not if they were offered £10 per month. In Victoria East the rent was about £3 per family for a year. The Civil Commissioner, W. F. Liddle, thought that a farmer housing 300 people could receive £500 per year.[211] Such sums were welcomed by most farmers. The wealthier ones could say no, but many of them had, like Bowker in 1840, been economically dependent on it in the past. Some of the black peasants had considerable assets, though, which meant that they could survive without labouring for white farmers. In Peddie some of the peasants had apparently even bought a "grantee" farm for £1,000.[212]

---

[206] Commission on Native Affairs, 1865. App. 2. T. Leppan, Bedford, pp. 28-29.

[207] Commission on Native Affairs, 1865. App. 2. W. C. Stapelburg, p. 52.

[208] Commission on Native Affairs, 1865. App. 2. J. B. Evans, Graaff-Reinet, p. 58.

[209] Commission on Native Affairs, 1865. App. 2. Graaff-Reinet, pp. 60-62.

[210] Commission on Native Affairs, 1865. App. 2. W. M. Bowker, Albany, p. 4.

[211] Commission on Native Affairs, 1865, W. F. Liddle, Civil Commissioner, Victoria East, p. 132.

[212] Commission on Native Affairs, 1865. App. 2. J. Stirk, Peddie, p. 46.

Labour relations on Wellwood

On the Rubidges' farm Wellwood in Graaff-Reinet there were 54 people in total in 1875. Of these 10 were white, 34 were black and 10 were coloured. The majority of the whites belonged to the Rubidge family; only two were employed as labourers. The rest, that is, the black and coloured people, were labourers of various sorts.[213] As we have seen, not all farmers could afford such a large labour force, which means that the Rubidges were relatively wealthy.

There are some references to wages paid to labourers during this time. Payments were often irregular; some were paid monthly, others not. A man called Barend was paid 10s. monthly in 1877. The following year a man called Skip was paid £4.16s. for eight months, thus also about 10s. per month.[214] Some were paid as families, or husband and wife, which meant higher wages; Matika and Katje were, for example paid £4.6s. for six months, thus 15s. per month and Klaas and his family was paid £1 per month.[215] Other labourers, like Stoffel, were paid considerably less: 5s. per month.[216] He was probably a young person, or relied more on other remuneration than cash. We can, however, conclude that cash wages varied between 5s. to as much as £1 per month for families.

According to the list of employees, there were four shepherds in 1875: Piet, 23 years old, Klass, 30 years old, Cobus, 48 years old, and Mentor, who was 13 years old. Mentor was the son of Cobus. Cobus and his family was hired in November of 1874, but had been employed there previously. Cobus was paid 10 shillings per month. Besides Mentor, he had another son, or young person who was his dependent, called August, who was 12 years old. August and Mentor were also paid wages, but slightly less: "2 goats each at the end of 6 months, & 2'/- per month".[217] Already at the age of thirteen a shepherd could thus accumulate his own stock. In this case it is, however, uncertain if Mentor actually received the wages himself, or if the wage of the son was paid to the father.

As the Rubidges in 1875 had 2,480 sheep and 768 goats it seems unlikely that they only had four shepherds. Such a ratio would mean that each shepherd was responsible for more than 800 small stock, which was a lot. A study of the diary for the year 1875 verifies the suspicions. There were, seemingly, six shepherds during that year, or at least references to people performing the work of shepherds. These were Cobus, Piet, October, Buiter, Old Damond and Booy. As Mentor was not mentioned there was a further discrepancy. At least

---

213 Rubidge accounts. Preparation for census 1875.

214 Rubidge accounts, 1877; Dec. 20, 1878.

215 Rubidge accounts, Sept. 10, 1879; April 30, 1876.

216 Rubidge accounts, Feb. 27, 1878.

217 Rubidge diaries, Nov. 24, 1874.

seven people worked as shepherds. Such a state of affairs leads to the conclusion that more people than those hired as shepherds were actually performing the work. Two of the shepherds left the farm during 1875, though. In October Charles Rubidge "[d]ischarged Cobus & family", and in November "Old Buiter left".[218] The same day as Cobus and his family left the Rubidges hired "a mantatee 'Boy'", possibly as a shepherd. Boy may have been the same man who was later called Booy, who took over a flock of sheep in November, but they could have been two different persons.[219] The shepherds were thus coming and going, but the number seemed to remain fairly constant. A farm such as Wellwood with about 2,500 sheep thus employed five to six shepherds yearly. Other farms of similar size may have had a few more or a few less, but overall there was most likely one shepherd per 500 sheep or small livestock.

The number of people actually working every day on Wellwood varied depending on the time of the year. During shearing time in September through December the demand for labour was at its highest, but also at other times there were peaks of labour demand, for example when dams were built. At such times additional labourers came to the farm and left when the work was done. In February 1875 a man called "William Adams came here in search of work at dams". Adams was subsequently hired and made a seemingly favourable agreement with Charles Rubidge. Five months later, "Adams finished his piece of work, received the balance of his money (£26) and left for town".[220] Adams was most likely included in the census list of the 54 people on the farm. Being on the farm for five months was a comparatively long time though. Several other labourers only stayed for short periods of time. At the end of July 1878, "[t]hree men from Bethesda came to work in the afternoon". It is unclear what sort of work they were hired for, but they finished it quickly; two days later Charles "[d]ischarged Bethesda lot".[221] Seasonal or occasional labour must thus be added to those who lived on the farm. The capacity to employ such labour varied between farmers, and those who could not afford it had to rely on harder exploitation of the labour force already on the farm. On Wellwood it appears that most additional labour was related to the building of dams, fencing and brickmaking.

It is not possible to establish an exact number of the additional labour force per year, but ten or fifteen people per year seems plausible.

It quickly becomes obvious that conditions in wool farming regions in the Cape were diversified. Some farmers, like the Rubidges and the Bowkers, had a comparatively large number of labourers on their farms. Others seem to have been struggling harder to find labour and could only report ten or less. Others

218 Rubidge diaries, Oct. 8, 1875; Nov. 10, 1875.

219 Rubidge diaries, Nov. 18, 1875.

220 Rubidge diaries, Feb. 24, June 11, 1875.

221 Rubidge diaries, July 31, Aug. 2, 1878.

still may have had only one or two labourers. The average seems to have been twelve. It is also obvious that the remuneration differed between farms. Cash wages thus varied from £12 per year down to £1 per year, depending on sex, age and occupation. Men received the highest wages; women and children considerably less, so age and gender and mattered in the same way as in Europe. A common feature of all farms was, however, the combination of cash wages and wages in kind. Food, housing and sometimes clothing made up a substantial part of the wages paid to labourers. Also grazing rights must be considered as wages in kind, and this practice was widespread and even constituted a critical feature of labour relations in wool farming. Successful farms like Wellwood and those less fortunate both depended heavily on the ability to allow the labourers' sheep, goats and cattle to graze on their farms along with their own stock.

Shepherds appear to have been in high demand, but were not necessarily better remunerated than general farm labourers. Based on the calculation provided by the Select Committee on Fences Bill in 1872, which stated that shepherds earned £18 per year, it seems like about two thirds of the wages were consisted of payments in kind. At least the wages to adult males, who earned around £6 per year on average in cash wages. Some of the shepherds seem to have been quite young, but children were usually not hired individually. As seen on Wellwood, the head of family, Cobus, was the one who was hired, not his son and the young dependent he cared for. After Cobus was hired the sons were, however, quickly given positions as shepherds. From what it seems, father and son did not work together in that case.

Wellwood, Graaff-Reinet (CA AG. 9448). Nineteenth century.

Leaving Wellwood and returning – two labourers on a mission

Labour recruitment was a crucial aspect of farming. On Wellwood it was common that families and single males arrived at the farm in search of employment. But there were other ways to recruit labour, primarily with the labourers as recruiters.

One of those who recruited was Tom, who had been involved in work with dam building in the mid-1870s. He made a substantial amount of money from work with dams, for example £20 for cleaning out a dam.[222] That was about twice as much as the average yearly wage for farm labour. Tom continued to work on dams with a man called Jack for a year and a half.[223] The wages paid to Tom, which was most likely more than £20 considering that he worked for a year and a half, would go a long way. A few days after he was paid his wages he "left for Kaffirland" together with Goliad.[224] "Kaffirland is present day Transkei, and was not formally annexed to the Cape Colony at the time. We do not know what the two labourers did in "Kaffirland". Three months later Tom

[222] Rubidge diaries, March 24, 1874.

[223] Rubidge diaries, June 12, 1875.

[224] Rubidge diaries, June 16, 1875.

returned to the farm and in October, Goliad was also back on Wellwood.[225] This indicates that they had no intention of staying away from Wellwood for long. And judging by the diaries, they were expected to return. Tom continued to work on Wellwood for the remainder of the year, but in April 1876 he was given leave and "left for Kaffirland to fetch his wife".[226] Apparently he had left his wife, Jena, there at some point, or found another wife. As there is no mention in the diaries of Jena leaving the farm, it is possible that he was in fact bringing a second wife to the farm. Although Tom was formally a migrant, he wanted his family to be on Wellwood, while he himself worked there. His strategy might very well have been to bring the wife to the farm in order to make even more money, accumulate cattle and be able to move back to "Kaffirland" as an independent peasant with a household of his own.

When Tom returned to Wellwood in May he did not just bring his wife, but came in the company of three or four other men. They arrived on May 24, and on May 25 two of them, Skip and Jan, started to work.[227] Skip had probably worked on Wellwood previously, but the others seemed new. Going to "Kaffirland" was apparently also a form of labour recruitment. Tom, who was employed on the farm, thus acquired additional labour for the farmer. Two years previously, in 1874, Goliad had also gone to "Kaffirland" to fetch his wife. He left in February and stayed away almost three months. In the beginning of May "Goliad returned from Kaffirland with a wife & another man & woman [...]".[228] At least one of them, the man, November, was working a month later. There was thus room for additional people who were brought to the farm. For those who were not hired, there was room, but no wages or rations were paid.

Colonel Stanford, Chief Magistrate of the Transkeian Territories, explained in the early twentieth century that farmers used to send one of their old servants "through Kafirland [...] and he would tell the natives that his master wanted some servants, and would give him a good name, and would go back with a family or two according to his requirements".[229] We do not know if Tom and Goliad were ordered to bring labourers to the farm, but the Rubidges did at least not object. Tom, who was paid very high wages, seems to have been one of the "old servants" who was trusted to find new labourers. This gave him a position of status, especially if those he recruited were his family members or relatives. They would be dependent and indebted to him. There were probably

---

225 Rubidge diaries, Sept. 26, Oct. 7, 1875.

226 Rubidge diaries, April 9, 1876.

227 Rubidge diaries, May 24, 25, 1876; Rubidge accounts, 1876.

228 Rubidge diaries, Feb. 19, May 9, 1874.

229 Select Committee on Farm Labour Supply, 1907. Evidence of Col. Stanford, Chief Magistrate, Transkeian Territories, p. 13.

expectations from family members that Tom, who was already hired, would help others to find work and earn money or cattle.

Owning stock – a blessing and a curse

Ownership of stock was important to labourers. It gave them some independence from farmers and it was often a prerequisite for marriage. In 1875 there were 2,480 sheep, 500 goats and about 50 head of cattle on Wellwood. Almost all the sheep were owned by the Rubidges, but some of the goats and cattle were owned by black and coloured labourers. At some points the numbers could increase rapidly when new people were hired. Several times families came to the farm with large numbers of stock. For example, the family of five men and eight women who arrived in 1874 had 322 sheep, one goat and cattle. Also Danster, who was hired in 1879 together with his son Klein Danster, brought 126 sheep and 15 goats to the farm. He and his son were hired for a heifer each for six months.[230]

It was unusual for labourers to have such a large number of stock, though. Most of them only had a few, but work on a farm was a way to accumulate cattle. Mr. Vermaak in Burghersdorp mentioned a black family that stayed on his farm for six years. When they arrived they about eight cows, but when they left they had 72 head of cattle, more than 500 sheep and a dozen horses. Vermaak always paid them in stock.[231] Many also chose this before cash wages. On Wellwood in 1875 a man called Coffey "left with 10 goats having taken 3 in payment of one month's wages [...]".[232] One month's wages were thus equal to three goats, at least to Coffey. While Coffey received both cash and animals, others settled with animals. Bye [?], who was hired later the same year, "agreed to work 6 months for a mare".[233] Based on the monthly wage, a mare was thus worth 18 goats. Cash wages were not particularly favoured among the labourers, but it is likely that the farmers had an advantage in negotiations. And it seems like the wages were highly negotiable. When the shepherd Matika and his wife had finished their first six months in 1879 they decided to stay and "agreed to take cattle in lieu of money".[234] The Rubidges could clearly pay cash wages, which perhaps was the original agreement in this case, but they did not object to paying in cattle.

---

230 Rubidge diaries, April 29, 1874; Dec. 26, 1879.

231 Select Committee on Supply of the Labour Market, 1879. Evidence of Mr. Vermaak, MLC Burghersdorp, p. 14.

232 Rubidge diaries, Feb. 15, 1875.

233 Rubidge diaries, May 28, 1875.

234 Rubidge diaries, March 25, 1879.

The system with cattle as payment and grazing rights benefitted both farmers and labourers. Many times it was an advantage for labourers to have a lot of stock. Their oxen could be used as draught animals and it gave them independence. If conditions were not satisfactory they could leave the farm and find a new one. Samuel Laubreker[?], a farmer in Graaff-Reinet, had two men, Andries and Hermanus, who stayed on his land but who were not employed. In August 1874 Laubreker did, however, approach Andries and told him "he must engage himself to me and let my goats run with his". Until then Andries and Hermanus had seemingly been cash tenants on the farm, but this was to end. Laubreker said he would pay a cash wage and rations to Andries. But before he started his employment, Andries left the farm with Hermanus and the stock. Apparently they also took some of the farmers' stock. He went in search of the men and found them "close to Aberdeen, about 6 hours from my farm". The two were trekking with their father, who was "in charge of their stock".[235] The father had apparently not been living on the same farm as Andries and Hermanus, but was involved in trying to find a new place for the stock.

Labourers with stock were, however, not welcome everywhere, especially when the stock was not in good condition. In 1877 a large black family came to Wellwood "to hire, but stock being brandsick could not come to terms".[236] Brandsickness, scab, was quite widespread, and particularly among the flocks of black peasants. They had less access to dipping, which protected both sheep and cattle from brandsickness. The family who sought grazing and employment on Wellwood would thus have been more attractive as labour without the stock. But despite this they kept the animals. Maybe they tried to find grazing with other farmers, who were more dependent on attracting new labourers. Selling the stock was not an option. Being without means of production would have meant being completely proletarianized, which was worse than owning stock that suffered from brandsickness. Other farmers, particularly the poorer ones, of whom there were many,[237] probably welcomed also brandsick stock, if there was no other labour to be found or if they required draught animals. Farmers who took on labourers with stock in bad condition probably had an advantage since they could negotiate for low wages, but labourers clearly tried to find new employers if they were not satisfied. It is even likely that many labourers agreed to work for only grazing rights, as long as it enabled them to keep the animals and thereby hopes of becoming independent peasants in the future instead of being completely proletarianized.

---

[235] CA 1/GR 2/95 Part I. Proceedings of Court Cases. Magistrate Graaff-Reinet. Andries and Hermanus, Aug. 28, 1874.

[236] Rubidge diaries, Feb. 11, 1877.

[237] Bundy, C 1979; 1986, Dubow, S 1982.

Shearing time

Shearing is the harvest time for wool farmers. It is a point in time when the investments into the farm will give results. Shearing requires great skills and experience.

Michael de Jongh notes that shearing during the late nineteenth century was largely done by migrants who travelled between farms on foot with their belongings. Soon they started to use donkey carts as means of transportation. During the early twentieth century people in the Karroo started to refer to them as the *Karretjiemense*, the donkey cart people.[238] The men were skilled shearers and the families appear to have accompanied them wherever they went. Their history is largely yet to be written, but popular knowledge about them is widespread. However, there is little evidence that shearing on Wellwood during the nineteenth century, or even the first half of the twentieth century, was performed by nomadic people. Instead, Wellwood relied on other shearers. In at least one instance, from 1877, the Rubidges "went to look for shearers" in nearby New Bethesda.[239] During the twentieth century shearers from New Bethesda seem to have been hired frequently on Wellwood. These shearers did not appear to be migratory, quite the contrary; they lived in New Bethesda and from there they were recruited by farmers in the surrounding area.

Shearers were usually black or coloured. Nothing indicates that white people were occupied as shearers. Apparently, quite a few of the shearers during the nineteenth century were former farm labourers, who chose to become migrant shearers. De Jongh argues that the migrant shearers were to some extent remnants of nomadic Khoi and San peoples, whose unwillingness to settle in one place created problems for farmers who wanted a steady labour force on their farms. But the migrant shearers were welcomed by farmers as their mobility suited production demands; shearing was only conducted during certain times of the year, which meant that farmers did not have to sustain them for a whole year.[240] During the shearing, which lasted for about a month or sometimes more, the shearers stayed on the farm. They were probably given rations during this time in addition to their cash wages, it occurred on Wellwood at least.[241] Shearers were in that regard not different from the other labourers.

De Jongh argues that shearers, at least those belonging to the Karretjie people, were a rural underclass, largely due to their lack of land ownership. In relation to the white farmers that is, of course, true, but the term underclass has little analytical value when investigating production and groups of labourers.

[238] De Jongh, M 2002, p. 448.

[239] Rubidge diaries, Oct. 20, 1877.

[240] De Jongh, M 2002, p. 448.

[241] Rubidge diaries, Oct, 14, 1901; June 1, 1906.

The shearers, along with all labourers, constituted a labouring class, which was qualitatively different from the capital owning class of white farmers. However, shearers were more skilled than other labourers and may have been paid better wages. Their skills gave shearers more freedom and influence over their labour than farm labourers.

The wages paid to shearers varied depending on the number of sheep shorn. In 1890 T. P. Theron in Richmond estimated that shearers could earn 10 shillings per 100 sheep. And as "a man can shear from fifty to seventy-five sheep in a day, [...] they generally bring home a good deal of money".[242] On a farm with 2,000 sheep that would have meant £10, which seems to be what was paid on Wellwood. In October 1885 the Rubidges paid £9.8.10 in total "for shearers".[243] There were definitely not more than 2,000 sheep on the farm at the time, indicating that 10 shillings per 100 sheep appears to have been the going rate. But that rate was probably not paid everywhere. We know that wages on Wellwood in general were higher than the average. Theron's estimate was probably therefore the highest rate paid, meaning that shearers could earn up to 10 shillings per 100 sheep. Compared to farm labourers, who earned 10 shillings per month on average, shearers were definitely not paid low wages. But shearers could only earn such amounts during certain times of the year.

On Wellwood the main shearing took place from September through November every year, but there were some variations.[244] Occasional shearing was done at other times during the year. There was never any trouble finding shearers, although they did not always show up for work when expected to. In 1885 the Rubidges started shearing on October 1 with seven shearers. About three weeks later they shore with only five shearers as the rest had "not returned". The missing shearers had probably been employed on another farm in the area. However, the following day Richard Rubidge "[e]mployed two new shearers", and could continue the shearing with the same number of people.[245] A similar thing occurred on Jan van Niekerk's farm Albertvale in Bedford. He started shearing with fewer shearers than he wanted as the "other men who promised to come did not come".[246] Due to their skills, the shearers were highly sought after and it may have created competition between farmers. Crais argues that a skilled shearer could shear a sheep in less than 10 minutes, while it could take one hour for a beginner.[247] This meant that they had a position of power in relation to farmers, which labourers usually did not have. In that

---

[242] Select Committee on the Labour Question, 1890. T. P. Theron, Richmond, Cape, p. 49.

[243] Rubidge accounts, Oct. 28, 1885.

[244] Rubidge diaries, 1875. For example, shearing started Oct. 1 and was finished Dec. 21 or 22.

[245] Rubidge diaries, Oct. 1, 19, 20, 1885.

[246] CL PR 3418, Van Niekerk diaries,Nov. 13, 1895.

[247] Crais, C 1992, p. 154. Crais does not give a source to that information, though.

regard they were thus also more independent than the other labour force on farms.

The shearers were characterized by a higher degree of proletarianization than farm labourers; they were paid cash wages although they also received rations, but mainly, their skills were their main asset. It is possible that they owned sheep or cattle or had a small peasant holding, which sustained them during the low season. Van Onselen's example with Kas Maine, who shore for some farmers, while being a tenant and conducting agriculture of his own, proves that such a practice was possible.[248] However, as wool farming was more extensive in the Cape than on the Highveld, it was easier to make a living as a shearer there. The proletarianization of shearers also seems to have generated a sense of unity, which was not seen amongst farm labourers. They managed to bargain collectively with farmers. Shearers were not organized according to trade union standards, but as they travelled and were hired in groups, they seem to have bargained collectively with farmers. This probably increased their wages.

Apart from the shearers, also the labourers on the farm were involved in the shearing. And it seems as if they were paid extra for this work. For example, in February 1886 five of the Wellwood labourers were paid cash for shearing. They earned between 10 and 17 shillings. One of them, Isaac, was also paid an additional 12/3 for "taking in wool".[249] These labourers, who probably earned around 10 shillings per month, could thus increase their income considerably through shearing. Shearing involved many other activities than just cutting the wool, such as classing, sorting and packing. These work operations, which we will examine in more detail later, were crucial to a proper shearing. Paying the labourers extra wages might have been an indication that the Rubidges valued this work highly.

The shearing clearly meant additional people on the farm, which increased the farmer's expenses. One example is from the Halse family in Sterkstroom. They had at least 3,000 sheep on the farm Carnarvon. In April 1888 there were as many as "20 men shearing wool" on the farm.[250] It is uncertain if that meant 20 shearers, or if some of the farm labourers were included in that number. However, shearing could obviously include a large number of people and it was beneficial to the farmers if some of the labourers were skilled enough to shear. But, following de Jongh's argument, those who were good shearers did probably not stay on as farm labourers as they could make more money being full-time shearers.

The manner in which shearing was conducted during the nineteenth century gave the Cape clip a bad reputation on the London wool market. For example, it was too short as many farmers shore twice a year and there was a lack of

248 Van Onselen, C 1997, pp. 108, 259.

249 Rubidge accounts, Feb. 14, 18, 25, 1886.

250 CL MS 17507, 17508, Halse farm diary, April 24, 1889.

sorting different qualities of wool from each other. This lowered the price on Cape wool.[251] Kraaling and trekking similarly contributed to foreign particles being stuck in the wool. These particles could be removed through proper cleaning of the wool after it was shorn. Dubow argues that the competitive situation among merchants, who paid similar prices for both high and low quality wool, was a main reason for poor wool quality in the Cape. Merchants were outside the sphere of production, and could not change it to any great extent.[252] But it is important to note that there were farmers who had realized the importance of proper shearing and handling of wool, for example in Beaufort West, according to Noble.[253] The Rubidges were also concerned about quality, and a shearing shed was built on Wellwood in the 1860s.

After having finished shearing a flock it was sent back to grazing. However, it was important to dip the newly shorn sheep. Charles Rubidge noted in 1867 that the sheep should be dipped two to four months after shearing.[254] This was probably the practice also later. The dip protected the sheep against various infections, for example scab and paralysis tick. According to Noble, dipping tanks seem to have been common among the successful farmers, at least in Beaufort West.[255] These tanks were permanent, probably made out of stone, and enabled the sheep to walk through the dip. During the walk, labourers pushed the sheep down under the surface to make sure they were properly dipped. On Wellwod a dipping tank was built in 1858.[256]

During the nineteenth century the most common dip seems to have been tobacco, which was used on Wellwood. According to Charles Rubidge, 25 lbs. of tobacco should be mixed with 100 gallons of water.[257] Some of the tobacco was used for rations to labourers. There was thus a double usage for it. In addition to tobacco, also sulphur was used for dipping on several occasions on Wellwood.[258] Although homemade dips were functional, a new product emerged on the market during the end of the century: Cooper's dip. Cooper's dip was a mix of arsenic and sulphur, which was to be mixed with water. It was produced in England for the first time in 1852. It was primarily designed to prohibit scab in sheep.[259] Cooper's dip was used on Wellwood at least as early

---

[251] Dubow, S 1982, pp. 26-27.

[252] Dubow, S 1982, pp. 27-28.

[253] Noble, J 1875, p 134.

[254] NL MSB 406, Charles Rubidge Collection. Letter, Oct. 18, 1867.

[255] Noble, J 1875, pp. 133-34.

[256] CL MS 6189, Old Extracts from Old Wellwood, 1867.

[257] NL MSB 406, Charles Rubidge Collection. Letter, Oct. 18, 1867.

[258] Rubidge diaries, May 13, 1874; Feb. 19, 1895; April 28, 1896.

[259] www.dacorumheritage.org.uk/coopers.htm (2012-11-26)

as 1890, but sulphur continued to be used alongside of it and Cooper's and salt was also used.[260]

The introduction of Cooper's dip in Cape wool farming marked an important step in the development of scientific management of sheep. As it enhanced the health of the sheep, and thereby the quality of the wool, it was a fundamental productive force in wool farming. A new compulsory *Scab Act* was passed in 1894 compelling farmers to dip their sheep.[261] Having sheep with scab or other diseases could mean great losses for farmers and being able to prevent it was a profitable investment. The access to a proper dip also stratified various sheep owners, especially between white capitalist farmers and black peasants. The sheep of white capitalist farmers became healthier, and their wool of better quality than that of black peasants. However, it is important to note that also the sheep of farm labourers were dipped in order to prevent the spreading of scab and other diseases. When a new labourer arrived at Wellwood, his sheep were invariably dipped before sent to grazing. This, of course, meant that farm labourers could not only accumulate sheep while being employed, but also enhance the quality of their stock. From the farmer's point of view it was therefore also beneficial as a way to attract labour.

---

260 Rubidge diaries, April 25, 1896; March 29, 1900.

261 Beinart, W 2008, p 154.

CHAPTER 6

Imperial Relations, 1880 – 1910

Imports and exports of capital

We have seen that Cape wool farming originated from sheep imported from Europe and Australia. Some of the sheep were bought by the Government, who facilitated for farmers to buy pure bred sheep. Imports of sheep constituted an essential part of the transnational production of wool. At the same time it reinforced the relationship between the Cape and imperial Britain, making the Cape wool farmers crucial members of the wool producing community in the Empire. But individual farmers did not only depend on government aided imports and supply of sheep; some of them made great efforts to improve their own flocks by importing on their own.

In 1861 Charles Rubidge went to Europe and purchased "30 ewes and some Rams [sic] from M. Gaurin France".[262] As he went to France it seems as if he went to Rambouillet, from where a famous merino breed comes, although it is not stated. Charles and his son Richard undertook a similar journey to Europe in 1873, when they visited England, France and Austria. In France they visited a sheep sale where Charles bought two rams.[263] Visiting Europe in order to buy livestock was surely an unusual venture for most Cape farmers. The journey was long and expensive, and it could not have been undertaken by the average farmer. Some may not even have had an interest in travelling such a long distance in order to find sheep. After all, the sheep came to the Cape in any case. The fact that Wellwood was a stud farm must have been an important reason for the Rubidges to visit places like Rambouillet. In the style of successful breeders, they wanted to find the best specimens for future breeding. These journeys must have been important for the future success of the farm, and especially the one in 1861, which brought more than 30 sheep to the farm.

But the journey to Europe did not only consist of sheep purchases. When they arrived in England in April 1873 Charles and Richard Rubidge visited a

---

[262] CL MS 6189, Old Extracts from Old Wellwood, 1861.

[263] Rubidge diaries, Aug. 1873 (June 12.).

textile factory. A man named Fawcett "showed us over the whole of the cloth factory of Mathew & son [...] in which he is a clerk".[264] Apparently Charles and Richard Rubidge were interested in seeing a place in England where the wool produced in the Cape, some of it perhaps from Wellwood, became textiles, that is, a finished commodity in a long chain of production and transport. The peripheral farmers, who produced the raw material, thereby had first-hand knowledge of the production in the end of the commodity chain in the core in England. Although this interest may have been shared by many other wool farmers in the Cape and all over the British Empire, few colonial farmers ever got a chance to see a textile factory at this time. There were no textile factories in the Cape in the 1870s, and it would take a long while until the first ones were established, and even longer until there was a textile industry in South Africa. Farmers in Australia and New Zealand were even further away from the core of the textile production of the Empire in West Yorkshire in England. During the twentieth century South African farmers went on organized trips to Europe studying production in textile industries and agriculture.[265]

The Rubdiges surely realized that much of the future of their endeavours on Wellwood was decided in places like Mathew & Son. The sale of finished wool commodities, and the money generated therefrom, was the foundation of the imperial wool industry. Acquiring knowledge about the production process in a textile factory – the different labour processes like cleaning, dying etc., and the requirements on the raw material for various purposes – was therefore a vital part of improving the production of wool on Wellwood. Being able to visit textile factories and be given tours most likely gave them an extra advantage to other farmers who were not as aware of the demands of textile producers. And, equally important, it probably also gave them extra incentive to follow through with the changes of production that had already started a few years back.

We have seen that the amount of fencing was not extensive during the 1870s, and some of the fences were even made of stones. It is apparent that the prerequisites for wire fencing increased considerably during the latter half of the 1880s.

264 Rubidge diaries, Aug. 1873 (April 29).

265 *Farmers' Weekly*, June 1; July, 13, 27, 1927.

Table 7. Imports of fencing material, wire, total and from top five exporters (£).

	1886	1890	1895	1896	1900	1905
Total	14,492	77,376	80,106	114,346	50,051	100,042
UK	13,435	61,785	41,081	54,493	18,082	37,566
Germany	719	3,063	18,781	15,801	531	1,142
Natal	706	2,432	2,792	3,519	49,998	
US	92	10,026	13,389	33,200	27,383	51,228
Belgium			3,433	6,412	3,957	6,461

Source: Statistical Register of the Colony of the Cape of Good Hope 1886, p. 102; 1890, pp. 103,128; 1896, p. 120; 1900, pp. 122, 160; 1905, pp. 137, 164.

The fencing material imported to the Cape clearly accelerated after 1886. At that time duties on fencing material had been lowered by the government in order to promote fencing. The demand subsequently increased. The amount of money spent quadrupled between 1886 and 1890. We can almost talk of a fencing revolution during the decade between 1886 and 1896. During the Second Anglo-Boer War around the turn of the century the imports were clearly reduced, and the British imports seem to have been redirected through the colony Natal instead of imports directly from the UK. After the war things were back to normal in wire imports, but the US became a large supplier, challenging the British dominance.

Much like the wool, which was sent to Britain, fencing wire was a colonial product, at least during the 1880s and early 1890s. Dubow states that during the 1860s and 1870s the British invested £100 million in their colonies and that some of that capital must have found its way to the Cape and the wool producing areas.[266] As seen in table 8 the British exports continued throughout the century. But instead of only referring to "investments" or "export of capital" our analysis will benefit from being more specific. Although a general British investment in all sorts of trades was done, it is apparent that wire for fencing was one such commodity, which the British expected a return from. This was the essence of imperialism. The British bought wool from the Cape long before wire fencing appeared in the Cape, but once it had started, the British clearly found this particular form of colonial "investment" worthwhile. Thus, at first the merinos were exported from Britain to the Cape, which became the start of the commercial wool industry. Then, half a century later, the wire for fencing became the next contribution to the expanding wool farming in the Colony for export of wool back to English factories.

The various improvements made in the Cape wool industry in the form of fencing and water supplies had a positive effect on wool production and

---

[266] Dubow, S 1982, p 13.

exports. The decades between 1870 and 1890 the amount of exported wool doubled. The wool price peaked in 1875, and the following years farmers saw the price falling. But the amount of wool exported continued to increase the following decades, although there were fluctuations some years.

Table 8. Wool exports from the Cape 1870 - 1896, and UK share 1886-1896 (per cent of lbs.).

Year	Lbs.	£	To UK
1870	37,283,291	1,669,518	
1875	40,339,674	2,855,899	
1880	42,468,662	2,429,371	
1885	39,432,562	1,426,108	
1886	47,454,153	1,590,432	80%
1890	65,655,917	2,196,040	92%
1895	65,632,613	1,695,920	89%
1896	73,442,598	1,874,555	95%

Source: Statistical Register of the Colony of Cape of Good Hope, 1886, p. vii; 1890, p. v; 1896, p. xiv.

The falling wool price was a setback for farmers. Increased production may have caused a lowered price, but the reverse could also have been the case; farmers produced more to retain the same level of income when the price fell. We have noted previously that the bulk of the Cape wool went to Britain and that the initial success of wool farming relied on demand from British textile manufacturers. This continued also during the last decades of the century. But more interestingly, the British share of wool exported from the Cape increased towards the end of the century. The imperial power strengthened its relation to the Colony, and the Cape's dependency on Britain subsequently increased. Cape farmers were more than ever in the hands of Bradford textile capital.

Viewing the exchange of wool for wire from a trade balance perspective it seems as if the British Empire made a considerable loss. The sums gained from the wire trade were next to nothing compared to the millions spent on buying the colonial wool, in 1890, for example more than £2 million. But such a perspective disregards the international division of labour in the capitalist world-economy. Britain had become an industrial society during the mid-nineteenth century, moving away from farming, including production of raw material for industrial refinement. The wool produced domestically within the UK decreased after the 1840s, and considerably after the 1870s and 1880s.[267] Buying the wool from the colonies meant that focus could be on production of

[267] Kirk, T 1980, pp. 228-29; Jenkins & Ponting, 1982, p. 188, 204; See also Hobsbawm, E 1994, p. 20.

finished commodities and the profits made there were more than enough to cover up any deficit in the trade balance; British exports of textile manufactured goods in 1885 valued almost £19 million, in 1890 £20 million and in 1895 £19 million.[268] Buying wool from colonies was much cheaper than buying domestic wool. The export of capital in the form of wire was therefore an indirect investment in production of raw material used for finished textile commodities. Wire made possible the creation of camps used for rotational grazing, which increased the quality of the raw material, the wool, which in turn enhanced production of finished commodities in Britain.

The British share of wire imports into the Cape, however, decreased in favour of imports from primarily the US. There were thus other actors involved, who were not residents in a state which was a colonial power in Africa. But the US textile manufacturers were also buyers of Cape wool. The US share of the wool decreased from 12 per cent in 1886 to 9 per cent in 1890 and to 4 per cent in 1896. However, US textile capitalists were still the second largest buyer of Cape wool behind the UK. Also in that case it was thus an exchange of wire for wool, and the US capitalists started to challenge British interests in southern Africa. The international division of labour was most clearly seen with Britain and the Cape, but also the US textile industry made profits from colonial wool. Furthermore, the US domestic production of wool was considerably larger than the British one. Unlike the Cape, the former colonial areas in North America turned their wool into finished commodities instead of shipping it abroad.[269]

The wool for wire trade must be seen in relation to another form of capital investment: the railways. Between 1870s and 1890 the amount of railway in Cape increased, which was the case also in India and other colonial areas. According to Luxemburg the railways were exports of capital from core to periphery. The introduction of railways in the Cape was directly related to the mining industry in the north. However, it affected also other sectors as the access to markets became easier. Before 1885 the railway reached wool districts such as Cradock, Queenstown, Beaufort West, De Aar, Hopetown and Graaff-Reinet.[270] When the railway between Port Elizabeth and Graaff-Reinet opened in 1879, Richard Rubidge noted that it was a "[b]ig event in G.R. [...]".[271] It is difficult to estimate how much the railway actually benefitted the wool production. The railway was at least not an immediate success. The line through Graaff-Reinet was not profitable for some time after the line north went through Cradock instead. The competition from ox wagons and transport

268 Jenkins & Ponting, 1982, p. 222.

269 Jenkins & Ponting 1982, p. 186.

270 Smith, K 1976, p 83.

271 CL MS 6189, Old Extracts from Old Wellwood, Aug.27, 1879.

riders also proved to be tough.[272] Wool was not a commodity that deteriorated by not being sold immediately. The time from shearing to sales and thereby income for farmers was accelerated, though. In the 1930s Sidney Rubidge noted what the railways meant in terms of transport time. Before the construction of the railway a trip from Graaff-Reinet to Port Elizabeth by ox wagon took about 10 days. Sidney Rubidge's first trip by train took 14 hours.[273] The railway obviously revolutionized transports. But it also incorporated Cape wool farming more closely into world capitalist production. The railway in Graaff-Reinet connected Wellwood, through Uitenhage where wool washing was conducted, and the export port in Port Elizabeth, to London's wool market and ultimately textile production in Bradford in England.[274]

Although the railway was primarily a result of the impact of mining, wool farmers were active in the decision making about its extension. Richard Rubidge attended a railway meeting in 1895.[275] The following year he "took list for signature to Bloemhof & Middlewater, in favour of Railway station near to Tromphs [?] kraal".[276] Later the same year he could report that there were "[g]reat doings in Graaff-Reinet in connection with [...] the GR Middelburg Railways extension".[277] There was at that time no extension of the line north of Graaff-Reinet. The railway north to Middelburg Road was opened by Sir Alfred Milner in 1898. The railway thus not only reached the mine fields, it was also extended to small wool farming towns such as Middelburg. The railway line through Cradock was, however, the one where most transports to the north passed.[278] The railway, although in competition with transport riders and ox wagons, brought the wool farmers closer to the British Empire, both regarding wool exports and wire imports for fencing. So let us see how farmers in the Cape reacted to becoming more entwined in the capitalist world-economy.

Sharing costs

Fencing in various areas throughout the Cape had been underway for some time at the end of the 1880s. A *Fencing Act* in 1883 compelled farmers to share fencing costs where they had mutual boundaries. According to witnesses to the *Select Committee on Fencing or Enclosing of Land* in 1889 a substantial amount

272 Smith, K 1976, p. 80.

273 Rubidge diaries, July 28, 1936. He does not mention when he went on his first trip.

274 For the importance of railways in expanding capitalism, see Engren, J 2007.

275 Rubidge diaries, Feb. 22, 1895.

276 Rubidge diaries, March 23, 1896.

277 Rubidge diaries, Aug. 15, 1896.

278 Smith, K 1976, p. 85.

of fencing had been undertaken. But not only wire fencing. John Frost, M. L. A. from Queenstown, had fenced fifty to sixty miles, stone walls and wire fencing, mostly wire fencing. "The first fence [he] erected was with iron standards and strainers, and they cost about £100 per mile, including gates."[279] Arthur Douglass in Grahamstown had "erected about forty miles of post and wire and stone wall fencing".[280] Similar to the Rubidges in Graaff-Reinet, both these farmers used a combination of stone walls and wire fences. The price on wire explains why stone walls were still in fashion and continued to be built. Despite this, Douglass reported that there was a lot of fencing being done in the Albany area.[281]

Paying £100 per mile, like Frost had done, was very expensive, but the price had dropped considerably since he erected his first fence. At the end of the 1880s he estimated that fencing cost £50 per mile.[282] Also John Laing in Beaufort agreed that fencing had become cheaper the past couple of years. When he first started to fence the cost was about £80 per mile, but "fencing can now be done for £40 to £50 per mile [...]".[283] Despite the reduced prices the costs of fencing were large. But the advantages were great. According to Frost fencing would pay in the Karroo, where each sheep required two morgen of land instead of three, as in Queenstown. According to Frost it "would pay the owner of such land better than it would pay me, because sheep tramp about the country, and have to be brought home every night". He further suggested that, once kraaling and trekking had disappeared, it would only take a couple of years before "the farmer, instead of having to take two morgen of land for one sheep, would be able to double his stock."[284]

Frost, who belonged to the group of very wealthy wool farmers in the Cape, of course, had few problems with financing his fencing. Most farmers in the Karroo, who had larger farms, and less money, would not find it cheap at all. But Frost insisted on declaring fencing as valuable and profitable also for them "as the expense of fencing is considerably reduced in proportion to the extent." Frost did, however, admit that it would be hard on poorer Karroo farmers initially to fence, but they would recoup themselves within a few years.[285]

The material used was important, and played a significant role. John Laing in Beaufort used "thoroughly good sneezewood poles, which I plant twelve

[279] Select Committee on Fencing, 1889. Evidence by John Frost, C. M. G., M. L. A., Queenstown, p. 9.

[280] Select Committee on Fencing, 1889. Evidence of Arthur Douglass, M. L. A., Grahamstown, p. 22.

[281] Select Committee on Fencing, 1889. Evidence of Arthur Douglass, M. L. A., Grahamstown, p. 23.

[282] Select Committee on Fencing, 1889. Evidence by John Frost, Queenstown, p. 15.

[283] Select Committee on Fencing, 1889, Evidence by John Laing, M. L. A. Beaufort, p. 20.

[284] Select Committee on Fencing, 1889. Evidence by John Frost, Queenstown, p. 15.

[285] Select Committee on Fencing, 1889. Evidence of John Frost, Queenstown, p. 15.

yards apart". After that "I lace the wires two yards apart, and the number of wires being six, and the height of a fence, as a rule, four feet six inches". According to him, such a fence cost about £40 per mile."[286]

Although Karroo farmers owned larger farms than others, there was at least one advantage regarding fencing. Arthur Douglass in Grahamstown claimed that the cost of fencing was larger near the sea. The salt air, which eroded fences close to the coast, was not a problem further inland: "[a]s soon as you get in the karroo, [...], you can use No. 6 or No. 8 steel wire and put up an effective fence." But also other material affected the price. Douglass, who farmed "in rather broken country and considerable bush [...]", mentioned that he had to put poles close together and instead of paying £40 as in the Karroo, he paid £80 per mile. If the poles were too far apart and "as soon as the wire rust at all, I think the fence would be liable to go to pieces [...]". This was obviously a problem for a farmer who wanted to have a long-term strategy for the farm. A "boundary fence ought to be of so solid a nature as to last for a quarter of a century".[287] As Douglass pointed out, good quality wires and poles would be profitable in the long run. But many farmers tried to save money and used cheaper materials, both wires and poles, which proved to create even more costs as such fences did not last long.[288]

Evidently, the last years of the 1880s were characterized by much fencing among Cape farmers. There was an increasing consensus that it was a good investment both for the individual farmer and the Cape Colony as a whole. But some of them appear to have had objections. According to John Laing, fencing "would be the best investment a man could make if he had not to borrow money". Those farmers who had little access to capital were thus forced to go to the bank, which some of them probably were reluctant to do. Furthermore, Laing pointed out that there was much fencing being done in the Beaufort area, but that the present act was imperfect as the term of payment between neighbours was fifteen years.[289] This lowered incentives for progressive farmers to start fencing as it would take more than a decade before they had been reimbursed.

In Graaff-Reinet the Rubidges and their neighbours managed these relations fairly well. In the mid-1880s the Rubidges had fenced a large part of Wellwood, but it was uncertain how far the neighbours had reached. Apparently there was a stretch of fence that the neighbour "du Toit does not pay for 874 yards". Du Toit on the farm Dasjesfontein did thus not have to fence that stretch of his farm. He could save some money by not sharing the costs. But the fenced

[286] Select Committee on Fencing, 1889. Evidence of John Laing, Beaufort, p. 19.

[287] Select Committee on Fencing, 1889. Evidence of Arthur Douglass, M. L. A., Grahamstown, p. 22.

[288] Van Sittert, L 2002, p. 100.

[289] Select Committee on Fencing, 1889. Evidence of John Laing, M. L. A., Beaufort, p. 20.

border between the two farm was considerably longer, more than 6,000 yards.[290] Du Toit and the Rubidges presumably came to an agreement on that fence, and du Toit probably paid the neighbour after the accounts were made. But he did not actually have to do anything such as hiring labour, buying wires, measuring and planting poles. Being in the right neighbourhood was thus an advantage, but it pressured also those who did not consider farming development as important to become progressive. In the worst case, this pressured the poorer farmers into bankruptcy or to the point where they had to sell their farms. Changing the farms was thus beneficial only to those who could afford it. The ability to invest into farms was in turn based on how much wool farmers could sell to British textile manufacturers. The pressure on poorer farmers was an indication that capitalist production of wool meant structural rationalization. There was a limited amount of profits for farmers to compete over, which meant not all could prosper and be "progressive".

For those white farmers who bordered on the areas of black people, further problems arose. Laing thought that the difficulty was "that in many native locations you have no legally constituted body to represent them, and it would be difficult to call upon them, under the Act, to pay or become liable for fencing".[291] The fundamental issue that disturbed white farmers was the lack of private ownership of the land belonging to black people. No individual could take on the responsibility or cost of fencing as the land was not owned by any individual, but was communal. These issues created great difficulties in a region where private ownership of land was relatively new. As Hobsbawm argues for the Scottish case, lack of private ownership of land stood in the way for capitalist farming.[292]

The lack of fencing around native locations was threatening to farmers in more ways. It made trespassing and illegal grazing easier and meant that disease could spread more easily among sheep. The lack of fences enabled sheep to wander around quite freely. Even without trespassing consciously it was thus possible that sheep of black and white people became mixed up if they grazed close to each other. The fences clearly remedied the situation and kept the different flocks apart. But the spread of disease was not stopped altogether. John Frost claimed that fences "certainly reduces the chances of infection; but my sheep, for instance, may come near those of my neighbour and touch against them through the wire fence".[293] Not even a fence could thus make farmers feel safe.

290 Rubidge diaries, Feb. 18, 1886.

291 Select Committee on Fencing, 1889. Evidence of John Laing, Beaufort, p. 20.

292 Hobsbawm, E. J. 1980, pp. 8-11.

293 Select Committee on Fencing, 1889. Evidence of John Frost, Queenstown, p. 17.

Combination of farming practices

Between 1891 and 1904 the area covered by fences in the Cape increased vastly: from 4 million morgen to more than 12 million. This was a crucial period in the fencing of the Cape. The leading districts regarding fencing in 1891 were Somerset East (316,326 morgen), Cradock (235,268 morgen) and Albany (217,615 morgen). In 1904 Somerset East (563,805 morgen), Cradock (527,438 morgen) and Graaff-Reinet (521,268 morgen) were at the top of the list.[294] All these were large wool producing districts.

Van Sittert has demonstrated that the Fencing Act was first implemented in the Eastern Cape and then spread to the north, west and the south.[295] Fencing of course improved possibilities of producing more and better wool, which resulted in higher profits for the farmers in these districts. But fencing in those districts was also caused by the fact that they were the leading wool producers already before fencing started. Farmers there had accumulated capital and had a desire to invest in new technology and implement capitalist relations. It is thus not surprising that these were the first areas to implement new legislation. However, implementing new legislation and investing in fences does not necessarily mean that farming practices changed at the same rate, which indicates that labour relations remained unchanged.

On Wellwood some of the camps were used for cultivation and also for horses, cattle and ostriches. Furthermore, the building of new kraals on Wellwood also suggests that kraaling and trekking remained a vital part of wool farming. Unless we analyse actual farms we cannot tell if and how farming practices and labour relations changed.

The witnesses to the Select Committee on Fencing in 1872 argued that the creation of camps would save farmers the cost of having shepherds; fences would make them redundant. Some estimated large savings, more than £100 per year, although those figures could be debated. However, the general idea with a fence was to replace human labour power with technology and in the process create better conditions for a profitable wool industry. But the hopes among farmers to replace shepherds were not fulfilled.

294 Cape of Good Hope Census 1904, pp. 506-07; 1891, pp. 456-57.

295 Van Sittert, L 2002, pp. 102-04.

Table 9. Shepherds and sheep and shepherds/pastoral farmer in the Cape 1875, 1891 and 1904.

Year	Shepherds	Sheep (million)	Sheep/shepherd	Shepherd/farmer
1875	17,233	10.9	633	2.0
1891	38,869	16.7	430	2.5
1904	34,093	11.8	346	1.98

Source: Cape of Good Hope Census 1875, p 185,xiii ; Cape of Good Hope Census 1891, p 304-05, 438. Cape of Good Hope Census 1904, pp. 344-45, 478.

Between 1875 and 1891 the number of shepherds more than doubled. The increase was partly a response to increasing sheep numbers, but the ratio between shepherds and sheep also changed; each shepherd became responsible for fewer sheep, which was contrary to expectations. Furthermore, as the number of sheep per farmer also increased, we can conclude that farmers had no problems finding labour and that the practice of using shepherds in fact increased along with fencing during the late nineteenth century. Around the turn of the century the number of sheep and shepherds decreased, and the trend of each shepherd taking care of fewer sheep continued. As the number of shepherds per farmer was reduced, it appears that farmers had trouble finding labour.

The dramatic increase in shepherds during the late nineteenth century, although it was related to overall expansion of the industry, could be seen as reflecting only the growth of those farmers who did not fence. The witnesses to the Select Committee in 1872 surely expected shepherds to disappear, as did most others, and we can therefore not be sure how the changed production of wool actually affected the shepherds. Archers argues that the reason for the continued use of shepherds was the prevalence of jackals.[296] That is a likely explanation, but in order to find out, we will have to return to a farm like Wellwood, where we can follow the relationship between shepherds, jackals and fences more closely.

In 1875 there were four people enlisted as shepherds on Wellwood according to the list of employees, but that was inaccurate. An analysis of the diaries revealed that there were at least seven references to shepherds or people performing the work of shepherds during that year. This discrepancy also gives cause to some doubt regarding the census figures for the whole Cape, but if there was an underrepresentation everywhere it is still possible to use them comparatively.

Unfortunately, there are no other lists of people on Wellwood during the late nineteenth century. We will thus have to rely on the diaries. According to these,

[296] Archer, S 2000, p. 692.

the number of shepherds did not decrease at all the first years after 1875; in 1880 there were references to at least six shepherds on the farm: Klein Adam, Danster (cattle), Old Jan, Matika, Claas and Old Booy.[297] One of them, Old Jan, was discharged and replaced by Matika. There were thus at least five at any given time. As we have seen, the late 1870s was not characterized by excessive fencing and creation of camps, which could explain why nothing seems to have changed. Contrary to this, the Rubidges invested more heavily in camps during the 1880s. Subsequently, in 1885 there were only references to three shepherds Jan, Jolly and Tom,[298] which suggests that a drastic change had occurred during the first half of the decade. One of them, Jolly, was even discharged during the year.[299] But these assumptions are quickly proven wrong. The following year, in 1886, there were seven shepherds mentioned: Old Jan, Tom, Soul, Jan, "Man", Uithalder [?] and Alwyn.[300] An additional five years later there were again only three shepherds referenced, but in 1896 there were at least six shepherds according to the diaries.[301] If anything, the number of shepherds on Wellwood had not changed much at all during the 1880s along with the creation of camps. The exact sheep number on Wellwood during this period is unknown, but there were probably 2,500. Farming practices did thus not change at all, even among those farmers who were at the frontline regarding investments in new technology. Shepherds, not wires and poles, still remained the principal guards of the sheep.

In 1889 John Frost in Queenstown had noticed "during the last three or four years, that the destruction by wild animals is so much on the increase that I have been compelled for the first time since I have been living in the Queenstown division to kraal my ewes and lambs constantly".[302] The advantages of fencing were great, but not "quite so great as they would be if we could destroy all the vermin".[303] Worst among the vermin was the jackal.[304] The jackals could not be kept out of the camps constructed by wires; they easily went through the fences. Therefore, shepherds were still required. While the jackal intrusion was definitely an important reason, perhaps even the most important one, it does not suffice as an explanation. Wellwood can be used to illustrate.

297 Rubidge diaries, April 30, June 21, Oct. 27, Nov, 14, Dec. 14, 1880.

298 Rubidge diaries, Jan. 16, March 16, Dec. 19, 1880.

299 Rubidge diaries, May 5, 1880.

300 Rubidge diaries, Jan. 3, 7, 21, March 16, Aug. 14, Sept. 22, Nov. 5, 1880.

301 Rubidge diaries, Feb. 9, 24, March 14; Jan. 27, Feb. 15, March 16, April 8, Oct. 5, Nov, 4, 1896.

302 Select Committee on Fencing, 1889. Evidence by John Frost, Queenstown, p 18.

303 Select Committee on Fencing, 1889, Evidence by John Frost, Queenstown, p. 10.

304 Select Committee on Fencing, 1889, Evidence by John Frost, Queenstown, p. 18.

Judging by the Rubidge diaries, jackals were not a big problem during the 1880s. The Rubidges, who had about five or six camps, could thus easily have fired the shepherds and saved money on labour. But they did not. As seen, they started building new kraals, which testifies to their intentions of continuing that practice. Although some camps were not used for sheep, most of them were. But shepherds herded them also in camps, which means that two practices were used at the same time: fencing and shepherding. This happened without interference from jackals. We must therefore seek answers in the actual labour process of shepherding. It is there that we will find why they were indispensable.

The shepherd had three major duties: to guard the sheep, bring them to grazing and bring them to water. While the two first ones could be taken care of in fenced camps, the third one could not in a satisfactory manner.

We have seen that a lot of effort was put into building dams on Wellwood, and there were probably five or six during the 1880s. They thus equalled the camps more or less. Having water in each camp was a precondition for farming sheep with rotational grazing. The dams on Wellwood probably fulfilled this requirement to some extent, but were all depending on rain water. If drought struck, or even if the rains stayed away for some months, which they could without conditions being even close to a drought, there would be problems. Considering this, it is easier to comprehend why shepherds were still required in quite large numbers. While Wellwood was worse off than many other farms due to the lack of spring water, the development of dams had made it equal to the general average in the Cape, if not better, as far as water supply was concerned.

Although dams functioned fairly well, a more reliable method was required. This was created through drilling for water and the use of windmills. For the Cape as a whole there were very few windmills during the last decades of the nineteenth century. In Graaff-Reinet there were only a few in 1891, but at least one of them was situated on Wellwood as Richard Rubidge was out in the veld and "[o]iled windmill" already in 1885. [305] The windmill was probably pumping water from a well nearby, but there was apparently a problem with its depth; later the same year a mason called Hamilton had "finished deepening well".[306]

There seems to have been only one windmill on Wellwood for a long time. One problem with this method was that water had to be found underground, which may have proven to be difficult on the farm. In any case, the windmill did not affect shepherding practices to any great extent. At least not as long as there was only one. Relying on windmills would also prove to be hard. A year

---

[305] Rubidge diaries, Jan. 15. 1885

[306] Rubidge diaries, May 2, 1885.

after the well was deepened, the windmill was "out of order".[307] New technology also required new skills and it does not seem like the Rubidges or farmers in general were able to repair the windmills on their own. Jan van Niekerk on the farm Albertvale in Bedford also brought a man to the farm "to look at my windmill".[308] Skilled labour would thus have to be called upon in order to get the water to start running again. Similarly, in 1890 on Wellwood the windmill was "damaged", suggesting that there was only one windmill, and that it could not be relied upon.[309] As with all machinery, maintenance was important. Richard Rubidge at first seems to have taken care of this himself, but in 1891 he found assistance as he "[s]howed Coetzee how to oil windmill".[310] Coetzee was probably an Afrikaner who acted as foreman on the farm. As he was given the task to take care of the crucial and expensive machinery he was at least trusted and in a position of some status.

The unreliable windmills did, however, mean that the dams were still the best way to secure water. A lot of time and money went into building them also during the 1880s. Yet another dam was completed in 1886; in February Richard Rubidge seemed satisfied when they "[f]inished off dam after over two years work".[311] Instead of focusing only on jackals as the cause for the continued use of shepherds, we have reached further by also including the actual labour process on wool farms. As seen, water supplies in the form of windmills were not at all widespread at the end of the nineteenth century. Wells and dams were more frequent, but it is questionable if they supplied water to every camp where sheep grazed, so a shepherd would still have to trek them. Furthermore, many camps were used for other things than sheep. It was more important to fence in lucerne, barley and mealies than the sheep on the successful farm Wellwood. Other farms could not have differed much from that practice.

Jackal-proof fences

While there were few incidents where sheep were taken by jackals on Wellwood during the 1880s and early 1890s, their presence was felt on other farms. Various methods were used in attempts to eradicate them. Poison, traps and hunting were all tried to a greater or lesser extent, but neither of them worked. The only thing that could keep the jackals away was jackal-proof fences.

---

[307] Rubidge diaries, June 5, 1886.

[308] CL PR 3418, Van Niekerk diaries, July 4, 1895.

[309] Rubidge diaries, Sept. 28, 1890.

[310] Rubidge diaries, March 24, 1891.

[311] Rubidge diaries, Feb. 12, 1886.

The ordinary wire fences, which have been described briefly, were usually strung with four to six wires, and were about one and a half metres tall. The spaces between the wires were thus wide, which made it possible for the jackal to enter an enclosed area. Stringing the wires closely together, leaving only a decimetre or two between them, could prohibit jackals from entering. But that method would be expensive. Farmers would have to use at least eight, and maybe ten, wires in order to create a fence that would keep the jackals out. Thus double the cost. Another type of fence was therefore required, a fence that would be tight enough to keep jackals out, but not be twice as expensive as the ordinary wire fence. The solution was a netting fence. The netting fences were in use in various parts of the world during the late nineteenth century. Farmers in Australia had faced similar problems as the ones brought on by jackals in the Cape.[312] The netting fence had thus been in use for some time when jackals appeared as vermin in the Cape. In southern Africa there were, however, no netting fences around. Consequently, they would have to be imported.

There was no massive import of netting fences during the late nineteenth century. Only in 1909 do they appear as a special post in the *Statistical Register*. Netting fences worth roughly £13,000 were imported that year, almost all of it from the UK.[313] Compared to the imports of regular wire worth about £115,000 that year it was only a fraction, but it is noteworthy that investments in netting fences started to make a mark at that point. Around twenty years had passed since farmers had started to feel threatened by jackals, which seems like a long time.

No domestic production of netting fences seems to have been conducted during the decades around the turn of the century. The Cape farmers thus again had to rely on developments in other parts of the world. Apparently, machines that constructed netting fences were constructed around the turn of the century, which made them considerably cheaper.[314] Their implementation on a large scale in the Cape did therefore not take place before the first decade of the twentieth century. But some farmers did not wait for the price to go down, or for government subsidies. The Rubidges were most likely among the first farmers in southern Africa to implement this new technology. During the winter of 1896 Richard Rubidge reported that he had "[p]ut netting to wire fence at windmill corner".[315] There may have been previous netting fences on Wellwood, but this was most likely the first one. Seemingly, the netting was attached to the existing wire fence. The netting was thus not completely functional on its own. Perhaps it was meant only as a complement. In any case,

---

312 Beinart, W 2008, p. 209, 220.

313 *Statistical Register*, 1909, p. 100.

314 Beinart, W 2008, p. 220. Does not say when machines were built, but they were in use by 1905, see *Agricultural Journal* 1905, vol xxvii, No 3, pp. 360-71.

315 Rubidge diaries, July 24, 1896.

the quality of the net was not as good as would be required. Neither does it seem to have covered a large area, although the windmill corner may have been of some length.

The windmill corner seems to have been chosen for a reason. We can expect that the Rubidges regarded it as a place where jackals could easily enter the farm. Furthermore, the windmill corner must have been a place where sheep gathered to drink water. As there was only one windmill at the time on Wellwood, it may have supplied several adjoining camps with water. If so, sheep from two, or maybe even three camps would have gathered on a fairly small area of the farm to drink. Such a place was easily found by the jackals. Jackal-proofing this particular part of the farm was thus probably a response to an increased threat from jackals there. The new technology implemented in water supply was thus not only beneficial; it also gave rise to new problems. When sheep drank water from dams they were more spread out. Mechanical water supply brought them together, which made it easier for jackals to find and catch them.

Van Niekerk in Bedford, seems to have been even earlier than the Rubidges to implement netting fences. In 1895 there was much activity on the farm. In June, van Niekerk went out to a place on the farm to inspect a man called Harkoff, who "was getting on with the Netfencing". Presumably, van Niekerk was more threatened by jackals than the Rubidges were. During 1895 and 1896 only one sheep was, however, reported having been caught by a jackal on Albertvale.[316] Only the day before the dead sheep was found, the fencing work was finished. On September 11 van Niekerk went to the flock which grazed where the fencing was done and "looked over the last 1300 yards of net fencing from Harkoff. I paid him by cheque £9.15.6."[317] Unlike the Rubidges, who had only fenced a corner with netting, van Niekerk covered a much larger area. In fact, he covered an entire camp. At the beginning of the following month the camp was brought into use as he sent a flock of 815 sheep to this area, which was "enclosed with netwire".[318]

Jackal-proof fencing was evidently implemented during the 1890s, but on a rather limited scale. Few farmers could afford the fences at that point. Many were probably also unaware of their existence. Before the early twentieth century the jackal-proof fences were not advertised or covered in the *Agricultural Journal*, although descriptions of homemade "netting" fences appeared.[319] Nevertheless, the implementation of netting fences was important. It demonstrates that farmers were ready to invest in this new technology. Hiring a few more shepherds to protect the sheep would have been cheaper in the short

316 CL PR 3418, Van Niekerk,diaries, Sept. 12, 1895.

317 CL PR 3418, Van Niekerk diaries, Sept. 11, 1895.

318 CL PR 3418, Van Niekerk diaries, Oct. 2, 1895.

319 Beinart, W 2008, p. 220.

run than buying expensive netting fences, but since the aim was to practice rotational grazing, investments in new fences were considered profitable in the long run.

On Wellwood the jackals definitely had a greater impact during the beginning of the twentieth century than they had in the 1890s. Perhaps the worst incident was when a jackal killed eight sheep in one day in 1900.320 On other occasions a single sheep, or perhaps two, were killed. But also other vermin proved to be threatening: a "red cat" also killed eight sheep in one day.[321] As a response to the threat from vermin more jackal-proof fencing was erected on the farm. In 1900 the camp in front of the house was enclosed with netting and also in 1905 a jackal-proof fence was erected. But the first years of the century there were very few jackal-proof camps on Wellwood, perhaps only one, which was mentioned in 1905.[322] Instead, a combination of netting and wires appears to have made up the enclosures on the farm. The price on netting was still high even for farmers like the Rubidges. There was thus still a dependence on shepherds.

If we once again analyse the references made to shepherds on Wellwood we find that nothing had changed since the 1890s. In 1900 there were seven shepherds mentioned, in 1901 there were four and in 1905 there were six. Despite the use of shepherds it is, however, obvious that rotational grazing was practiced on a large scale. In 1900 there were five camps used.

Disruption, recovery and destruction of a colonial industry

During the 1890s the Cape farmers were supported in their fencing activities by the Government, primarily due to the rinderpest epidemic. The pest most affected the stock belonging to black peasants, but also white farmers suffered losses. The Cape Government, however, wanted to prevent the disease from entering the Colony and subsequently wanted to fence the border. The Second Anglo-Boer War 1899 - 1901 contributed to fencing in the Cape. The British fenced the border in order to keep Boer commandos out of the Colony. But the war also disrupted the advancements made by farmers as many fences were destroyed.[323] The number of sheep also decreased from 16.7 million in 1891 to 11.8 million in 1904. For wool exports, the disruption caused by the war was not as severe as the loss of sheep numbers indicate, though.

---

[320] Rubidge diaries, May 31, 1900.

[321] Rubidge diaries, Jan. 11, 1900.

[322] Rubidge diaries, Dec. 30, 1905.

[323] Van Sittert, L 2002, p. 104.

Table 10. Cape wool exports.

Year	Lbs.	£
1895	65,632,613	1,695,920
1896	73,442,598	1,874,555
1897	60,255,417	1,496,779
1898	73,732,926	1,766,740
1899	69,289,606	2,183,904
1900	27,671,036	837,809
1901	65,209,699	1,489,246
1902	79,327,850	1,930,227
1903	65,524,078	1,817,932
1905	63,473,934	1,887,459
1907	77,469,254	2,490,297
1909	102,345,698	2,820,716

Source: *Statistical Register*, 1896, p. xiv; 1900, p. xv; 1905, p. xx; 1909, p. xix,

The export of wool was more or less unchanged except for the year 1900. We clearly see that also during the 1890s there were fluctuations in export figures. A high point was reached in 1896 and 1898. The war meant a setback, but only for one year, 1900. Next year the export had returned to pre-war figures, and in 1902 a new record was reached, although the wool price had dropped. Increased production generated a lower price, or reversely, low prices caused farmers to produce more to maintain their income. The causality is uncertain, but the relationship is evident.

These figures do, however, correspond with those of the British textile industry. Beginning in the 1890s there was a decreased production and export of textiles in Britain. There were several reasons for this, but a main one was the competition from the US textile industry. Especially the tariff on imported textile products to the US, which was meant to spur domestic textile production in the US, affected the English textile industry. In 1890 British exports to the US made up 25 per cent; in 1900 only 9 per cent and in 1910 only 7 per cent. But during the early twentieth century British exports turned up again, much because of exports to other parts of the Empire; in 1890, 22 per cent of exports went to the Empire, in 1900 it had risen to 33 per cent and in 1910 as much as 40 per cent.[324] British textile capital thus exploited imperial relations in order to find an outlet for their products when textile manufacturing in the US threatened their markets. Core and periphery within the Empire were thus brought more closely together also in regards to sale of finished products. This upturn affected Cape wool farming and exports were

[324] Jenkins & Ponting 1982, pp. 222, 235-43.

soon larger than ever before. In 1909 the Cape exports increased by 25 per cent compared to the previous year and reached 100 million lbs. Similar tendencies were apparent also in Australian sheep numbers, which was reduced from more than 100 million in 1890 to about 50 million in 1905.[325] The problems experienced by farmers in the Cape around the turn of the century was therefore more of a setback in the global, or at least the imperial, production of wool and textiles. A disturbance in the production of finished commodities in Britain was thus felt throughout the wool producing communities of the Empire.

The Cape wool farmers, and those in Australia and New Zealand, could barely have managed without the British textile industry. But its role started to decrease at the expense of textile capital in the US and other European countries. In 1909 Cape farmers exported more than 100 million lbs of wool, but only about 60 per cent of it was sent to the UK. Primarily Germany had become a large buyer by then, purchasing about 33 million lbs. In 1909 the UK again bought as much wool as before the downturn of the industry, more than 60 million lbs., which indicates that the textile industry there had recovered. But what caused Cape wool farmers to export record amounts of wool was an increased demand from outside the UK. This marked the beginning of both the diminished role of the British Empire in the Cape and South Africa, which was confirmed by the creation of the Union of South Africa in 1910, and the Cape farmers' reliance on other markets than the imperial one. Although the Cape farmers had initially been indirectly bound to textile manufacturers in Britain, their position was definitely one of less dependence by 1909. They had not freed themselves from colonial ties, as the UK was still the main buyer of their wool. But Cape farmers' ability to sell also to others meant that they could actually increase the sale of their wool. Capitalism as a transnational production system, not the British Empire in itself, was the crucial structure for wool farming.

However, there was a more important change in the wool exports from the Cape during the last decades of the nineteenth century and the beginning of the twentieth. In the late nineteenth century wool-washing was a widespread industry in the Cape. Noble mentioned that from Cape Town to Aliwal North there were washeries. The centre was, however, in Uitenhage, on the Zwartkops River, where there were ten washeries.[326] Apparently, the soft and alkaline water made it suited for washing, but the proximity to Port Elizabeth was also important for the growth of the industry in Uitenhage. The railway between Port Elizabeth and Uitenhage opened in 1875, probably directly as a result of

[325] Beinart, W 2008, p. 12.

[326] Noble, J 1875, p. 177.

the wool washing. According to Noble £200,000 had been invested in the washeries, where about 200,000 bales per year were washed in 1875.[327]

Washing and scouring meant a further step in the commodity chain and enhanced the value of the wool. Capital in the periphery clearly used wool washing as a means to accumulate capital from their position in relation to the core in Britain. They had access to raw material, which was demanded elsewhere in the world. Until 1870 washed and scoured wool made up two thirds of the wool exports from the Cape.[328] In 1886 washed and scoured wool constituted 24 million lbs of a total of 47.4 million lbs., thus about half. But the washed and scoured wool brought £1.1 million of the total of £1.5 million. In 1895 washed and scoured wool made up about 25 per cent of the total wool exports: 16 million lbs. of a total of 65.6 million lbs. The income from scoured and washed wool was about 40 per cent of the total: £712,082 of £1.7 million. During the early twentieth century the industry collapsed. In 1909 washed and scoured wool only constituted 3.8 million lbs. of a total of 102 million lbs. and brought in £201,268 of a total of £2.8 million.[329]

Beinart correctly notes that the decreased value of wool exports from the 1870s was not so much a result of decreased production, but the destruction of wool washing, which meant that grease wool became the principal export.[330] However, he does not mention why wool washing disappeared. Obviously, manufacturers were more interested in buying grease wool as it was cheaper, but for a long time they bought washed wool. If we look into the production process in textile factories we may find a likely answer. New technology in washing, especially a process known as carbonising for removal of vegetable matter, became more widespread during the late nineteenth and early twentieth centuries.[331] Washing in factories in Europe thus became more profitable and the process of washing of wool was subsequently moved from periphery to core. In order to maintain their income from wool, farmers were forced to produce more grease wool. Such a relocation of a part of production meant that the manufacturers increased their control over the production process. Within the commodity chain of wool, the role of the Cape as producer of raw material was further entrenched, while production of finished commodities became concentrated in Europe.

---

327 Noble, J 1875, p. 177.

328 Beinart, W 2008, p. 13.

329 Statistical Register 1886, p. vii; 1896, p. xiv; 1909, p. xix.

330 Beinart, W 2008, p. 13,15.

331 Jenkins & Ponting 1982, pp. 214-17.

CHAPTER 7

Perspectives on the Rural Class Struggle

Farm labourers and peasants – capitalist expansion

Wool farming undoubtedly includes other forms of labour than shepherding. We have already seen that fencing, dam building, lucerne cutting and weeding, shed building, windmill repair and shearing were all crucial parts of a successful wool industry. The development of the total farm labour force around the turn of the century is therefore crucial to the analysis.

Table 11. Farm labourers and peasants in the Cape 1891, 1904 and 1911.

Year	Farm labourers	Peasants
1891	57,825	489,037
1904	85,854	757,066
1911	89,195	749,589

Source: Cape of Good Hope Census 1891, pp. 18-19, 304-05; Cape of Good Hope Census 1904, pp. 344-45; South Africa Census 1911, pp. 8, 564-65.

While the shepherds decreased in number along with the sheep between 1891 and 1904, the farm labourers increased considerably. Unfortunately, we cannot determine which sectors of farming the labourers were involved in. Thus, for example wine and fruit farming, more than wool, may have caused the increase of farm labourers. However, we should assume that at least some of these were occupied on wool farms. There is a discrepancy between the number of people enumerated as farm labourers and as "workers on farms". In 1891 there were 180,443 persons enumerated as workers on farms in the Cape. More than 75,000 of these were white, which means that they were mainly family members of the white farmers. But 103,682 black and coloured people were enumerated as workers on farms.[332] They were most likely tenants, sharecroppers or casual labourers, who were not regarded as employed

[332] Cape of Good Hope Census 1891, pp. 446-47.

labourers, but that category probably also included domestics. The actual black and coloured labour force on farms was thus almost twice as large as the 57,852 labourers in 1891. In 1904 there were 210,942 workers on farms. More than 88,000 of these were white, 122,279 where black and coloured.[333] The black and coloured farm labourers thus made up 69 per cent of the total labour force in their group, which indicates increased proletarianization. In 1911 there were 223,216 workers on farms. 82,281 were white, 140,935 were black and coloured.[334] Thus farm labourers made up about 64 per cent of the labour force. Equally interesting, the number of peasants increased quite drastically too, although their share of the population was more or less the same in 1904 as in 1891.

The Cape Government tried to weaken the back peasantry during the late nineteenth century. Starting in the 1880s several location acts had been passed. These determined the number of tenants that a white farmer was allowed to have on his farm. Too many tenants resulted in a fine for the farmer. These measures were not successful, though. In 1894 the *Glen Grey Act* was passed. In essence it restricted the area a black man was allowed to own to only a few morgen, and was thus called the "one-man-one lot" system.[335] As the area allowed for each person was limited, a subdivision of the land begun.

Restricting the area allowed for each person of course made it difficult for black people to accumulate wealth, either through stock or cultivation. Even those who had plots of their own thus found that their peasant farming was not enough, and were forced to seek employment on white farms to be able to survive. But more importantly, it disrupted the pre-colonial system of production, which was based on the gendered and generational division of labour. The small areas allowed for each person could not sustain a family consisting of one male head of family, one or several wives, brothers and sisters of the head of family or the wives and their combined children. Instead only a man and a wife, and small children, could be sustained on such a plot if it was big enough. Those who could not be sustained, i.e. the ones who had no household of their own, were also forced to become labourers. We can expect that a portion of those who were peasants in 1904 had become farm labourers in 1911. The peasant's share of the population decreased from 31 per cent in 1904 to 29 per cent in 1911. The trend with a vastly increasing peasant population thus culminated during the first decade of the twentieth century, which suggests that the increase between 1891 and 1904 to a large extent was caused by the implementation of individual tenure among the black people in the Eastern Cape. The Glen Grey Act can therefore be seen as the beginning of the end of the pre-colonial South African peasantry.

---

[333] Cape of Good Hope Census 1904, pp. 496-97.

[334] South Africa Census 1911, pp. 1346-48.

[335] Bundy, C 1979, p. 135.

This development can most clearly be explained through the words of Rosa Luxemburg. She asserts that the capitalist system is dependent on other modes of production, but simultaneously consumes them.[336] This was exactly the case with the peasantry in the Cape. The capitalist sector, which required labour, drew peasants away from their pre-colonial and pre-capitalist system of production, which weakened the peasantry. The establishment of capitalist relations of production was a central part in this, but we have seen that labour relations were not what we call capitalist. Instead there was a mixture of cash wages and wages in kind and grazing rights. Neither were the labourers totally proletarianized; they owned means of production in the form of sheep, goats and cattle, and many of them were migrants who owned plots of land outside of the white farming districts. This caused problems for some farmers. In Barkly East the "labour supply throughout the district has been fairly maintained, [but] the slump being felt during the winter months, when a majority of the Natives return to Kafirland for the harvest operations".[337] Apparently, a large share of the farm labourers in Barkly East were migratory, and thus only worked in the capitalist economy for parts of the year when they did not have to work on their own land.

To talk of semi-proletarianization is perhaps more accurate, but also difficult, as it presupposes a certain deterministic development of labour relations. We must therefore focus on the actual labour relations instead of getting caught in terminology. To paraphrase Mike Morris, the labour relations in wool farming can probably best be described as *proletarianizing*,[338] not halfway to a predetermined goal, or halfway from a distinct past. Much like capitalism itself, the labour relations were in a process, and were constantly changing. We know that the labourers were proletarianizing as they were continuously dispossessed of their means of production, and forced into labour outside of the family unit. The labour force in wool farming was more proletarianized than that in other rural sectors, where various forms of tenancy was common. This had been the case since the first half of the nineteenth century, which means that it is difficult to talk of a transition from pre-capitalist to capitalist wool farming in the Cape. Instead, there was increasing capitalist farming.

Those who worked on wool farms definitely took part in the capitalist world-economy. They did so in the peripheral part of it. As Wallerstein notes, there are various modes of labour, as he puts it, within the capitalist world-economy.[339] In the core, in English factories, the proletarian cash wage system was dominant. In the periphery, on Cape wool farms, there was a combination of labour relations. Grazing rights, cash wages, rations, and in some cases

---

[336] Luxemburg, R 2003, p. 397.

[337] Blue Book on Native Affairs 1909, Barkly East, p. 15.

[338] Morris, M, 1988, p.67, argues that "capitalism is always in a process of proletarianising".

[339] Wallerstein, I 1979, pp. 16-17.

tenancy, combined to form the remunerative practices. In between these two, along the commodity chain of wool, there were variations, but cash wage labour dominated the transports and management of the wool, to a greater extent in Britain than in the Cape. Although private capital was the main actor in the imperial wool industry, the state also had a crucial role to play. It was a medium and an agent for the expansion of capitalism, providing structures for accumulation of capital in the periphery and facilitating it both through loans to farmers and through building railways and roads. The role of the state will be analysed more closely in the following chapters, where aid to farmers through legislation will be focused.

Resistance to change – the class struggle intensified

Despite the increased number of black people being forced out to work on the farms of whites, the farmers were not satisfied with conditions. Some even complained that they had difficulties finding labour. A Select Committee was appointed to investigate the matter of farm labour supply in 1907.

It was evident that many farmers depended on various forms of tenancy. The racialized class struggle between farmers and peasant families who became labour families constituted the central factor in the formation of labour practices. Colonel Standford, chief magistrate for the Transkeian Territories, declared that the most common practice among farmers in the Eastern Province was to allow black families to stay on their farms. The wages paid were small, but "the natives have the advantage of a bit of land being given to them to cultivate and of running a certain quantity of stock, and they remain on the farms, and from these families the farmers draw their labour supply".[340] The family labour system was seemingly quite crucial to farmers. Getting the labourers to stay seems to have been a major concern. In Barkly East Frank Powrie said that they usually hired labourers for "six months and either pay them in sheep at the rate of one sheep per month or in cattle; [...]." But there were also other forms of remuneration: "If we hire for cash as farm servants we pay 15s. to 20s. and sometimes 12s. per month. [...] Yes, we feed them, and of course they have the advantage if they have stock of running them on the farm owner's property."[341]

Arthur Fuller, Stutterheim, agreed and stated that in the Eastern Province farmers had difficulties "in getting anything like a continuity of labour, except he is prepared to offer big inducements to the natives in the shape of squatting

---

[340] Select Committee on Farm Labour Supply, 1907. Evidence of Col. Walter Standford, C.B., C.M.G., Chief Magistrate, Transkeian Territories, pp. 1-2.

[341] Select Committee on Farm Labour Supply, 1907. Evidence of Frank Powrie, M. L. A., Barkly East, p. 35-36.

rights".[342] He explained, however, that "those who have no land under the Glen Grey Act may be induced to come [as shepherds]". The measures taken by the government were thus helpful to the farmers as they forced people into labour. But "[y]ou would have to offer him a plot of land to cultivate for himself and family, and allow him to run a certain number of stock".[343] The labourers were clearly still not interested in becoming proletarianized; they held on to their stock. They did not avoid labour in the capitalist sector, as they had to survive, but to some extent they worked there under conditions they themselves approved of. Holding on to the cattle was one way of resisting the capitalist system as it meant that they had some access to means of production and were not completely proletarianized. Maintaining the gendered and generational division of labour was another. Many labourers thus came in families to stay on the farms, not as single migrants.

However, the families constituted a problem in some cases. Viljoen in Hanover said that "we do not allow any of them on the farm who do not work. The women and children also get work, and they get paid for it."[344] But there were some problems with the family labour system, mainly that some women were not interested in domestic work, at least according to Viljoen: "In the villages there are enough women, but usually they will not work, and then we cannot take their husbands either, because we cannot support the wives and children if they will not work."[345] The wives of farm labourers usually worked in the household of the farmer, but it seems like there was a tendency among some families to withhold the labour of women from white farmers. It is likely that male labourers who were not proletarianized, and thus had stock and land to cultivate on, wanted the women to work for them and not the farmer. Beinart presents a similar case of a Transvaal tenant who stated that "I must work for the baas [...] I buy a woman to work for me".[346] Women were clearly subordinated both to their husbands and the farmers. The gendered division of labour seemingly managed to continue also when male peasants became involved as labourers in capitalist farming.

The wages paid to shepherds and labourers were thus not enough for the whole family. And neither were the rations. Viljoen said that a shepherd gets "[a] rib or so of mutton and a piece of bread two or three fingers thick in the morning, and in the evening a pound or so of flour more or less". That was not

---

342 Select Committee on Farm Labour Supply, 1907. Evidence of Arthur Fuller, M. L. A., Stutterheim, p. 49.

343 Select Committee on Farm Labour Supply, 1907. Evidence of Arthur Fuller, M. L. A., Stutterheim, Kei Road, Komgha, East London, p. 58.

344 Select Committee on Farm Labour Supply, 1907. Evidence of Dirk Viljoen, M. L. A., Hanover, p. 65.

345 Select Committee on Farm Labour Supply, 1907. Evidence of Dirk Viljoen, M. L. A., Hanover, p. 67.

346 Beinart, W 2001, p. 56, (quoting Bradford 1987).

sufficient for the whole family: "If you hire a man you are forced to feed his women and children, although they do not work. They cannot live on the food you give the shepherd."[347] From Viljoen's statement it definitely seems as if farmers at least occasionally were forced to feed also those who did not work.

Wages did not seem to exceed the levels of the 1870s. Some of the problems to attract labour were definitely caused by that. Colonel Warren in Stutterheim declared that "[t]he highest wages I give is £1 per month per man, but I feed his wife and children, and give him grazing for 10 or 12 cattle and a piece of ground to plough, [...]". In order to create incentives for his labourers and make them more inclined to come to his farm, Warren also offered "a suit of clothes once a year, but even with this it is difficult to get boys to work."[348] Paying higher wages was certainly not possible for all farmers. But even those who could, like the Rubidges and several of the witnesses to the Select Committee, were entangled in the system of family labour and the combination of cash wages and grazing rights. The resistance from the labourers to convert to only being paid cash wages thus continued to keep the labour practices intact and relatively unchanged. Simultaneously it must have been beneficial to those farmers who were well off. As they did not have to spend large amounts of money on wages they could focus their attention and money on improving their farms.

The enormous amount of fencing being done during the 1890s and the early twentieth century must be seen in this context. If all the money that was spent on fences had gone into wages, there would not have been as much trouble to find labour. To some extent it thus seems like the poorer farmers decided wage levels and labour practices. Those who could not pay much cash wages were the ones who were most dependent on giving grazing rights and rations. The wealthier farmers did of course not have an interest in paying substantially higher wages than what was necessary to attract the number of labourers they demanded, and as long as they paid only fractionally more than the poorer farmers they could attract labourers. Some of the complaints to the government were thus probably a way of ensuring political support for their endeavours without having to pay higher wages. However, as long as the farm labourers had access to cattle, sheep and goats and could resist the pressure from capitalist farming, the labour practices seemed difficult to change.

---

[347] Select Committee on Farm Labour Supply, 1907. Evidence of Dirk Viljoen, M. L. A., Hanover, p. 67.

[348] Select Committee on Farm Labour Supply, 1907. Col. William Warren, C. M. G., M. L. A., Stutterheim, p. 79.

Two-legged jackals – relations between farmers and shepherds

Another form of resistance by the labour force was stock thefts and injuries to sheep. The intrusion of jackals into wool farming areas offered an opportunity for labourers and shepherds to cause problems for farmers. The jackals, which followed in the wake of intensified capitalist farming, therefore also changed the way farmers and shepherds interacted.

On Marthinus Goedhals' farm Ordonnantie in Graaff-Reinet an incident involving a shepherd was brought to the magistrate. According to Goedhals, his shepherd Peppermint Siko had lost eight sheep and killed one sheep in the kraal. Apparently Siko had reported to his master Goedhals that a sheep "had fallen in to a stump in the kraal" and was wounded in the belly. Siko explained that a jackal had entered the kraal, but when Goedhals asked how it came in there, Siko could not say how. Goedhals accused his shepherd of having inflicted the wound himself by using a keerie. After a few days the sheep died, whereupon Goedhals warned Siko not to do it again. Some weeks later when Goedhals was counting his sheep he saw another sheep that had been beaten. According to Goedhals the shepherd Siko told him that he had beaten the ewe. Yet another sheep from Siko's flock was found dead in the veld some days later. It had a hole in the side that was several inches deep. Another shepherd on the farm, Christian Weinnand, stated that Siko had told him about injuring the second time. He then told the farmer what he had heard.[349] Any solidarity between the two shepherds did not seem to exist. Weinnand might have objected to the injuring of sheep, but he did not tell Siko this. Instead he reported to the farmer, Goedhals, which indicates that relations between master and servant were stronger than class relations between shepherds. Loyalty to the farmer was surely also reinforced when labourers were allowed to have stock on the farm.

Despite being supported by his wife, Leah, who also blamed the jackal, Siko confessed to having killed and beaten at least one of the sheep, but there is no explanation why he did it. He did not eat any of the dead sheep, injuring them was therefore only a way of inflicting pain upon them, which may have been directed at the farmer Goedhals. Since he initially blamed the jackal there is reason to believe his motive originated in self-interest. By showing that the sheep were threatened he could demonstrate that a shepherd was necessary. In the midst of fencing, and the beginning of jackal-proof fencing, shepherds must have seen that their work operations were disappearing. The fences had been around for a relatively long time, but shepherding was still the dominant practice, and became even more important after the jackals had appeared. The

[349] CA 1/GR 2/132 Part II. Magistrate Graaff-Reinet. Peppermint Siko, Nov. 9, 1895.

introduction of jackal-proof fences changed conditions, though and implied that farmers could manage without shepherds. Blaming jackals for injuring sheep can therefore be seen as resistance towards the developments within wool farming. Much like the Luddites, who damaged machinery, shepherds like Peppermint Siko caused damage to capital in the form of sheep in order to justify their own existence.

Thefts were not something only farmers were affected by. Those labourers on farms who had sheep, goats or cattle of their own were also at risk of being exposed to theft. January Mei, a shepherd at the farm Louwskraal in Graaff-Reinet, had two sheep stolen from him. The sheep were his possession. They were stolen by a man called Salmon Kok, who herded goats on the same farm. Mei explained: "I had placed my sheep in the kraal with the kids, and told [Kok] to let them remain there until my wife came to fetch them. [...] She came back and told me that the sheep were out of the kraal." Mei then went into the veld and eventually found his sheep, but discovered that one was missing. He followed the tracks of the sheep to Kok's house. Mei subsequently went to the owner of the farm and reported the matter. They searched for Kok, but when they found him he ran away.[350]

Kok, who herded the goats, clearly saw an opportunity to steal a sheep when they were in the same kraal as his goats. And it may have seemed like less of a risk to steal from a shepherd than from a farmer, but the punishment was more severe than in at least one case where a white farmers' stock was stolen: one year imprisonment with hard labour.[351]

As seen previously on Wellwood, the sheep of the labourers and shepherds usually ran with those belonging to the farmer. This must have been the case also on Louwskraal. January Mei did not only herd his own sheep, but also those of the farmer, but he kraaled them separately from those of his master. Such a separation may have been related to the risk of disease spreading from the sheep owned by the shepherd to those owned by the farmer. Instead of kraaling them with the larger flock, he put them with Kok's goats, while waiting for the wife to fetch them. As the wife was supposed to fetch them, women were also involved in shepherding, but mainly when aiding their husbands and in this case with the sheep owned by the shepherd.

The enclosed camps, which farmers came to rely on, were there to protect animals, but also to keep others out, which impacted the labour force. The farmer Jacobus Schemper in Graaff-Reinet found a servant of his, Aprekos, in

---

[350] CA 1/GR 2/132 Part II. Magistrate Graaff-Reinet. Salmon Kok, Nov. 15, 1895.

[351] CA 1/GR 2/132 Part II. Magistrate Graaff-Reinet. Salmon Kok, Nov. 15, 1895; See for example Dampie Samson, Nov. 18, 1895, who was sentenced to five months with hard labour for theft of stock from a white farmer; 1/GR 1/32 Part II. Adrian Ruiter Senior and others, Oct. 23, 1895. Adrian Ruiter Senior was sentenced to one year with hard labour for theft of stock from a white farmer.

his "ostrich camp [...]. The camp is enclosed with prickly pear & a wire fence."[352] Aprekos had apparently wandered about in the enclosure without permission, which suggests that farmers were afraid of thefts of eggs, and also slaughtering of birds. Ostriches were more expensive than sheep, and enclosing them without supervision of herds made them easy targets for theft. Entering the camp was therefore a serious offense of trespassing. Aprekos was sentenced to one month imprisonment with hard labour.[353] To establish and enforce private ownership of land was perhaps even more important with ostriches than with sheep. Being in the camp without stealing was seemingly not too serious, but farmers obviously found it serious enough to threaten the accumulation of capital.

The difficulties experienced by farmers in gaining control of the labour force also resulted in violence. Farmers wanted control over the labour force, and labourers wanted independence. In Carnarvon around the turn of the century few farms were fenced; only about 20,000 morgen were enclosed compared to more than 500,000 morgen in wool farming centres like Graaff-Reinet, Cradock and Somerset East. Other capital investments were also lacking.[354] This created a great dependency on shepherds, but as they herded sheep on large pastures they were often outside the reach of farmers' control during the day.

The lack of control during daytime could be made up for on their arrival back to the kraal. The overseer on the farm Mentjesberg in Carnarvon, Cornelis Herman, was convicted of having beaten a shepherd on the farm with a sjambok. The shepherd, April Wildsehout [?], and his wife had been on the farm for four months, living in a hut near a kraal. According to Herman the shepherd was mistreating the sheep. He stated that he "saw the Hottentot driving the sheep about", meaning that he chased them and threw sticks at them. As overseer it was Herman's responsibility to make sure the sheep numbers were correct and that they were in good condition. According to April, the overseer came every night to put the sheep in the kraal. Later that day he came to the kraal where April's sheep were standing and Herman "saw he had mixed up the sheep". April then became "impertinent" and Herman subsequently "gave him few cuts with the riem".[355]

According to April and his wife the overseer used a sjambok to hit April. However, the owner of the farm, Hendrik Jacobs, stated that there was "no sjambok on the whole farm". He confirmed that the shepherd had been beaten, though, as the overseer Herman came to him to report that he had used the

---

352 CA 1/GR 2/103 Part I. Magistrate Graaff-Reinet. Aprekos, 565/1880.

353 CA 1/GR 2/103 Part I. Magistrate Graaff-Reinet. Aprekos, 565/1880.

354 Cape of Good Hope Census 1904, pp. 506-07, 516-17.

355 CA 1/CAR 1/1/1/2, Proceedings of Court cases, Magistrate Carnarvon, Cornelis Herman, 9 May, 1901.

riem on April. These actions were evidently sanctioned by farmers. According to Jacobs "[t]he boy has been working badly for the last months. I have warned him but he takes no notice."[356] As Herman was convicted of assault we know that excessive violence was condoned by the authorities. There is no way of telling the frequency of such beatings, but judging by the above case it may have been common when farmers had few other means of control. Reduction of wages and rations was a possibility, but they were low to begin with and would starve the labourer. And it did not occur to Jacobs to fire April, probably because the supply of labour was rather limited. In Carnarvon in 1904 there were only 382 black and coloured "workers on farms" compared to 578 whites who were sustained by farming. As comparison there were 1,966 black and coloured and 1,266 whites on farms in Graaff-Reinet.[357] Farmers in Carnarvon must thus have been reluctant to fire labourers as they did not know if a new one would come to the farm.

The violent relations on farms were commonplace and also affected children of labourers,[358] but it was difficult for many shepherds and labourers to leave their masters. One way of avoiding exploitation was to run away. Servants absconding from service was perhaps not equally commonplace as violence, simply because there were few places to run to, but it still occurred. One shepherd who ran away from his duty was Koos Wiel, who worked on a farm in Carnarvon in 1901. On June 5th he disappeared from the farm without permission and before his service was ended. That day the farmer, Luberberg [?], went out to the veld to give food to his shepherd, but could not find him. Instead he found that Wiel had left "the sheep without any herd". Finding the sheep without a herd upset him, but it was worse that there were also 500 sheep missing. The majority of the sheep were found, but as many as 20 were irrecoverably lost. Wiel did not seem to bother about the sheep, and neither did he bother about the wage, 10 shillings per month, for the three remaining months on his contract. Conditions on that farm were apparently not tolerable to Wiel and instead of waiting three months for his wages he seems to have stolen an ox-hide at the time he departed from the farm.[359] The low wages and violent treatments contributed to the short-termed stays of labourers. Those who owned stock of their own had options besides running away, but the ones without capital in any form were left to be vagrants if leaving their master's farm.

---

356 CA 1/CAR 1/1/1/2, Proceedings of Court cases, Magistrate Carnarvon, Cornelis Herman, 9 May, 1901.

357 Cape of Good Hope Census 1904, p. 496.

358 Beinart, W 2001, p. 60; Select Committee on the Labour Question, 1890. Evidence of M. J. du Plessis, Queenstown, p. 45.

359 CA 1/CAR 1/1/1/2, Magistrate Carnarvon, Proceedings of Court cases, Koos Wiel, 16th July, 1901.

Composition of the labour force – generation and gender revisited

The shortage of labour supply voiced by farmers was seemingly an illusion, as the number of labourers increased between 1904 and 1911, although not by much. According to the 1909 *Blue Book on Native Affairs*, the labour supply in Cathcart was "equal to the demand" and in Cradock the labour "supply [was] sufficient for local requirements".[360] In Somerset East (Pearston) the labour supply was even described as "plentiful".[361] Also in Beaufort West the "labour supply [was] equal to the demand", but there was a difficulty in finding shepherds: "Shepherds are at times difficult to obtain, as Natives would rather work at odd jobs about the town than engage themselves as shepherds on farms". An answer to why there was a problem was, however, given: "Very low wages are paid to any class of labourer."[362] Farm labour was hard, and many seem to have preferred working in the town instead. The wages in Beaufort West were not specified, but examples can be given from other places. In Aberdeen the average wage to farm labourers and shepherds was 8 shillings in addition to rations of meat and meal.[363] In other places the wages were slightly higher. Both in Cathcart and Aliwal North the monthly wages, apart from rations and housing, ranged from 10s. to £1.[364] In Cradock the remuneration was differentiated depending on duration of employment: Those farm labourers and shepherds who were hired for six months were paid five sheep while their wives were paid two sheep if they worked as domestics. Those who were hired on a monthly basis were paid at another rate: the husband was paid 10s. and the wife 4s. Apart from that they also received "free rations, quarters and grazing".[365] Interestingly enough, also the women, not only men, were paid in livestock. As animals generally were connected to males it seems like the men received also the sheep paid to the wives. The wages were thus paid to the whole family, not individually.

Still, some farmers may have been unable to offer sufficient wages to attract labourers. As we have seen, wages were diversified depending on age and gender. In order to describe labour relations on farms more comprehensively, we must look closer at the age and gender composition of the labour force. The 1904 Census is the first one to offer that possibility.

360 Blue Book on Native Affairs 1909, p. 16.
361 Blue Book on Native Affairs 1909, p. 22.
362 Blue Book on Native Affairs, 1909, p. 15.
363 Blue Book on Native Affairs, 1909, p. 14
364 Blue Book on Native Affairs, 1909. Aliwal North p. 15, Cathcart p. 16.
365 Blue Book on Native Affairs, 1909. Cradock p. 16.

Table 12. Farm labourers (black and coloured) in the Cape, age and gender composition 1904.

Age	Male	Female	All
5-9	590	177	767
10-14	6,075	951	7,026
15-19	10,493	2,207	12,700
20-29	15,981	3,307	19,288
30-39	12,832	2,684	15,516
40-49	9,161	1,562	10,723
50-59	5,313	889	6,202
60-69	3,316	499	3,815
70-	1,862	231	2,093
Total	65,623	12,507	78,130

Source: Cape of Good Hope Census 1904, pp. 360-61.

The adult males, that is, those above than 20 years of age, were paid the highest wages as they were the most attractive labourers and their cost of reproduction was higher than for other categories. Adult males constituted 62 per cent of the labour force in the Cape, which indicates their central role. But it also indicates that other categories were important, which reduced wages. The youngest male labourers, those under 15 years of age, made up about 9 per cent of the labour force. Together with the male youths, those between 15 and 19, they made up 22 per cent of the labour force. Including the females under 20 years of age, they constituted 26 per cent. Many of these labourers were paid considerably lower wages, perhaps only half of the adult males. In Aberdeen the man and his wife were "as a rule [...] engaged at fixed rates, while their family are allowed to live with the parents on the farm in return for minor services rendered by the children [...]." Some of the children were however also "employed at fixed rates of remuneration in addition to their parents."[366] This enabled also poor farmers to attract labour, but not the sort they demanded.

The youngest children were clearly not crucial as farm labourers. There was probably no lack of children on farms, but the farmers did not want them except at labour peaks such as harvesting and shearing, and when occasional weeding was undertaken. They could not perform the work of young adult males. And besides, there were quite a few young male labourers around after the implementation of individual tenure for black people in the Eastern Cape. Most young children were thus seasonal or casual labourers, which did not make up a category in the census. But many children also worked for their fathers. Those labourers or tenants who had cultivation of their own, which was not unusual even in wool farming districts, had their children working on their

[366] Blue Book on Native Affairs, 1909, p. 14

own land. When the farmer required the labour of those children he made an agreement with the father. When that work was completed, the children went back to work on the family plot. Children were thus not idle for the most part and although they only made up ten per cent of the labour force, there were many more children who actually performed labour on the farms.

Women's share of the farm labour force remained more or less unchanged between 1904 and 1911 at twelve and thirteen per cent respectively.[367] It was to a greater extent young females who came to work on the farms of whites. Some of these were most likely seasonal or casual labourers, demanded mostly during labour peaks. Some must, however, have been working more regularly. As noted by Guy and others, women and young girls were responsible for agricultural work alongside of domestic work in pre-colonial societies. Being involved in farm labour was thus not unusual for females, but during the late nineteenth century women were mostly working in farmers' household, or on the subsistence plots on the farms. The gendered division of labour was thus only partially utilized by farmers. Reluctance among male labourers and tenants to allow their wives and daughters to work for white farmers was probably an important reason for this, but also the availability of male labourers.

There is strong evidence that the family system was the most prevalent. The ratio between males and females in the ages 20 to 49 was more or less even. Males in their twenties made up 24 per cent of the total male labourers, women 26 per cent of the females. Males in their thirties made up 19 per cent, women 21 per cent. Males in their fourties made up 12 per cent, women 14 per cent. It could of course reflect only labour demands from various age groups, but as they correlate it is likely that a large share of the males and females were from the same families.

While women and girls took part in general farm labour to some extent, shepherding was a male occupation. And it was an occupation for the younger children on farms. Let us therefore look closer at the composition of the shepherd labour force regarding age and gender in 1904.

[367] Cape of Good Hope Census 1904, p 344-45; South Africa Census 1911, pp. 8, 564-65.

Table 13. Shepherds in the Cape, age and gender composition 1904.

Age	Male	Female	All
5-9	1,590	58	1,648
10-14	7,699	217	7,916
15-19	5,539	134	5,673
20-29	4,027	102	4,129
30-39	4,215	88	4,303
40-49	4,171	76	4,247
50-59	2,995	33	3,028
60-69	2,115	21	2,136
70-	1,004	9	1,013
Total	33,355	738	34,093

Source: Cape of Good Hope Census 1904, pp. 360-61.

It is obvious that people under 20 years of age were crucial as shepherds. They made up about 45 per cent of the shepherds. The children under fourteen years of age were especially important as shepherds. We saw that only 9 per cent of the male farm labourers were under fourteen years of age, but for shepherds that group made up 27 per cent of the total.

At the same time we should note that also older people were involved in shepherding. The shepherds between 30 and 49 years of age were actually about half as many as those under 20 years. The majority of the shepherd labour force was thus either between five and nineteen or between 30 and 49 years old. Many of these probably belonged to the same family, that is, they were fathers and sons. A father and two sons was seemingly a popular model for shepherding. They may not necessarily have worked together; we have seen several examples from Wellwood and other farms that children around the age of fourteen and younger were in charge of their own flocks. But the recruitment of shepherds to a farm most likely relied on the exploitation of these family ties. Thus, the father was hired, and his sons were also given herding duties.

Shepherd's hut. (CA J1651). Shepherd's hut on a Beaufort West farm, probably 1890s.

The relative absence of women from the labour force on farms does not mean that they had no place in economic life. Quite the contrary, their efforts were crucial in the family economy and in reproduction of labour; they were the ones who upheld pre-colonial and pre-capitalist production by working on family plots along with young children when men and older boys sold their labour to white farmers. It is evident that women made up the largest segment of the peasantry, especially those who were in their twenties.

Table 14. Peasants (black and coloured) 1904.

Age	Male	Female	All
5-9	32,260	31,527	63,787
10-14	56,390	56,793	113,183
15-19	46,622	54,007	100,629
20-29	67,715	106,067	173,782
30-39	47,932	68,838	116,770
40-49	36,004	45,883	81,887
50-59	22,612	28,272	50,884
60-69	14,158	17,428	31,586
70-	10,983	13,454	24,437
Total	334,676	422,269	756,945

Source: Cape of Good Hope Census 1904, pp. 360-61.

The peasantry probably consisted also of those who were tenants of white farmers, but who did not work directly for the farmers; the categories were somewhat fluid. But it is nonetheless evident that when peasant boys turned fifteen years old, they left for the capitalist economy to a greater extent than girls did. Until then they were more or less even in numbers and worked for their parents on the family plot, presumably according to a gendered and generational division of labour. After they turned fifteen it seems like boys were forced out of the peasant household by economic reasons. The location acts and the Glen Grey Act must have been the primary reasons for this, but also the demands on the labour of young men from the capitalist sector. Viewing the peasants who were in their twenties, the pattern becomes even clearer. It was the women who took responsibility for the peasant household and the subsistence agriculture and pastoralism. Some 61 per cent in that age group were women. After the age of 30, the ratio between men and women became more even again. When males had reached 30 the demand for their labour in the capitalist sector decreased. If we compare the peasantry with thc farm labourers we see that the group who were between 15 and 30 most frequently left peasant life to become labourers. But the age of 30 could also have been the time when many of the farm labourers had earned enough money or cattle, or both, to be able to find a homestead of their own and return to the peasantry.

Viewing the occupations of black people a distinct pattern emerges. The young males, i.e. those between 15 and 30, were the ones who took part most actively in the capitalist sector. The females in that age group stayed at home and took care of the peasant household and production along with the youngest children, i.e. boys and girls under 15 years of age. When adult males around the age of 30 had earned enough money or cattle to establish a new homestead and a family, many of them left the capitalist sector. But all along the generational divide more men than women took part in the capitalist sector, which meant that women and young children were responsible for peasant production, which can be seen as subsistence production to a great extent. The partaking in the capitalist sector was seemingly a strategy among the black peasants. To some extent it was forced upon them, but it also created an opportunity for the peasant family to earn money or cattle, which enabled them to remain on their plot of land as independent peasants instead of becoming proletarianized labourers on the farms of whites.

Accumulation of capital, accumulation of stock

Capital expansion was clearly evident in wool farming. But it expanded to an even greater extent in the mining industry. The competition for labour created problems for quite a few farmers. In De Aar "[t]he scarcity of labour is becoming very marked [...], and I can only put it down to the recruiting by Labour Agents for the Mines".[368] There is no way of estimating the total number of people being recruited by the mines, but in some districts we know. For example, in Fort Beaufort 720 black people left the district, "the majority going to the mines".[369] An even larger number left Queenstown for the mines: 4,666 black people "were contracted here during the year".[370] It appears that the gold mines in the Witwatersrand in the Transvaal were not the primary object for many of the migrants to the mines. In Barkly West the "Natives of this district will only go to Kimberly and the neighbouring mines, and to the River Diggings".[371] Apparently the treatment of the labour force on the gold mines caused many to avoid them: This was not "entirely due to indolence; they seem willing enough to labour, but rather anywhere else than the mines in the Transvaal [...]". Bad treatment in the Witwatersrand mines was the main reason, black people instead preferred the mines in Kimberly and the orange River Colony, and even German South-West Africa.[372]

The influence of the mining industry, both gold and diamonds, was generally considered to be the main reason for the difficulties in attracting labour in farming. But losing labour was not inevitable or unavoidable. Work at the mines was not favoured by black people; they only went there because of the higher wages. Consequently, the expanding mine industry accentuated stratifications between farmers. In a sense it sorted out those who were not equipped for capitalist farming from those who were. Those who were not equipped for capitalist farming stood the risk of being turned into labourers.

Carnarvon was one district were the expansion of capital had not reached as far as in the leading wool districts. The rate of fencing was, for example, very slow compared to districts like Graaff-Reinet, Somerset East, Cradock and Colesberg. Only 66,000 morgen was fenced in Carnarvon compared to more than 600,000 in each of the above mentioned districts in 1911.[373] Consequently, the Resident Magistrate of Carnarvon reported that labour "supply was not equal to the demand". However, "[t]his alludes chiefly to the poorer class of European farmers. The most advanced farmers appear to have experienced no difficulty in obtaining the labour necessary for the proper carrying on of their farming operations." The Magistrate suggested that the difficulties in finding labour was due to the fact that many black people had left Carnarvon for work in asbestos mines in Prieska. Yet another form of mining thus affected poor farmers in Carnarvon. But the difficulty to acquire farm

368 Blue Book on Native Affairs, 1909, p. 16.

369 Blue Book on Native Affairs, 1909, p. 16.

370 Blue Book on Native Affairs, 1909. Queenstown, p. 21.

371 Blue Book on Native Affairs, 1909. Barkly West, p. 15.

372 Blue Book on Native Affairs, 1909. Glen Grey (Bolotwa), p. 17.

373 South Africa Census 1911, pp. 1255-57.

labour to the offered wages was not only caused by an expanding mining industry: "This district has also been drained of labourers to a considerable extent by farmers in the Fraserburg and Sutherland district, where it is reported they receive higher wages".[374] Labourers did thus not favour mining over farm labour per se; they favoured higher wages. The Inspector of Native Locations in Clanwilliam, another district where farmers complained that they could not get enough labourers, explained the situation in a most clarifying way: "The wages given by the farmers are very small, consequently they have, in a way, to suffer through their own doings".[375]

The stratification of farmers was seen also in those districts where wages were higher. In Fraserburg (Williston) the wages were between 10s. and 15s. per month. There was a "constant demand for shepherds at that rate; in fact, labour is so scarce that Europeans are compelled to employ their little sons and daughters to herd the sheep." Some farmers suffered more than others: "It might well be said to be the exception, rather than the rule, to see a Native on the smaller farms." The larger farms did not appear to have experienced the same problems. The labour force in Fraserburg was to a large extent migratory and did not stay for long periods of time. The Acting Assistant Resident Magistrate did not assume that it was caused by low wages or harsh conditions, but was "inclined to think that the food – meat and bread, year in, year out [...]" was a main reason along with the "terrible monotony of the open veld [...]".[376] We can at least assume that the open veld could be endured given a sufficient amount of money or stock as remuneration.

The stratification of farmers in wool producing areas had been prevalent since the arrival of British settlers to the Cape Colony. Afrikaners were generally poorer and many of them transformed into a bywoner class. Similarly, as described by Dubow, the crisis in the wool industry in the 1860s and the upturn during the following decade reinforced the hierarchy among farmers. Those who were equipped for capitalist farming and exports to Britain managed the crisis better and could secure labour even in a state of economic depression.[377] Bundy has described how poor whites existed in the Cape already during the 1860s, half a century before "poor whiteism" became a concept. Expanding capitalist farming was a main reason for stratification, according to him.[378] But it is also important to note that it was a result of capital expansion in the world-economy. Thus, the same process which brought white settlers to the Cape, and made some of them prosperous and wealthy, caused others to succumb under the pressure of increasing debts and low profits. Only those

---

[374] Blue Book on Native Affairs, 1909. Carnarvon, p. 16.

[375] Blue Book on Native Affairs, 1909. Clanwilliam, p. 16.

[376] Blue Book on Native Affairs, 1909.Fraserburg (Williston), p. 17.

[377] Dubow, S 1982, pp. 30, 58-60.

[378] Bundy, C. 1986, pp. 108, 112, 116.

who could accumulate enough capital and had foresight managed to continue with their farming operations. This was a crucial part of capitalist expansion, that is, the establishment of capitalist relations of production in the capitalist periphery, wherein labour became a commodity that could be sold and bought for money.

Expansion of capital and expansion of capitalism may seem like interchangeable concepts, but there are important differences. Expansion of capital is essential to expansion of capitalism, but preludes it. Before there is accumulation of capital there cannot be capitalist relations of production. In the Cape wool industry the capitalist relations of production were established early, even before there were fences and windmills on the farms, but the privatization of land, guaranteed by the state, and imports of sheep to the Colony constituted the initial stages of capital expansion. And most farmers relied on a system of more or less grazing rights, wages in kind, and relatively little cash wages. The poorer farmers who appeared in the early twentieth century could surely have acquired labour, but they could not buy it. Giving up parts of their farms to tenants, who performed labour in exchange for land, would have secured labour, but would have made the white farmers half-sharers instead of capitalist farmers. Along with the implementation of fences and windmills the capitalist relations of production increased, as the capital accumulated in the hands of farmers, i.e those who bought labour. Not only fences, but also land accumulated in the hands of whites.

The establishment of capitalist relations of production facilitates capital accumulation. A cash economy, which was spurred by the mining industry, and a state structure, which implemented legislation aimed at forcing peasants to find labour in the capitalist sector, enhanced prerequisites for accumulation of capital among farmers. At the same time, however, there was an accumulation of capital along the wool commodity chain. Also transport riders, shipping companies, wool brokers and textile manufacturers in Britain profited. But it was an unequal distribution of capital. Farmers in the Cape only gained access to a part of the profits produced in the British imperial wool industry. In 1910 the value of South African wool exports was £3.8 million while the value of British exports of wool textile manufactured goods alone the same year was £25 million.[379] In addition to that we must include the value of production for the home market in Britain, which was also considerable. Transnational wool production was thus definitely more beneficial to textile capital in the core than to peripheral farmers, and, as seen, far from all farmers benefitted at all, quite the contrary. As the production of finished commodities created higher value than the production of raw material, more profits were made in the core. The unequal distribution of capital within the world-economy clearly affected many

[379] *Annual Statement on Trade and Shipping* 1910; Jenkins & Ponting 1982, p. 222.

of the Cape farmers profoundly as they could not compete with mines and other farmers and found themselves in trouble to find labour.

Several important legislative measures had been implemented during the early twentieth century, which also contributed to accumulation of land in the hands of whites. The location acts during the late nineteenth century also aimed at this, but were not efficient. The *Location Act* of 1909 reinforced the previous legislation and also established a stricter definition of bona fide labourer, thereby aiming to limit the number of black people on white farms who were not employed as labourers.[380] The Government desired capitalist labour relations as opposed to the semi-feudal nature of the tenancy which characterized some parts of the Cape. However, despite government efforts and the expansion of capital in wool farming, the labour practices were not characterized by proletarian cash wage labour. Grazing rights was a central feature of labour relations. In Barkly East "the majority of the Natives are located on farms, where they work for the farmer and depasture their stock", and in Colesberg "[f]armers usually allow their labourers who have small flocks to run these on their farms free of charge".[381] The animals were often accumulated while being employed on the farms. The Acting Resident Magistrate in Britstown stated that the "Kafir or Fingo as a rule, when employed as herdsman, accumulates some small stock, which the farmer permits him to let run on his veld [...]".[382]

But it was obvious that farmers did not want labourers to accumulate too much stock. In De Aar the majority of farmers did "not object to their servants having a few goats or sheep; but when they number over 50 they prefer to let them go, although a few of the larger farmers do not mind, say, 150 small stock, [...]". But labourers could not come to a farm with such numbers of stock; the farmers only tolerated it if "the Natives have accumulated them whilst they are in their employ, but will not start a Native with that number."[383] Accumulation of stock by labourers and tenants was seen as threatening by farmers, especially the poorer ones who could find themselves in a position where the labour force owned more stock than they themselves did. However, by spreading capital in the form of stock also to labourers, the farmers could manage to acquire labour also during times of harsh competition from the mining industry. After all, the black labourers wanted livestock for marriage and the possibility of establishing homesteads of their own. In King William's Town (Keiskama Hoek) the Assistant Resident Magistrate noted that the wasges earned by labourers in mining was used to buy cattle.[384] Mine

380 Bundy, C 1979, pp. 136-37.

381 Blue Book on Native Affairs, 1909. Barkly East, Colesberg, p. 10.

382 Blue Book on Native Affairs, 1909, pp. 10, 18.

383 Blue Book on Native Affairs, 1909. De Aar, (Chief Constable) p. 16.

384 Blue Book on Native Affairs, 1909. King William's Town (Keiskama Hoek), p. 12.

labour did only generate cash, but when the wage was received, many bought livestock.

Accumulating cattle and other livestock was not something all labourers were interested in though. In De Aar the "Hottentot very seldom collects more than 10 or 15 small stock, when he wants a holiday, or what he terms a rest. He then comes into the town and very soon finds himself without anything."[385] The "Hottentots", that is the khoisan descendants, who constituted a part of the coloured group were not, unlike the Xhosa or other black groups, involved in a societal structure, which favoured ownership of stock. Black people wanted to be peasants and some could use the livestock they received as wages to get married and establish a homestead. The coloured group was more involved in the white capitalist sector, and did not have families outside of it, as black people had in the eastern parts of the Colony, the place usually referred to as "Kafirland". The coloureds who were paid in livestock did thus not use it in order to establish homesteads of their own as free peasants, only to trade it for other commodities.

[385] Blue Book on Native Affairs, 1909. De Aar, (Chief Constable) p. 16.

CHAPTER 8

Capital Accumulation, Legislation and new Organization of Production

Shepherds, water and windmills, 1904 – 1911

The Second Anglo-Boer War caused considerable sheep losses for farmers, although the war was not as devastating for the industry as such in view of the continued exports. The increasing demand from the British textile industry, which increased its production a few years into the new century after a fifteen year decline, but also the German one, apparently created good opportunities also for the Cape farmers. It even increased to levels unseen before the Anglo-Boer War and more than 100 million lbs. of wool were exported from the Cape in 1909 compared to between 60 and 80 million lbs. during the 1890s and the first decade of the twentieth century (table 14, p 10).

As a result of the increased exports, the number of sheep in the Cape increased vastly between 1904 and 1911. Reversed, the increased number of sheep made possible more exports. In any case, the sale of wool was pivotal to farmers' ability to quickly increase their sheep numbers and accumulate capital. Along with the sheep, we can see that the number of shepherds once again became more numerous, but also that they were fewer relative to the sheep.

Table 15. Shepherds and sheep and shepherd/pastoral farmer in the Cape 1904 and 1911.

Year	Shepherds	Sheep	Sheep/shepherd	Shepherd/farmer
1904	34,093	11.8 mil	346	1.98
1911	42,582	17.1 mil	401	2.3

Source: Cape of Good Hope Census 1904, pp. 344-45, 478; South Africa Census 1911, pp. 564-65, 1208-09.

The trend seen between 1891 and 1904, that each shepherd became responsible for fewer sheep, was reversed during the early twentieth century. There was an increased demand for shepherds as the sheep numbers grew, but each shepherd took care of fewer sheep than previously. We identified the jackals, but also the low level of satisfactory water supplies to the sheep, as the major reasons behind the larger number of shepherds required during the late nineteenth and early twentieth century. Jackal-proof fences had started to become implemented during the 1890s, but on a very small scale. Windmills were more frequently seen, but not at all widespread at the turn of the century. So, let us view how the implementation of this technology developed during the first decade of the twentieth century.

Between 1891 and 1904 the number of artesian wells, which was the name used for boreholes, increased from 617 to 2,168 throughout the Cape. Both in 1891 and in 1904 the large wool farming district Middelburg took the top position. The number of artesian wells there increased from 76 to 156. Other districts with many artesian wells in 1891 were Fraserburg with 69 and Steynsburg with 41, both wool farming districts. In 1904 another wool district, Colesberg was second with 93. Wine farming district Stellenbosch was in third place with 89.[386]

The number of pumps (wind) similarly increased rapidly between 1891 and 1904 in the Cape, from 508 to 2,516. Hope Town with 41, Willowmore with 36, and Middelburg and Graaff-Reinet with 35 were the places where pumps were most frequent in 1891. Hope Town was leading also in 1904. The number had increased to 143. Britstown and Beaufort West were two other wool districts where farmers had implemented large numbers of pumps, 133 and 131 respectively.[387] It is evident that boreholes and pumps dominated in the Karroo where they became an increasingly important feature of wool farming.

The Rubidges probably only had one windmill during the 1880s and 1890s. The windmills were expensive, and they also required that water sources were found underground, which created further costs. In 1905 the Rubidges appear to have spent more energy and resources on this form of water supply, though. Two men, Jacob and Tom, began working on a well in March. They had been hired two days previously to sink the well "down to rock".[388] Another man, Crouse [?], also began working on a well in April. It may have been the same one as Jacob and Tom were working on. In any case, working with wells was quite slow, but proved to be successful; almost a month after he had started, Crouse apparently "found water at 43 feet". Two days later he "took the first 50 gallons of water out of his well".[389] If it was the same well all along, it took several months to find water through manual labour. A quicker way was to drill.

---

386 Cape of Good Hope Census 1891, p 456; Cape of Good Hope Census 1904, p. 506.

387 Cape of Good Hope Census 1891, p 463; Cape of Good Hope Census 1904, p. 517.

388 Rubidge diaries, March 14, 16, 1905.

389 Rubidge diaries, April 12; May 6, 8, 1905.

Due to the high costs involved in drilling for water, farmers in an area often had to organize themselves to buy or hire a machine collectively. This is what happened in Graaff-Reinet when the Rubidges and the neighbour on the farm Rockwood joined forces in 1905. One day in June Richard Rubidge reported that "Sidney & I drove over to Rockwood to see the boring machine at work".[390] The farmer on Rockwood was the first to have access to the machine, and the Rubidges took an interest in the activities there: In July Richard Rubidge mentioned that "Sidney & I rode over to Rockwood to see borehole tested [...]". The result was thoroughly noted: "750 gallons per hour".[391] When water had been found on Rockwood, it was subsequently time to start looking for water on Wellwood. Some weeks later, at the end of June, two men, Victor and Gert, went "over to Rockwood to fetch Boring machine". It was not transported easily, only the next day the "[b]oring plant arrived".[392]

The Rubidges were apparently eager to start working with the machine, and it also required a lot of labour. The day after the machine had been transported to the farm, "[a]ll hands at getting water for boring machine". Fortunately, there was some water on the farm already, which could be used, presumably for cooling the machine. Those who had no water at all could, seemingly, not use a machine to find it either.[393] There is no record of when they found water or how, but it was evident that the boring machine made certain people redundant. At the end of August, Crouse, the man who had sunk wells some months earlier, was "here to look for work". He did not find any, and seems to have been somewhat desperate; only four days later "Crouse again here to look for work".[394] He was seemingly not hired that time either, at least not for sinking wells. The Rubidges had replaced him with the machine.

We do know that water was eventually found. Towards the end of the year a new Samson windmill was purchased and taken into use. Also that time the entire labour force was involved as "[a]ll hands at drawing up windmill tower which was placed in position".[395] The Samson was an American windmill, used in the dry areas in the West. But now it had found its way to a farm in the Karroo, where it was to provide water for sheep. We can assume that the Rubidges intended to use also the new windmill for several adjoining camps and would attract both sheep and jackals. At the end of the year a man called Paul thus "finished his netting fence round new [...] mill plant".[396] The windmill was presumably jackal-proof.

---

390 Rubidge diaries, June 10, 1905.

391 Rubidge diaries, July 10, 1905.

392 Rubidge diaries, July 29, 30, 1905.

393 Rubidge diaries, July 31, 1905.

394 Rubidge diaries, Aug. 25, 29, 1905.

395 Rubidge diaries, Nov. 18, 1905.

396 Rubidge diaries, Dec. 30, 1905.

Measures like these characterized much of the Karroo during the first decade of the twentieth century. The census figures illustrate well the rate of implementation of windmills and boreholes. The 2,168 boreholes (artesian wells) in the Cape in 1904 increased to 7,513 in 1911. Wool farming districts in the Karroo like Colesberg with 428, Cradock with 455 and Middelburg with 385 wells were at the top. In Graaff-Reinet, where the Rubidges contributed to borehole figures, the number was 177 in 1911. The frequency of boreholes in Graaff-Reinet was not extraordinary, but there had been a considerable increase since 1904 when there were 45 boreholes in the district. The windmills did not follow the development of boreholes, but still almost doubled between 1904 and 1911 in the Cape, from 2,516 to 4,671. In Graaff-Reinet there were 116 windmills in 1911 compared to 70 in 1904. That was less than half the number in Cradock where there were 266 windmills in 1911. Middelburg with 228 and Willowmore with 218 windmills were also among the most advanced districts regarding water supply.[397] Wool farming was definitely changing the rural areas. The first decade of the century was definitely prosperous for wool farmers, who could turn some of the money gained from exports into capital in the form of windmills and a mechanical water supply. But access to water was still a problem.

The water supply on Wellwood was greatly improved by the implementation of the Samson windmill in 1905. However, there were still areas on the farm where the lack of water caused problems, especially in the mountainous areas. In September a flock of sheep "from Alidan's fountain" had to come down to the homestead "for water".[398] Two weeks later the procedure was repeated and Sidney Rubdige sent labourers to clean the fountain.[399] These problems seem to have continued throughout the year, and may have been worsened with the arrival of the summer heat in the Karroo. However, this did not stop the Rubidges from allowing trekkers to use their water. In December a "trek with 200 stock took water here". The trekkers seem to have outspanned where the fountain dams had caused problems some months before. Sidney Rubidge seemed somewhat concerned the following day when he went to the mountain and counted ewes. While there he concluded that the "water supply nearly finished. Trek with 800 sheep and over 200 donkeys in Kloof".[400] The custom in the Karroo – which implied helping fellow farmers with water and sometimes food – probably affected his decision to let the trekkers use his water. The decision may have caused him further problems though. A few days later some of the sheep had to be taken from the mountain again and he sent Speelman to bring down the ewe flock to the "shed", as the water supply was

397 South Africa Census 1911, pp. 1262-63.

398 Rubidge diaries, Sept. 10, 1910.

399 Rubidge diaries, Sept. 24, 1910.

400 Rubidge diaries, Dec. 8, 9, 1910.

not functioning in the "Magnum camp" on the mountain.[401] The situation appears to have been very serious, and Sidney himself took part in repairing the water supply, he went along with the labourers "up to Kloof to clean out fountain dams at top & found water very low".[402] The unreliable water supply in areas like the mountain camps on Wellwood meant that farmers required people who could trek the sheep from the mountain to the homestead or other places on the farm where water was more easily accessible. Still, the implementation of windmills and jackal-proof fences provided opportunities for increasing sheep numbers, and to some extent it reduced the dependence on shepherds.

Jackal threat, shepherds and netting around 1910

Shepherds were also still required in order to combat jackals. The jackal threat caused farmers to kraal their sheep, but shepherds were also important in combating the vermin.

The amount of netting fences in the Cape was limited during the first decade of the twentieth century. The netting fences only appeared as a post in the *Statistical Register* in 1909. Netting worth about £13,000 was imported that year, almost all of it from the UK.[403] Overall, the effects of the jackal-proof fences at that time should thus not be overestimated.

On Wellwood there was at least one netted camp in 1905, but it was a small one. Jackal-proofing was focused on camps near the homesteads and at water places. The high price for netting was presumably a reason for the low frequency of jackal-proof fencing, but also the low frequency of attacks from jackals. But incidents occurred, and not even netted camps were always helpful. In January 1906 two "Cape sheep (rams) caught by jackall [sic] or rooi-kat in netting camp".[404] Farmers in Graaff-Reinet as in other places started cooperatives to combat jackals. Richard Rubidge attended one of these meetings in 1906.[405] In 1910 a cooperative effort was conducted on Wellwood. The Rubidges and the neighbours on the farm Paardekloof fenced a stretch of the mutual boundary.[406] We do not know if netting was used, but as Wellwood was already enclosed with wire it seems likely that the boundary was at least fortified.

---

401 Rubidge diaries, Dec. 13, 1910.

402 Rubidge diaries, Dec. 19, 1910.

403 Statistical Register 1909, p. 100.

404 Rubidge diaries, Jan. 17, 1906.

405 Rubidge diaries, Nov. 12, 1906.

406 Rubidge diaries, Oct. 19, 1910.

The Rubidges had been relatively spared from jackals during the first decade of the twentieth century, but in 1910 jackals became a larger threat. From October to December 1910 six sheep were killed by jackals on the farm, some of them even in kraals.[407] Neither did netting camps stop jackals: in November a lamb was "caught by jackall [sic] in small netting camp". As both kraaling and jackal-proof fences did not stop the jackals other methods were tried; the Rubidges subsequently "laid out about 30 poison baits around camp".[408] Poison was one method of killing jackals, which was frequently used in the Cape. Another method was trapping them. The ones responsible for the trapping were the shepherds and their families. In August 1910 a "[s]hepherd's wife from mountain kraal, brought down rooi-jackall's (sic) skin". The shepherd's wife may have been responsible for the actual setting of traps, or it may have been a task shared by the shepherding family. In any case, before she left the homestead Sidney Rubidge gave her another trap.[409] Shepherds and their families were seemingly the ones responsible for a large share of the jackal eradication. In order to make sure the shepherds did not overstate jackal numbers, which could facilitate for them to steal sheep, farmers traded skins for new traps.

Although the extent of jackal-proof fencing during the first decade of the twentieth century cannot be determined, it was clear that overall fencing continued to characterize wool farming areas in the Cape. The 12 million morgen enclosed in 1904 increased to more than 19 million morgen in 1911. The extent of enclosed land in the whole newly established Union of South Africa was 34 million morgen. It was evident that the expansion of capital was most clearly visible in the Cape. In 1911 the leading districts were Hope Town with 794,739 morgen, Somerset East with 771,745 morgen and Cradock with 730,158 morgen, all of them in the Cape.[410] Although the extent of fencing had increased also in these districts since 1904, the rate of fencing was slowing down compared to the previous decades. This was also seen in Graaff-Reinet, where 637,972 morgen was fenced in 1911 compared to 521,268 morgen in 1904 and 190,276 morgen in 1891.[411] The land in the leading wool producing districts in the Karroo was more or less fenced up in the first decade of the twentieth century. The expansion of capital had started to slow down, but the accumulation of capital continued to increase. Certainly, this development affected labourers, tenants and peasants in the wool producing districts of the Cape. We will now look closer at how.

---

407 Rubidge diaries, Oct. 2, 3, 1910.

408 Rubidge diaries, Nov. 4, 1910.

409 Rubidge diaries, Aug. 17, 1910.

410 South Africa Census 1911, pp. 1255-57.

411 South Africa Census 1911, pp. 1255-57; Cape of Good Hope Census 1904, p 506-07; 1891, p 456-57.

The Fencing Act of 1912 – impacts on wool farming

After the creation of the Union of South Africa in 1910 the newly formed Government realized the importance of the wool industry for the country. It is true that gold was the foremost bearer of revenue to the new Union, but wool brought in £3.8 million in 1910,[412] and it dominated the rural areas. In 1911 the *Grootfontein Agricultural College* was consequently founded, with the specific aim of assisting the wool industry. The college was situated in the centre of the wool farming regions in Middelburg in the Cape Province. The purpose of Grootfontein College was to conduct research specifically on wool farming and sheep, and to provide education for farmers. During the first decade the number of students attending the College was low, though, and the education was perceived as too theoretical.[413]

Many of the leading politicians at the time were also wool farmers, which reinforced the role of farming in the Union. In 1912 a *Fencing Act* was voted into effect.[414] There had been previous acts in the four provinces, but the act of 1912 set a national legislative framework for fencing. The purpose of the act was to facilitate for farmers to fence by subsidizing joint purchases of fencing material. Wool farming was a priority and fenced farms were a precondition for a prosperous wool industry.

The Fencing Act of 1912 did not include jackal-proof fences, i.e. netting fences. We should therefore assume that the act was not primarily aimed at the capitalized farmers. Their farms were to a large extent already enclosed and subdivided into camps with wire, as seen in the Blue Book on Native Affairs in 1909 and also on Wellwood. The act was therefore aimed at those who had not been able to fence their farms at all, or only to a limited extent. It is possible that the state did not afford to subsidize the expensive netting fences, but the jackals had caused problems for farmers since the 1890s and there was a consensus that netting fences were the best means to combat them. Ordinary wires could be used for creating camps and practice rotational grazing, but farmers would still have to kraal their sheep at night and continue to rely on shepherds. The Fencing Act of 1912 was therefore not progressive in terms of creating preconditions for a new way of farming. However, the Fencing Act facilitated for all farmers to improve fencing on their farms.

The Rubidges may have been inspired by the new legislation to some extent. In 1913 Sidney Rubidge took over as proprietor of Wellwood. He continued in his father's footsteps as a progressive farmer. The boundary was already enclosed and five or six camps as well. But in May 1913 "Victor & self walked right around boundary of camp behind randt to inspect fence, with view of making it

---

412 *Annual Statement on Trade and Shipping*, 1910, 4:63.

413 Beinart, W 2008, pp. 247, 258.

414 *Agricultural Journal* 1910, vol xxxvii, no 6, pp. 681-85; Beinart, W 2008, p. 224.

thoroughly jackall [sic] proof". The camp called Behind Randt was fenced with ordinary wire, which did not keep jackals out. However, Sidney did not cover the entire camp with netting, as would be expected when making it jackal-proof. Instead he "[d]ecided that West Side required 3 more barb wires, South Side 2 more barb & East Side 4 ft netting & 1 barb above". In order to keep jackals from digging under the fence, the "[w]hole length to be packed" with stones. Especially the places where the ground was uneven facilitated for jackals to dig under the fence. The fence required in total 3,000 yards of netting, 43 rolls of barb wire, 70 standards and 20 poles and the cost was "estimated between £105 & £130."[415] The decision to implement netting only in certain places definitely kept costs down. His decision to use barb wire instead of netting was presumably influenced by the 1912 Fencing Act, which meant he would be subsidized for the 43 rolls of barb wire. The 3,000 yards of netting he would have to pay in full. The places where he added additional wires were probably already strung with many wires, which meant that they may have been equally good as netting fences. In general, however, netting fences were preferred by farmers. The 1912 act seemingly created incentives to add wires to existing fences instead of implementing netting.

The decisions to accelerate fencing, particularly jackal-proof fencing, on Wellwood, definitely seems to have been at least partly induced by the act of 1912, but it was to some extent also a response to a greater threat from jackals. As seen, several sheep had been caught by jackals. Furthermore, in early August 1913, one of the shepherds informed that three young rams had been caught by a jackal.[416] The amount of jackal-proof fences on Wellwood was clearly not enough to keep the jackals away. In 1914 the Rubidges even made their "[f]irst attempt at jackall [sic] drive in big camp, [...]". Hunting jackals was a method used throughout the Cape, with varying results. On Wellwood it did, however, not seem to work: In all, they "mustered some 20 men, with assistance from Woodcliff, but found no trace of anything".[417] A better method was to continue to improve the jackal-proof fences, which was also done.

At the end of 1913 the mountain area was to become enclosed. Sidney Rubidge met with a man called Pienaar, who was probably a neighbour, on the mountain and arranged with a fencer to fence for 8s. per 100 yards.[418] The mountain constituted a boundary area of Wellwood, which means that it was partially fenced already. But at the same time the cost would be shared with the neighbour. It was not stated that the camp was to be netted, but we should assume that the Rubidges at least wanted to jackal-proof it with wires, which was facilitated by the new legislation.

---

415 Rubidge diaries, May 31, 1913.

416 Rubidge diaries, Aug. 4, 1913.

417 Rubidge diaries, Jan. 27, 1914.

418 Rubidge diaries, Dec. 30, 1913.

As long as the boundary of the farm was not jackal-proof, the jackals could still enter the farm. While several camps had become jackal-proof on Wellwood, the boundary was not, which meant that jackals still posed a threat on Wellwood, and in 1914 Sidney Rubidge decided to start jackal-proofing the whole farm, not only the camps. Together with some of the labourers on the farm he started to work on the boundary fence "from ostrich camp corner on main road side, making it proof along ground".[419] The material used was not netting; about a month later the farm assistant "Billy & boys finished adding wires along ostrich camp boundary fence".[420] And two days later "Billy & 3 boys at fence along main road again putting in laces".[421] Making the entire farm jackal-proof was a long term project, and it took several years before it was done. It is, however, important to note that it started in 1914, and that netting fences were not primarily used although they made up a part of the new fences.

Shepherds and grazing rights

The increased creation of jackal-proof camps on Wellwood had implications also for the labour relations. Van Sittert claims that fences were "a spatial projection of power" and had "transformative effects on social relations" in the countryside,[422] which is true. But he does not say how the relationship between farmers and labourers changed. There were two major changes; firstly, the fences reduced the number of outstations and shepherds on Wellwood to two in 1913,[423] and secondly, which is more interesting, they changed the practice of grazing rights.

One of the shepherds, Bosslandt, arrived at the farm in early 1913 and took a flock of sheep to "Kloof Kraal" on the mountain, which is where his family also lived.[424] A few days after Bosslandt was hired, Sidney Rubidge inspected his work. Counting sheep was done regularly, but it was perhaps even more important when it came to new shepherds. There was no reason to worry, though, as Sidnet Rubidge was "very satisfied with new herd".[425] The other shepherd was called Dial, whom Sidney sent with "ewe flock, 683 in all, to Allidan's fountain [...]".[426] Allidan's fountain was also in the mountain area, but appears to have been separated from the "mountain", where Bosslandt

419 Rubidge diaries, July 21, 1914.

420 Rubidge diaries, Aug. 29, 1914.

421 Rubidge diaries, Aug. 31, 1914.

422 Van Sittert, L 2002, p. 96.

423 Rubidge diaries, March 10, 1913. Reference to "both outstations".

424 Rubidge diaries, Feb. 10, 1913.

425 Rubidge diaries, Feb. 13, 1913.

426 Rubidge diaries, Feb. 17, 1913.

herded his sheep. Some months later the flock from Allidan's fountain was replaced, though, as "Dial brought ewe flock down, which drove to camp behind randt, after catching out 80 near lambing".[427] The move of the sheep indicated that they would not be herded any longer, but were to run in the camp "behind randt". And it seemed like there was no demand for two shepherds; in August there was only one shepherd left on the farm, as "Dial and Betty left".[428] However, in November Sidney had hired a new shepherd, Janavaries, who went "with 438 ewes & 123 lambs to Alidan's fountain".[429] There were thus still two areas where sheep were herded, but altogether it indicates that the demand for shepherds was greatly reduced compared to the early years of the twentieth century, when as many as five shepherds seem to have been on the farm. The jackal-proof camps were thus deemed safe enough to allow the sheep to run free in them.

As fencing went on, it was also obvious that the farmers were less interested in tenants and labourers with much stock. James Flanaghan, representing the Komgha Farmers' Association, stated that they were "very much opposed to having natives in our district [...]". The reason was that "natives" brought their stock with them, which were infested with ticks. "Many farmers are now carrying large flocks of merino sheep and we feel that the more natives we have in the district the worse it is for the farmer." Flanaghan did of course not want black people to disappear from the district altogether, only those who had stock. He recognized that "[...] we must have labour, but it must be paid labour."[430] W. R. Warren in Stutterheim clarified the matter, saying that "as sheep farmers or stock farmers it does not pay us to have natives mixed up among us because we know that they make depredations on our stock".[431] F. C. Bousfield, also in Stutterheim, explained that there was a difference between pastoral and agricultural farmers. His "experience is that where sheep farming is concerned the farmers have no time for the native, but where agriculture is concerned, I think the white farmer and the native get on very well together".[432]

Wool farmers, who were involved in the "wool for wire" trade with British capital, could thus manage better without tenants and labourers with stock than agricultural farmers could. But that was also a result of the actual production

---

[427] Rubidge diaries, June 17, 1913.

[428] Rubidge diaries, Aug. 14, 1913.

[429] Rubidge diaries, Nov. 8, 1913.

[430] Natives Land Commission, 1916. Vol II, Appendix IX. James Flanaghan, Komgha, pp. 162.

[431] Natives Land Commission, 1916. Vol II, Appendix IX. W. R. Warren, Stutterheim, p. 177.

[432] Native Land Commission, 1916. Vol II, Appendix IX. F. C. Bousfield, Stutterheim, p. 177.

process. Agricultural farmers were more dependent on seasonal or casual labour, which could be acquired from tenants or half-sharers on the farm, for harvests than pastoralists were. The wool farmers who had fenced their farms were not interested in the produce that black tenants could offer. The wool of their sheep was usually inferior to that of the white farmers' merinos. The crops that tenants could produce were probably of more interest, but in most wool districts the environment did not allow any large production of crops. And land on wool farms was not geared towards cultivation, but for sheep. The white farmers could not afford to completely deny the labourers grazing rights, but they definitely desired to do so. And although grazing rights still occurred even on successful farms like Wellwood, the practice was changed by fencing.

While the two shepherds seemingly herded quite a few of the Wellwood merinos, around 1,000 altogether, it was also clear that the stock belonging to the labourers were concentrated in one of those areas: the mountain. The following examples will illustrate.

In March the two labourers Kleinbooi and Piet left the farm. Sidney Rubidge paid them and then "sent them to fetch their stock on mountain". They left with quite a few animals; Piet had "14 goats & 2 Cape sheep" and Kleinbooi had "48 goats, 16 sheep & 4 head cattle". However, already the same day replacements were on the farm: A black man called "Willem & his Fanny [?] began work, [...]". Also Willem had stock, and it was sent to the same area where Kleinbooi's and Piet's stock had been grazing: "dipped his 8 sheep & let him take his stock 25 goats & 8 sheep to wether flock on mountain".[433] In May the labourer Julie and his family was hired, they also arrived at the farm with stock. The day after he was hired, "Julie took his stock 10 goats & 12 Capes to wether flock on mountain".[434]

Labourers were not the only ones who brought stock to Wellwood. In June 1913 Bill Hartzenberg came to Wellwood "to offer his services as assistant on the farm".[435] Hartzenberg's services were apparently required on Wellwood, and less than a week later "Bill Hartzenberg brought his luggage & stock here [...]". In all he had "43 small stock (20 Capes 20 goats) 3 cows & 1 mare". Also the farm assistants were thus in possession of stock, but not necessarily more than some of the labourers. But the wages were clearly better for assistants than for labourers; "Hartzenberg began work at £3 per month".[436] The position as farm assistant was more or less reserved for whites, usually sons of farmers, who did not have a farm of their own, but who could perhaps aspire to have one after serving as farm assistant for some years. The labour force was thus stratified along racial lines, as the position as farm assistant was only held by

433 Rubidge diaries, March 19, 20, 1913.

434 Rubidge diaries, May 20, 1913.

435 Rubidge diaries, June 16, 1913. Also called Billy Hartzenberg.

436 Rubidge diaries, June 23, 1913.

whites. But the stock belonging to the farm assistant was not separated from that of labourers: As with the other labourers, Sidney "[s]ent Hartzenberg's stock to mountain flock".[437]

Placing the stock belonging to labourers and farm assistant on the mountain could, of course, have been a coincident, but later that year it was evident that the area used for grazing rights for labourers was restricted; in December 1913 Sidney Rubidge "[r]esorted all stock on farm", which revealed the composition of flocks. Of these he sent 472 sheep, mainly merinos, to the camp "Behind Randt". These sheep did not seem to be herded. Neither were the prime stud animals herded: "Sent 75 select [...] Ewes to run in upper-house enclosure". In only two places was there a mention of flocks being herded. In one case he sent a flock of 810 sheep comprised mainly of ewes with Janavaries to Allidan's fountain. The other case was the flock which he "[s]ent to mountain with Bosslandt" which consisted of "445 sheep, excluding 8 small lambs, comprising 350 merino wethers 16 Capes from behind randt, & about 79 Capes belonging to Billy & servants".[438] It seems like the stock belonging to labourers were on the mountain, which was the poorest veld and where they could not run free.

Bill Hartzenberg and the rest of the labour force could thus not negotiate to get their stock to run among the best stud merinos in the jackal-proof camps. Their stock was kraaled and trekked on the mountain according to the old way of farming. Although the farmers had to give in to labourers' demands on keeping stock of their own, the relationship between the two was clearly not equal. The sheep of the farmer were obviously valued higher, and the farmer had the power to treat them better. They thus ran in the jackal-proof camps without being herded. Labourers were not able to get their sheep to run free, which was the prescribed way of increasing the health of sheep and the quality of wool. Those sheep that farmers considered of good quality, he bought, usually at very low prices; when July was hired Sidney "bought 4 goats 95 bastard sheep for £4.2/-", thus only fractionally more than 1s. per head. Similarly, some months earlier Sidney made an exchange with a man called "SwartBooi, giving young [...] heifers in exchange for 16 boergoats & buying 4 others at 5/".[439] These sheep and goats were used for rations, but also for further trade. As labourers desired ownership of stock, the animals could be used for remuneration. This practice rendered labourers some cash or cattle in return, but concentrated the best sheep in the hands of farmers.

---

437 Rubidge diaries, June 24, 1913.

438 Rubidge diaries, Dec. 5, 1913.

439 Rubidge diaries, May 17; Feb. 17, 1913.

The Oudtshoorn family – old relations withering away

Even though the stock of labourers was herded instead of running free, the ownership of stock enabled labourer to keep their families together and preserve the generational division of labour. Others were in dire straits.

In May 1913 "Jan Oudtshoorn here begging for work […]". Sidney "gave him section of road […] to repair for 13/-".[440] Jan Oudtshoorn had been on the farm previously, working with fencing along with his son in 1901. At that time he also worked with the sheep and one day "turned up at 11 am to help with dipping & shearing".[441] In 1901 he stayed on Wellwood for some months with at least one of his sons. Besides helping his father with fencing, the son, Hans, also carried out deliveries in 1901: Richard Rubidge "[s]ent Klein Hans Outshoorn to Bloemhof for post", more than once.[442] At that time the generational division of labour appears to have been in full operation. The father, Jan, arrived at the farm and at the same time his son Hans assisted him in his work with fences, but he was also ordered to run errands for the Rubidge family. But Jan was a casual labourer, coming and going.

Some twelve years later, the Oudtshoorn family was still together. After Jan had finished his work with the road in June he and his family stayed on the farm or at least close by; less than a month later "[t]wo sons of Jan Oudtshoorn […]" were involved in making "clay for repairing clay walls".[443] The Oudtshoorn family seemingly had masonry skills and the generational division of labour was exploited by Sidney Rubidge; he, like his father Richard had done in 1901, gained access to the sons of Jan through him. Yet another month later "Jan Oudtshoorn finished with clay wall and left".[444] One of his sons, Andries, did, however, remain on the farm. The day after the clay wall was finished, he started constructing breeding paddocks.[445] The system of family labour was thus used to gain access to the labour of Jan's sons, but when he left, one son remained.

The son, Andries, must have been an adult, or at least old enough to be able to manage himself. He did not seem to have any stock, neither did his father. Staying on the farm on his own definitely shows that he had a desire to be independent, but could also have been a strategy among those labourers with few means of production. In essence, they were proletarianized to an extent not seen among labourers who owned stock and who left the farm as a family. The Oudtshoorns, who had no stock, therefore had less possibilities of holding the

440 Rubidge diaries, May 30, 1913.
441 Rubidge diaries, May 16, 1901.
442 Rubidge diaries, Oct. 22, 1901.
443 Rubidge diaries, July 3, 1913.
444 Rubidge diaries, Aug. 7, 1913.
445 Rubidge diaries, Aug. 8, 1913.

family together, and were forced to take employment where they could find it. The farm, in this case Wellwood, had completely replaced the family as a productive unit.

At least one of Jan Oudtshoorn's sons thus stayed on Wellwood, while he himself went elsewhere. But Jan did not stay away for long. In September he returned to Wellwood together with a man called Windvogel. The following day "Jan Oudtshoorn & Windvogel undertook clearing away old hedge along top side of young grove for £4". The wage was fairly large considering he was only paid 13 shillings to repair a road some months earlier. Clearing away the hedge, which consisted of aloes and prickly pear, thus appears to have involved a lot of work and took more than a month to complete. But he did not work with his son Andries on the hedge. The same day that Jan started working again on the farm, Sidney "[p]aid off Andries Oudtshoorn & dismissed him".[446] The Oudtshoorn family split up again as Andries left the farm. But he did not stay away for long either. At the end of October he was back, this time with stock of his own, as Sidney "[d]ipped 9 goats with kids & 2 Capes of Andries Oudtshoorn & bought some at 8/-".[447] Dipping Andries' stock implied that he would be on the farm for a longer period, although this is not stated. In any case, while being away Andries seems to have accumulated some stock, even enough to be able to sell some of it.

The Oudtshoorns were apparently casual labourers, without stock on the farm, until Andries arrived with his animals. The father, Jan, returned to do some more work, but seems to have finished in November, when Sidney "[p]aid off Jan Oudtshoorn & Piet, having finished reaping".[448] The Oudtshoorn family is therefore highly interesting as it demonstrates a case where the son Andries, not the father, was the one who had access to stock. The family labour system, which rested on the father's access to his family's labour through ownership of stock, was in that case suspended. Sidney Rubidge chose to hire the son Andries for a longer period, while the father was sent away as a casual labourer without stock or his son's labour power to offer to other farmers. Such a state of affairs was probably unusual at that point in time, but it indicates that things had started to change among the rural labour force. As young men could earn money or stock of their own, their dependence on their fathers was clearly reduced. The family labour system thus started to wither away under the pressure of capitalist farming.

[446] Rubidge diaries, Sept. 3, 1913.

[447] Rubidge diaries, Oct. 27, 1913.

[448] Rubidge diaries, Nov. 26, 1913

Men on the mountain – the last shepherds and the first camp walker

In January 1914 the grazing area on the mountain was enclosed, creating another camp on Wellwood. The last grazing area on the farm was thereby enclosed. Presumably it was jackal-proof, although not with netting, as it seems. And there were still shepherds on the mountain, Janavaries and Bosslandt. Before the year was over, none of them remained on the farm, though, and Sidney Rubidge had increased his control over the labour force and the production process.

One day in February, Sidney went to the mountain and searched Janvaries "hut and found paraffin tin of beer, one full of mealies brewing and two other tins full of ration mealies". The beer, so called kafir beer, was a frequent matter of disturbance to farmers, and had been for a long time. Brewing was outlawed. The illegal nature of the activity caused Sidney to send the farm assistant "Billy to Bethesda for Police".[449]

The shepherd Janavaries was subsequently arrested and brought to Graaff-Reinet. He was brought before the magistrate two days afterwards. Sidney also went there and later the same day he "returned with Janavaries, having paid his fine of £5, the alternative sentence being 1 month in jail".[450] Paying the fine instead of going to jail was frequently done in the Cape at this time, provided the convicted could pay. If it was a labourer, the farmer often paid the fine, as in this case. Having a labourer in jail was of no use to the farmers, and they were therefore often willing to pay the fine. Paying the fine obviously made Janavaries indebted to Sidney Rubidge. He was even £5 in debt, which probably represented five or six months' wages. This practice clearly strengthened Sidney's position in relation to Janavaries, who would have to work off his debt for another half a year. The incident did not cause Sidney to distrust his shepherd, though. Janavaries was back on the mountain a month later herding his flock of sheep.[451]

The shepherd Bosslandt, who was hired in early 1913, and was favoured by Sidney Rubidge, decided to leave the farm in May 1914, and came "down with wethers [...]" from the mountain. It did not seem like he brought any stock of his own to the farm, but during his time on Wellwood he must have accumulated some; he was "leaving with 35 sheep, 8 goats and 1 donkey".[452] Instead of convincing Bosslandt to stay, Sidney Rubidge had already arranged

---

449 Rubidge diaries, Feb. 8, 1914.

450 Rubidge diaries, Feb. 10, 1914

451 Rubidge diaries, March 21, 1914.

452 Rubidge diaries, March 25, 1914.

with a new shepherd to take care of the sheep, as he gave the flock to a black man called Johnas.[453]

Johnas, or Jonas, was hired only two days prior to Bosslandt's leaving Wellwood, indicating that Sidney Rubidge prepared for a shift of shepherds. Also Jonas came with a family and stock. Jonas, his son George and his daughter Jessie were hired. They brought with them 47 head of stock, made up of 32 sheep and 15 goats, which were all dipped.[454] One shepherding family was thereby replaced by another. The son of Jonas, George, was probably quite young, but he was of use both to his father and to Sidney Rubidge. He probably worked with his father on the mountain and initially he was involved in minor herding duties, such as looking for lost stock and trekking them. Two months after he was hired Sidney Rubidge noted that "George [was] back from mountain & reported having found 13 of the missing young rams, also brought 2 more cows down with calves".[455] Some months later he s entrusted to herd sheep on his own. But as he was quite young, he was ordered to take care of the easiest flock, the lambs in the mountain camp.[456]

The arrival of Jonas and his family may have created an abundance of shepherds on Wellwood. In early May Janavaries came down with came down with his flock of sheep as the "water having given in at fee-Kraal – sent flock to lie at shed 'Kraal'".[457] The problem with the water supply took a couple of weeks to repair, but when it was done it was not Janavaries who took the sheep back. Instead Sidney sent "herd Jonas back to feekraal with flock".[458] After his coming down, there is no further mention of Janavaries, and we must assume that he was involved in other work than shepherding. Jonas and his son George seem to have been the only shepherds left on the farm.

However, a new shepherd, called Johnson, came to the farm and "agreed to work for no pay, & to receive only mealie rations. [...]". Johnson was apparently desperate not only to find work, but also a place to stay at: "He even offered to hand over his 3 head sheep if we would only keep him". Sidney exclaimed his astonishment over this state of affairs, but also had an answer as to why: "To such a state of reduction has the price of labour dropped, first, owing to ostrich feather slump, but chiefly owing to Great European War".[459] The ostrich feather slump, which started in 1912 after feathers were no longer in fashion in Europe, was felt throughout the farming areas of the Cape, and according to Sidney Rubidge created a situation where labourers begged for

---

453 Rubidge diaries, March 25, 1914.

454 Rubidge diaries, March 23, 1914.

455 Rubidge diaries, May 22, 1914

456 Rubidge diaries, Oct. 10, 1914

457 Rubidge diaries, May 2, 1914.

458 Rubidge diaries, May 27, 1914.

459 Rubidge diaries, Aug. 26, 1914.

work. The First World War reinforced the slump in ostrich feathers, as most European countries focused on other imports than feathers. In all, it created a situation where labourers begged for work, at least according to Sidney Rubidge. However, a few months earlier some labourers on Wellwood did not seem to be in need of taking any work as they declined to undertake repair work for £5. 10s.[460] That was before the outbreak of the war.

A few months later, Johnson was in trouble, and was replaced. Instead Sidney hired a man called Andries, "who I know to be a good herd" [...]" to replace Johnson, "who after pleading to be hired and doing so well with sheep which were in a poor state when given him, ended by causing so much trouble & anxiety [...]". The problem was that Johnson had allowed 270 sheep from his flock to escape from the camp, "some of which were found quite [a] few miles away. Several of which died from exposure & also eaten by jackals."[461] We do not know why Johnson allowed the sheep to run away, but he was obviously regarded as neglectful. And his case demonstrates that proletarianization could happen also when working on a farm. As he had handed over his sheep to the Rubidges on his arrival and agreed to work only for rations, he probably left the farm without either stock or wages, and was even worse off than when he came there. When Johnson came to Wellwood he at least had some stock to offer to those who wanted to keep him and give him rations. After his time on Wellwood, he could only offer his labour power.

Perhaps as a consequence of the incident with Johnson, and also other incidents with jackals killing Wellwood sheep, Sidney tried a new method. There were evidently jackals in the mountain areas, sometimes in the camps, but certainly outside of them. As the sheep herded by Johnson had run out of the camp, there was obviously a hole in the fence somewhere, which allowed sheep to get out. Such holes would allow also for jackals and other vermin to enter the camp. Therefore, controlling the fences was pivotal to the practice of rotational grazing in jackal-proof camps. Several times Sidney and others had ridden around camps on horseback, controlling fences, as in December 1913, when he "[r]ode netting fence Behind randt & found it in perfect order".[462] But the camps were large, some comprising more than a thousand morgen, which meant that controlling them took a lot of time and effort, if done by the farmer. Sidney therefore decided to create a new occupation on the farm.

In December 1914 Sidney Rubidge "[h]ired single man Jacob for a months [sic] trial to live in hut in mountain camp & walk the fences every day".[463] The first so called camp-walker had been hired on Wellwood. As it was a new position, Sidney apparently wanted to try it first, as Jacob was hired on trial for

460 Rubidge diaries, Jan. 26, 1914.

461 Rubidge diaries, Nov. 10, 1914.

462 Rubidge diaries, Dec. 11, 1913.

463 Rubidge diaries, Dec. 8, 1914.

a month. Jacob may have taken over the hut used by shepherds previously, but we should assume that the sheep in the mountain camp were still herded. However, Jacob represented a new form of labourer, who was to replace the shepherd. Unlike the shepherds, who worked with animals and thereby performed the same work as past generations, the camp walker worked with fences. Through the hiring of Jacob, the labour force on Wellwood thereby lost further control over the production of wool. The skill of shepherds, which assured the well-being of the sheep, had been reduced to controlling the functionality of the fences.

CHAPTER 9

State Interference and Support to Farmers

War and wool

The First World War meant an upturn in South African wool exports. The amount exported did not change, but the price did. During the war there was a shortage of cross-bred wool in Europe, which was the main raw material for uniforms. Merino wool was therefore used to a greater extent, which benefitted farmers in South Africa.[464]

Table 16. South African wool exports 1910 - 1920.

Year	Lbs	£
1910	121,668,932	3,830,830
1912	161,974,684	4,780,594
1913	176,971,865	5,719,288
1914	133,981,317	4,238,205
1915	170,009,886	5,380,281
1916	136,405,125	6,601,657
1917	117,657,142	8,782,280
1918	115,634,498	9,689,630
1919	184,952,800	17,920,384
1920	119,504,747	15,988,103

Source: *Annual Statement on Trade and Shipping,* 1910-1920.

The war also meant that the relations between Cape and South African wool farmers and the British Empire were strengthened. In 1917 the British entered an agreement with the South African Government to buy all its wool at a fixed price, which was 55 per cent higher than the price one year prior to the war, the so called *Imperial Wool Scheme.* The same arrangement was made with Australia and New Zealand. South African farmers were not pleased with the wool scheme when they realized that the fixed price was lower than what they could

[464] *Journal of the Department of Agriculture,* vol 1, no 2, 1920, p. 271.

obtain for the wool through sales to the US and Japan. About one third of the accumulated wool was sold through this scheme, but some farmers parted from it; also the US and Japan bought large quantities at a higher price than under the Government scheme.[465]

While the wool exports fluctuated heavily during the war and the years after its end, the wool industry did not seem to suffer; the wool price increased considerably between 1915 and 1920. The exports for 1919 were also a record as almost 185 million lbs. was shipped from South Africa. Despite this apparent improvement, the annual report of the Department of Customs and Excise in 1920 argued that the future for wool farmers was bleak. The "superabundant supplies" of wool in Great Britain together with an end of orders from Japan and the US were seen as threatening the future for wool farmers.[466] The war also caused the ostrich feather slump.[467] Sidney Rubidge noted in 1918 that his income from ostrich feathers was reduced by about £400 compared to before the war. He estimated that in 1913 each bird would generate £6 and in 1918 only 16s. Such an extreme reduction in the value of ostrich feathers was most severe for those who had no other sources of income. Those who had sheep probably focused most of their attention on them: "Thus today a lower return is got per bird than for an average fleece from a merino wether."[468]

Also fencing was, however, interrupted by the war. Low supplies of fences and a price increase by "three or four times as much as was formerly paid" resulted in a decreased amount of fencing being done.[469] But a large number of the farms in the Cape were enclosed at the end of the war. In 1918, almost half the farms in the Cape, 15,035 out of 31,119, were "wholly fenced", while 12,823 were "partially fenced". Only about 10 per cent, or 3,261 farms, were "not fenced" at all.[470] Unfortunately, there is no indication of the amount of netting fences at that time, but in 1924 only 5,000 farms in the Cape were enclosed with netting. As the netting was not included in the Fencing Act they were more expensive for farmers to buy. Their spread was therefore limited. But there were other ways to jackal-proof camps, such as lacing with machines and by hand. This was probably used to a fairly large extent as well.

The main source of fences was still the UK. Ordinary fencing wire worth £777,367 was imported in 1920, whereof £369,220 worth came from the UK, thus about 47 per cent. The US was a larger exporter of fencing wire to South Africa in terms of weight (cwts), but at a lower price, £323,109 worth. More

---

465 *Journal of the Department of Agriculture*, vol 1, no 2, 1920, pp. 271-74 ; Garson, N. G 1980, pp. 77-78.

466 *Annual Statement on Trade and Shipping,* 1920, "Introduction".

467 Beinart, W 2008, p. 15.

468 Rubidge diaries, July 12, 1918.

469 *Journal of the Department of Agriculture*, vol 1, no 1, 1920, p. 68.

470 Agricultural census 1918, p. 9.

interestingly, however, the share of netting fences had increased considerably since 1909. Netting worth £219,264 was imported to South Africa in 1920, which was more than one fifth of the total value for all fencing, compared to £15,000 in 1909. Just like in 1909, nearly all the netting came from the UK; £212,253 worth came from there, which amounts to almost 97 per cent. While the US thus had become a competitor to the UK in exports of ordinary wire, the imperial power was the one supplying the new technology in the form of netting. The UK was not as dominant as during previous decades regarding imports of Cape and South African wool, in 1920 only 35 per cent of the South African wool was exported to the UK compared to more than 90 per cent in 1890. Japan, Belgium and the US together purchased 45 per cent of the South African clip in 1920.[471] Nevertheless, the UK still remained the most crucial actor for Cape wool farming as supplier of new technology, which was necessary for successful wool farming.

Clean wool – higher profits

The wool exports that generated income for farmers were enhanced due to the increased price during the war. However, there were many things that farmers could do to increase it as well. The most crucial measure was in regards to shearing.

Wool experts such as W. M. McKee claimed that shearing machines were vital for sheep farmers. Besides a faster shearing pace, machines also increased the yield of wool shorn. J. Pringle, a farmer in Bedford, claimed that shearing with machines resulted in 1 lb. more wool per sheep on his farm.[472] Despite these advantages, few farmers seem to have purchased shearing machines. A main reason was probably that the labour costs for shearers were quite low. Compared to Australia, where machines were frequently used, wages in the Cape were very low, a matter that in general slows down mechanization. Sidney Rubidge noted that in Australia the shearers were paid 45 shillings per 100 sheep in the 1920s. In the Cape the recommended price for shearing in 1930 was 10 shillings per 100 sheep, thus about the same as in the 1890s.[473] While the racial class division increased profits for farmers through low wages paid to the labourers, it also kept back some technological change.

Other factors than shearing machines were of greater importance for a successful shearing. Wool expert W. M. McKee meant that shearing in South Africa in general was done in a careless manner: "Any old shed or outhouse

---

471 *Annual Statement on Trade and Shipping*, 1920.

472 McKee, W. M. 1913, pp. 341, 343.

473 Rubidge diaries, Aug. 13, 1945; Bouch, R 1997, p. 105.

seems good enough to harvest the year's crop."[474] An initial measure was therefore to build a proper shearing shed, which was large enough for those who were involved, as "most hands are too cramped for space to do full justice to the wool". Most importantly, the "farmer should not do any manual work – he will be fully occupied with seeing to it that others do their work properly".[475]

A certain division of labour was of the essence for successful shearing. The practice at the time in South Africa was that the shearer picked up the shorn fleece and carried it to the skirting table. This meant that it took a long time to arrange the wool "so that skirting can be properly done". Instead, the wool should be shorn on stages. Firstly the smaller parts and the belly wool should be taken off. This would be picked up by another member of the shearing team and put in a basket.[476] According to McKee, the person carrying the wool appears to have been a youngster, indicating that there was room for young people also in shearing. Once the smaller parts had been shorn, the main fleece was next. It should be in one piece and after it was shorn off, be carried away by a person employed especially for this, usually called a fleece thrower. The fleece thrower was not a youngster as the task required certain skills and was of great importance to the shearing.[477]

The shearing process did not end with the wool being shorn off the sheep. Wool expert Charles Mallinson explained that keeping the wool clean was essential and measures could be taken during shearing in order to improve the wool. Firstly, farmers should make sure that no vegetable matter or dirt was stuck in the wool. Secondly, farmers should class the wool according to quality so that buyers, that is, the representatives of manufacturers, could find the sort of wool required for different purposes.[478] If wool was sold unsorted, the manufacturers would have to hire labourers to do it, which would increase their costs. Labour was considerably cheaper on Cape farms, and hiring labour for classing on farms reduced the overall labour costs within transnational production.

Apart from classing, the wool should also be baled properly. In 1918 there were 1,689 wool presses in the Cape, and only 556 in the other provinces combined.[479] Mallinson emphasized the importance of uniformity in bales. The shipping companies gave discounts to bales that were pressed and from at least 1915 the *South African Railway Company* offered a 10 per cent discount on all pressed wool.[480] Uniformity in bales facilitated both transports and purchases

---

474 McKee, W. M. 1913, p. 186.

475 McKee, W. M. 1913, pp. 188-89.

476 Mallinson, C 1915, pp. 83, 85.

477 McKee, W. M. 1913, pp. 192-93

478 Mallinson, C 1915, p. 86-87.

479 Agricultural census 1918, p. 73.

480 Mallinson, C 1915, p. 91.

of wool. Although the wool-presses were expensive, the discounts were an incentive for farmers to invest in them. In 1929-1930 the number of wool presses in the Cape had increased to 5,463 and in the Union to 7,738. During the first half of the 1930s very few wool presses were purchased. In 1936-1937 there were 5,596 in the Cape and 8,095 in the Union.[481] The Depression probably affected the willingness among farmers to invest in machinery, but it could also have been an indication that the presses were shared by several farmers.

The recommendations from wool experts were no doubt correct if farmers wanted to maximize their profits. The advice was also valuable for those who had little knowledge of wool and what happened to it on the global market. The extent to which these recommendations were adhered to is, however, more difficult to estimate. Some farmers invested in proper shearing sheds and other equipment, but others probably continued as they had done previously.

In 1923, the Rubidges bought a wool press for £36.[482] There may have been a wool press on the farm previously, but it was never mentioned. The price does not seem excessive, at least not compared to the great expenditure that was put into water supplies and fencing, which for some years exceeded £300. Of course, fences and water supplies were probably prioritized by most farmers as those implements were necessary for efficient farming. The wool press did not affect farming, only the price which could be fetched for the wool. But the pressed wool generated higher income as it was more attractive to buyers. During the 1940s adverts appeared in the *Farmers' Weekly* for "1-man wool presses", one sold by P. R. Dodds in Port Elizabeth.[483] The early models required more than one man to operate them, but improvements to the wool presses seem to have made them easier to handle, and manufacturers emphasized the efficiency of the new model. With the wool press shearing would thus become less labour intensive while also producing better pressed bales.

After shearing the sheep were still dipped in Cooper's dip. In 1925-1926 the Rubidges paid £27 for "sheep dip & disinfectant". The expenditure on dip and disinfectant thus exceeded wages to shearers, who were paid £19 in 1926. The ratio between the two demonstrates how important the low wages were for farmers' ability to improve the quality of the wool, and still be able to make profits. The dip only constituted a fraction of the total expenses of £3,863 on Wellwood for that year, but it was the equivalent of one shepherd or labourer per year. For many farmers such sums made a difference in the economy of the farm. The low wages certainly benefitted the poorer farmers. In that regard they were also aided by the state, but there was competition over labour.

---

481 Agricultural census 1929-30, p. 93; Agricultural census 1936-37, p. 113.

482 Rubidge diaries, Oct. 17, 1923.

483 *Farmers' Weekly*, Oct. 8, 15, 1947.

Sheep shearing (CA J1342). Shearing outdoors.

Fenced out

Subsequent to the creation of the Union of South Africa, the *Natives Land Act* was passed in 1913. The act was to divide the country into areas for black and white people. Black people would not be able to buy land in white areas, and the black reserves were largely held in communal tenure, meaning that black people could not accumulate land. Only about seven per cent of the land in South Africa was reserved for black people, indicating the actual aim of the law: to make sure that black people could not be independent of the white capitalist sector. They would thus be further induced to seek employment on land owned by whites. But the 1913 act also promulgated stricter labour relations, such as abandoning pure cash tenancy. Arrangements that did not include transfer of labour from the tenant were to be outlawed. The Natives Land Act was, however, reversed in the Cape Province in 1917. It was found unconstitutional as it hindered black people from qualifying for the vote through ownership of land.[484]

[484] Beinart, W 2001, pp. 10, 56-58.

But despite parliamentary objections to the act, its contents already affected black people in rural Cape. They found it increasingly hard to acquire land for their own farming ventures. In King William's Town the black peasants were clearly in a concerned state. Charles Modossi, giving evidence to the *Natives Land Commission* in 1916, said that "[a] boundary has been placed there dividing the Europeans from the Natives and has caused a great deal of trouble because our stock has no place to graze on". Modossi further explained: "Our stock is dying since that has been done and when cattle go over the border they are seized." The problem was not so much the farmers, as the state, which fenced the location. "They are fencing the ground now right to Berlin, it is said for grazing purposes, [...]". Modossi claimed that the black people in the area had not been consulted and "we would like to know whether the fence is correctly placed there. There is no room for us."[485]

In other parts of the Cape things were equally hard for black peasants. The process of dispossession was underway and caused severe problems for the black peasants. E. Gugutsha explained that "Palmvietvlei was taken from us. The men went away to the war and their place was sold to a farmer, then they moved to Snijklip. The farmer wants to fence it further. The other places are all fenced up."[486] The process of fencing, which was especially important in wool farming districts, as it made possible rotational grazing, was also a process of dispossession. As the old practice of kraaling and trekking with shepherds started to be replaced by rotational grazing, the entire landscape in the rural Cape changed. And with it, the relations between white farmers and black peasants who did not adhere to new methods of pastoralism and were not dependent on enclosed areas for grazing and capital accumulation. Quite the contrary, their farming was still to a great extent based on open pastures, where the stock could graze and enhance their accumulation. Enclosures were an obstacle for them, while they were an aid for the white capitalist farmers. Dispossession, which this process has been called by many, was a primary concern for the state.[487] As black peasants found it harder to continue with their peasant activities, they would be forced to labour in the capitalist sector. Not all of them went to wool farming areas for work, though.

Mallinson noted in 1919 that labour supplies in some of the large wool producing districts such as Graaff-Reinet, Middelburg, Somerset East, Colesberg and Cradock was "scarce" or "moderate". The labour supply was "fairly plentiful" in Aliwal North, Barkly East, Herschel and Wodehouse. In Albany, Cathcart, Stutterheim, Kingwilliamstown, Komgha and Queenstown

---

[485] Natives Land Commission, 1916. Vol II, Appendix IX. Charles Modossi, King William's Town, p. 155.

[486] Natives Land Commission, 1916. Vol II, Appendix IX. E. Gugutsha, p. 246.

[487] See Beinart et al. 1986.

the labour supply was "plentiful but of poor quality".[488] The reasons for the scarce supply of labour were not given, but it is likely that the mining industry and also the urban industries attracted black people from rural areas.

During the first half of the 1920s the farm labour force actually increased, but not in relation to the number of farms. The number of black, coloured and Indian labourers employed on Cape farms in 1918 was 150,168, or 4.8 per farm. In 1925 the number employed was 158,461 or 4.5 per farm.[489] Compared to the average of 12 labourers per farm according to the Commission on Native Affairs in 1865 it was a drastic reduction. But the figures for 1865 were based on a limited sample of relatively successful farmers. At the same time the entire farm labour force in 1918 and 1925 was with all certainty larger than 4.8 and 4.5. Only "employees" were enumerated, not tenants, bywoners or occasional labourers as it seems. Still, the farm labour force had increased since 1911 when there were 89,195 farm labourers and 42,582 shepherds and herds of all races, thus altogether 131,777 people employed on farms in the Cape. Counting only blacks and coloureds in the 1911 census, there were 120,450 people employed as labourers or herds.[490] The war years and the early 1920s was thus a period characterized by an increase of about 25 per cent of the rural labour force.

As seen, the demand for shepherds started to decrease in 1914 as more camps became enclosed. However, the shepherds were replaced with camp walkers, which is why the total labour force probably did not change to any great extent. The Rubidges also had considerably more labourers than the 4.8 average for the Cape in 1918. As many as 19 black and coloured people and 3 whites were recorded as labourers in April and May 1918. During shearing in October and November some extra males were also hired. These were not shearers, but probably worked with other operations such as packing wool. When shearing was over, not only the shearers but also the additional labourers left. The steady labour force seems to have been 10 black males, 4 black females and 3 white males, which was the number in January 1918.[491] Compared to 1875, when there were 14 male labourers, 4 shepherds and 3 females in domestic service, the total labour force had decreased somewhat. There were, for example, only two shepherds in 1918, Adrian and Jan. But also the number of general labourers had decreased. Around 10 or 11 male labourers seem to have been the average in the late 1910s.

Still, far from all farmers had an abundance of labour. We will have to return to the actual production to find out how they differed.

---

488 Mallinson, C 1919, pp. 5-6.

489 Agricultural census 1918, pp. 9-72; 1924-25, pp. 104,165-66.

490 South Africa Census 1911, pp. 564-65.

491 Rubidge diaries, July 22, 1918. Enumeration of labour force July 1917 – June 1918.

Inside the enclosed farm

Despite the relatively high level of enclosure in the Cape, the farming practices did not seem to change to the same extent. Measuring the number of farms that were wholly or partially fenced only indicated boundary fencing, not internal fencing into camps. Subsequently, to a large extent the farmers still practiced shepherding, and kraaling and trekking, not rotational grazing. D. H. R. Featherstone from Aberdeen mentioned in 1922: "There, inside his enclosed farm, the farmer still has his stock herded and the old work of loosening the soil, for the wind to blow and the rain to wash away, goes on just the same." The continued widespread use of shepherds had implications not only for the quality of wool, but the soil itself.

The old methods of farming, which was based on kraaling and trekking, had been criticized previously on a number of occasions. Many farmers had changed their practices, or were in the midst of doing it. But there were many who had not done enough, or nothing at all. When a drought struck the country in 1918 and 1919 it became evident that changes of farming practices were necessary. Large numbers of stock were lost, and with it, income for farmers. A *Drought Commission* was appointed. Its report was published in 1923. It found no evidence for any changes in rainfall. Instead the Commission argued that "only one conclusion can be drawn, namely, that the severe losses of the 1919 drought were caused principally by faulty veld and stock management".[492] Three factors were identified as central to the losses from drought: "kraaling of stock [...] inadequacy of the drinking water facilities, the destruction of vegetation and the resulting soil erosion [...]".[493]

Kraaling obviously necessitated trekking to grazing pastures, which deteriorated the veld. The paths along which the sheep walked eroded and dongas were formed, which in some cases turned into gulleys. When water came in the form of rain it washed away large parts of soil. But even those farmers who had created camps and practiced rotational grazing experienced problems if drinking places were too far apart. The Commission noted that "the farmer loses much of the benefit of having abandoned kraaling, if his stock have still long distances to travel to water". These problems were probably experienced all over the Cape, but one particular area was mentioned: "In the North-west of the Cape Province, the unfortunate animal cannot get water every day, but has to go alternate days without water – at such great distances do the drinking places lie from the grazing grounds." Farmers in the North-Western Cape had accumulated less capital than those in successful districts like Graaff-Reinet, Cradock or Middelburg and consequently their water supply was lacking in both quality and quantity.

---

[492] Drought Commission, 1923, p. 5.

[493] Drought Commission, 1923, p. 4.

Many of these problems could have been avoided through less intensive grazing, but that was not an option. Quite the contrary, farmers increased the number of sheep on their farms too much in relation to the carrying capacity. Instead of profiting from the quality of the wool, they went for quantity. Ultimately, the exploitation of the land struck back at those who did not farm progressively, with fences and without shepherds. Capital expansion in wool farming, represented by fences, was thus a vital factor behind the problems arising from drought. Not because fences caused losses, but because their existence made possible increased production and increased profits. Those who did not have fences exploited the land harder in order to compete.

The main reason for continued use of shepherds was the prevalence of jackals. The solution, once again, was jackal-proof fencing. D. H. R. Featherstone in Aberdeen argued that the "Government should pass a law prohibiting the Land Bank from advancing a fraction for fencing, except only for perfect jackal-proof, of the standard one sees in the Sneeuwbergen", the area north of Graaff-Reinet.[494]

The problem was thus not entirely a matter of having fenced farms or not, but more a matter of implementing the correct fencing, which was to be jackal-proof. However, farmers could not be entirely supported by the state in that regard, as netting fences were exempt from the 1912 Fencing Act. Still, the Commission "found that farmers in general were unaware of existing loan facilities for fencing and other purposes [...]", which means that farmers did not utilise the state support as much as they could have. The Committee recommended that the "Department of Agriculture take steps to bring this knowledge to the door of every farmhouse in the country".[495] In many respects, the farmers thus had themselves to blame for much of their problems. It was their inability to act progressively that created a situation where nature became an invincible enemy. But their problems were not simply a lack of will to act progressively, they also lacked capital. The two went hand in hand.

Farmers in the North-Western parts of the Cape seem to have been among those who suffered most. In those areas, "witnesses complained bitterly of the trek-paths. It would appear that there are persons, farmers who own no farm and pay no rent but who graze their stock along the trek-paths, raising large families the while."[496] These landless farmers, who only had their stock, constituted one part of the group of "poor whites". Not only were they in a poor state, but their existence as non-propertied farmers also caused problems for others: "The eradication of scab, and the fencing and paddocking of farms is greatly hindered by these trek-paths."[497] Trek-boers, who based their farming

494 Drought Commission, 1923. D. H. R. Featherstone, Basson's Kraal, Aberdeen, p. 179.

495 Drought Commission, 1923, p. 22.

496 Drought Commission, 1923, p. 72.

497 Drought Commission, 1923, p. 72.

on constant movement of both their stock and themselves, where not new to the Cape, they had existed since the nineteenth century and even before. But when capitalist farming became more widespread, it was evident that the old, non-capitalist, way of farming was counterproductive for capital accumulation. These farmers made up a large portion of the so called poor whites, who had existed as a social group since the 1860s. Their existence was an anomaly in the racial hierarchy of the country, but it was not until the 1920s that they were considered a social and political problem. Similarly, droughts were also considered a problem for the country when a large portion of the white population succumbed under its pressure.

The Drought Commission in 1922 was not the first recognition of droughts as a potential threat to the Cape or other parts of South Africa, but it was the first time that droughts were given attention to such an extent. The main reason was the evident relation between the drought and "poor-whiteism". The *Carnegie Commission*, which was appointed to investigate the "poor white problem", indicated a state of despair for many of the whites. According to the Commission, increased capitalist wool farming had displaced many white bywoners and small-scale farmers, who dependent on others for access to land.[498]

As poor whites could not support themselves by farming they had to find additional income. Some of the poor whites came to Wellwood in order to find work. For example, in 1927 "[p]oor white van d. Berg here on bike looking for work – offered to sink well where hand boring had failed [...]". He offered to do it at 3 shillings per foot, which Sidney thought was "too cheap".[499] There is no indication that he proposed to pay more, however. Later the same year a man called Vorster was hired to conduct fencing on Wellwood. Sidney Rubidge was satisfied with the work, which comprised 1,200 yards of fencing with eight wires. Vorster had been aided by his son and a coloured man, and was thus able to recruit labour both from his own family, but also outside it. However, Sidney was upset about the state of affairs in the country and asked: "Why should such industry (14 to 15 hr per day work) be performed by 'Poor Whites' as the term goes? Does not such industry deserve an uplifting of the position of these men? Oh sad poor country!"[500] It is a typical feature of capitalism that the poor whites first sold or lost their land and then sold their labour to sink wells and conduct fencing for others, the same investments they themselves could not afford.

---

[498] Grosskopf, J. F. W. 1932, p. 8

[499] Rubidge diaries, March 9, 1927.

[500] Rubidge diaries, Dec. 14, 1927.

The jackal-proof farm

During the 1910s and early 1920s the jackal menace, and the debate about it, was intensified, which can be summarized by a quote from the Drought Commission in 1922: "In conclusion, your Commission desires to again emphasize that the jackal is a dangerous menace to the State."[501] Between 1914 and 1923 the number of jackals killed increased more than ten times: from 5,091 to 57,492.[502] Still, the prevalence of jackals prevented the abolishment of shepherding. Also on Wellwood the jackals made their presence known, and to a much greater extent than previously. At the end of 1918 Sidney Rubidge summarized that 118 sheep had been killed by jackals during the year, thus about one every third day.[503] In the beginning of the early twentieth century that number did probably not exceed 20 per year. According to the *Vermin Extermination Commission*, "the direct losses caused to farmers by vermin can safely be estimated at 7 per cent per year." The losses in small stock "amount to over £1,000,000. The indirect losses, [...], including yearly damage to farm property through erosion and slooting, are estimated at over £5 million."[504] Incentives to combat the jackals were thus great.

Those responsible for combating jackals on Wellwood were the shepherds, of whom there were two in 1918: Adrian and Jan. Both of them seem to have been herding sheep on the mountain, which was heavily attacked by jackals. They caught some of the jackals by using traps and were paid on at least one occasion 10 shillings for a jackal.[505] But the jackals continued to kill sheep on the farm and although the Rubidges had abandoned kraaling, Sidney Rubidge even started to build a new kraal on the mountain to protect the sheep.[506] Besides the losses in sheep, an equally big problem with jackals was that the sheep could not run free. Apparently, in those areas where sheep could run free it was reported that the carrying capacity on a farm had increased by one third. Furthermore, the condition of merino sheep that ran free was greatly improved and the wool yield per sheep increased with two lbs. per year compared to those that were kraaled.[507] Creating jackal-proof camps was therefore of the essence.

Probably as a direct result of the threat from jackals, Sidney Rubidge decided to jackal-proof the mountain camp in 1918. At first he directed two of the labourers on the farm, "two Oudtshoorns", to conduct the fencing. He paid them 5 shillings per 100 yards. There was already a fence on the mountain, and

501 Drought Commission, 1923, p. 20.

502 Vermin Extermination Commission, 1924, p. 6.

503 Rubidge diaries, Dec. 29, 1918.

504 Vermin Extermination Commission, 1924, p. 5.

505 Rubidge diaries, July 15, 1918.

506 Rubidge diaries, July 10, 1918.

507 Vermin Extermination Commission, 1924, p. 4.

the Oudtshoorns were to fortify it, partly by adding a so called verandah hanging out over the fence.[508] The verandah was recommended by experts as it made it more difficult for jackals to jump over the fence.[509] But when Sidney inspected their work the following month, he "found it getting on very slowly".[510] Another fencer, J. Jacobs, was brought in, but he succumbed to the Spanish influenza. A man called Victor was instead hired to finish the work. Jacobs and Victor seem to have been white and were paid more: 7/6 per 100 yards. The cost of the material was not mentioned. Although the Oudtshoorns did not finish the fence, they completed the main part of it, "3,250 yards due to Oudtshoorns" and 2,350 yards was done by Jacobs and Victor.[511] Sidney Rubidge's decision to hire labour from outside to finish the work thus cost him extra. He did not seem to be dissatisfied with the quality of the Oudtshoorn's fencing, only the speed. When jackals killed a sheep every third day, time was of the essence.

When the mountain camp was finished, Victor was offered more work on Wellwood. He returned and began fencing another section of the farm of about 1,600 yards. Also at this section a verandah was deemed necessary. Victor was to "replace one barb wire from fence to act as verandah in conjunction with netting [...]".[512] The verandah apparently was popular on Wellwood. But verandah, or jackal-proof fencing in general, was only efficient if several farmers in the area did the same. Sidney Rubidge met with a neighbour, Hensley [?], at the boundary and they agreed that "netting fence be shifted to this side aloe fence [...]". Sidney was the one who arranged with the fence, but the neighbour would pay half the cost of both the labour and any additional material which was required.[513] Just like in 1886 when du Toit on Dasjiefontein benefitted from a fence that Richard Rubidge arranged, it was once again beneficial to be a neighbour to Wellwood. Half the cost would have to be contributed, but all practicalities were handled by Sidney Rubidge.

This particular fence proved to be more expensive regarding labour: "Agreed with Victor to erect new section at £1 per 100 yds & to cut off old at £1 per 100 yds."[514] The price, about three times as high as the rate for the mountain fence, may have been a result of the situation which emerged when neighbouring farmers shared the fencing costs. Victor and other fencers probably utilized the fact that farmers could get the fencing done for half the price. Fencers could thus negotiate for a higher price than on a fence which did

---

508 Rubidge diaries, Aug. 12, 1918.

509 *Journal of the Department of Agriculture*, No. 4 (Oct.), 1925, pp. 338-50.

510 Rubidge diaries, Sept. 28, 1918.

511 Rubidge diaries, Oct. 4; Nov 2, 12, 20, 1918.

512 Rubidge diaries, Nov. 27, 1918.

513 Rubidge diaries, Nov. 27 (?), 1918.

514 Rubidge diaries, Dec. 2, 1918.

not constitute a boundary. As the Fencing Act also facilitated joint purchases of fencing material for farmers who fenced a mutual boundary, all could gain from border fencing; farmers shared the cost, and were given a subsidy, and fencers in turn could charge a higher rate. To a large extent the state made it possible.

Wellwood was enclosed with netting in 1920. Most of the camps were probably also enclosed by then. The netting proved to be successful. The same year the last jackal for 26 years was shot on Wellwood. The jackal problem, which had existed on the farm since the 1890s, and intensified during the first decades of the twentieth century, was thereby to an end. Sidney Rubidge was enthusiastic about the effects of a jackal-proof farm. During the early 1920s droughts struck the Cape again. Towards the end of 1923, a drought year, he made some "remarks as a further testimony or rather revelation as to the miraculous results of netting camps & running stock free." He compared with previous droughts in 1903, 1908 and 1912 and concluded that those droughts "did not reach the severity of this present state, & yet from about 1200 head on the farm they were reduced in each instance to 800 & 900 head, whereas not only has nothing, out of 2,900 yet died, but prime ones are even found in some camps".[515]

These measures definitely improved wool production on Wellwood, and it would do the same on the national level if all farmers implemented jackal-proof fences. The Vermin Extermination Committee argued that if sheep ran free the state revenue would increase by £4,500,000 per year. After several years of pressure from farmers and officials, the Fencing Act was amended in 1922 and included also netting fences.[516]

Hermaans and his daughter

The increased importance of jackal-proof fencing meant a lowered dependence on shepherds. But they were replaced with camp walkers, who inspected the fences. As the jackal-proof camps spread out on Wellwood, their role became more important. But conditions for them differed from those for shepherds.

When Hermaans and his family of seven members arrived at Wellwood as the new camp walker in 1918 he was not without means. He brought with him 90 goats and 11 donkeys. Compared to most other labourers such a number of stock was large. It seems as if Sidney Rubidge was troubled by that. He therefore "[...] suspended decision & gave him temporary quarters at shed kraal".[517] It took almost two weeks for Sidney to make a decision. On March 12 he hired Hermaans as a camp walker at the rate of £3 per month, which was

[515] Rubidge diaries, Dec. 29, 1923.

[516] *Journal of the Department of Agriculture*, No. 4 (Oct.), 1925, p. 327.

[517] Rubidge diaries, March 2, 1918.

more than what other labourers were paid. But Hermaans was forced to give up some of his stock in return for the higher wage. Sidney Rubidge demanded "Hermaans to reduce his goats to not keep more than 30, while his donkeys would only be allowed grazing in outside veldt".[518] Compared to those labourers who had arrived at the farm with stock previously, Hermaans was in a worse position. He was forced to reduce his goats by one third, which was much. His donkeys could be used as draught animals, which is why he could keep all of them. But their grazing was limited to the "outside veldt", which was probably furthest away from the homestead and which did not interfere with the pastures used for sheep. He could have refused the offer, but evidently had few options that were better. He thus accepted being hired as a camp walker with a heavily reduced number of stock.

The case of Hermaans indicates that in wool farming grazing rights were not reduced because farmers were in crisis, as Morris argues for agricultural farmers on the Highveld.[519] The Rubidges were certainly not lacking cash or capital. Instead, the limited grazing rights were the result of a changed production in wool farming, where a new form of labourer had emerged, which was paid a higher cash wage and thereby had to accept less grazing. A week after being hired Hermaans sold 56 of his goats at a local sale in Graaff-Reinet.[520] The goats rendered him some money, perhaps even quite a lot, but he was on the way to becoming proletarianized. He had to keep on to the animals he had in order to still be somewhat independent from farmers. But selling the stock was not the only sign of changed power relations in wool farming. Also his family was affected.

When Hermaans was hired the agreement was that two of his daughters would work if necessary. They would get rationed and paid. However, when they had started picking almonds Sidney Rubidge made a deal with Hermaans that his daughters would be paid 7s. 6d. per month without food.[521] The input required from Hermaans family had thus increased since he was hired. Three of his daughters were working for the Rubidges instead of two. Such an agreement was a more intense exploitation of Hermaan's family, and in itself, the family relations of the labourers. But it could also have been favoured by Hermaans himself. We do not know who suggested that three daughters should work, but as an agreement was made, it is clear that both parties accepted it. Furthermore, also the remuneration was renegotiated; from cash wages and rations to cash wages and no rations. The new agreement meant that Hermaans received money for the work of three daughters instead of two, and perhaps at a higher

518 Rubidge diaries, March 8, 1918.

519 Morris, M 1976, p. 321-24.

520 Rubidge diaries, March 21, 1918.

521 Rubidge diaries, March 25, 1918.

rate in cash than before as they did not get rations. In other words, Hermaans' family was being proletarianized.

Such a contract was probably favoured by Hermaans over rations only, as that would not bring him a cash income. But being responsible for his daughters' food was a heavier burden on his own household, as the food had to be shared between an additional three people. This left him with the possibility of rationing the food in his own household. The daughters who worked were probably given a sufficient amount of food, but there were others, such as the wife and other children, who could be given less.

The system of family labour was thus not only exploited by farmers. Also the male labourers themselves could exploit their families. Or, more specifically, the system of family labour forced male labouring head of households to exploit their families, when their position in relation to the farmer was weakened. A gendered and generational division of labour made it possible for the father to increase the output of labour from his family when this was required. But doing so kept the family together as a unit. Unlike Jan Oudtshoorn, whose family was divided, Hermaans managed to keep his family together as he could control the labour of his daughters. The ownership of stock ultimately decided his ability to do so, which is what Jan Oudtshoorn lacked. But Hermaans' ownership of stock was threatened. He only had 30 of his goats left and his independence was severely reduced. Owning a large number of goats would have made it possible to withstand the demands from Sidney Rubidge on the labour of his family, but if he kept them he would not have been welcome on the farm. He could possibly have found other farmers who would take him and his family with all his stock. As he chose to stay with the Rubidges it is likely that he deemed the conditions on Wellwood better than the alternatives. After all, he received wages, and his daughters brought cash incomes. With that money he could buy stock in the future, and he would still be able to hold the family together.

Being a camp walker did not only involve controlling the fences; jackal hunting and trekking of sheep was also undertaken by Hermaans. When the herd Adrian and two others were taking out blaauwbosch in one of the camps, Hermaans was in town and came back "with 100 bought wethers from GR [...]".[522] The difference between a shepherd and a camp walker was thus not clear cut, perhaps because camp walker was a new position. It is possible that it was a position of some status as it involved the new technology in fences. Hermaans was paid £3 per month, which was considerably more than the average for shepherds. However, at the same time Sidney Rubidge demanded labour from his daughters and limited the amount of stock he was allowed to graze on the farm heavily. The higher cash wage and the restrictions on ownership of stock were two sides of the same proletarianization process which became noticeable on Wellwood as a result of jackal-proof fencing and

[522] Rubidge diaries, Dec. 14, 1918.

investments into water supply. The higher wage, of course, also indicates that camp walkers were valued highly by the farmers. In the absence of shepherds, the camp walker was the only one who could protect the sheep by making sure the technology was functional. Furthermore, the introduction of camp walkers who worked for higher wages indicates that a cash economy was becoming more important. The cash was perhaps used to buy livestock, but barter of animals and labour was beginning to be replaced by sale and purchase with money. The expansion of capital meant that capitalist relations of production, wherein labour was a commodity, became more noticeable.

Boundary riders and "piccanins" in the East

Wellwood was not the only farm where labour practices and relations changed as a consequence of new technology in the form of fences. Claude Orpen on the farm Avoca in New England in the Barkly East district stated that he had "boundary riders to see that my fences are kept in order". Controlling the fences was done "about once a month" on his farm.[523] Also Alfred Sephton in Barkly East had employed a man to inspect fences, but at much closer intervals: "It is rather rough country and he walks this fence every day along the whole of the border." If the fence was broken immediate action was taken: "He reports if there is anything wrong and a man is sent up to repair the damage. In the mean time he does it temporarily."[524]

The importance of having a camp walker or boundary rider was evident, as there was no other protection from either jackals or stock thefts, or sheep running away. Orpen thought that all farmers had camp walkers or boundary riders, which probably reflects the situation in his immediate vicinity, and perhaps the Barkly East district in general. But throughout large parts of the wool farming regions of the Cape the camp walker was most likely not commonplace. In some places they were probably even unheard of, as the jackal-proof fences were still far apart. The camp walkers signalled the progressive, capitalist farmers who could dispose of the shepherd, but who were forced to replace them with a man who inspected fences.

However, despite using camp walkers, Sephton still hired shepherds: "I have 9,000 sheep and I have a herd for every 800. These herds do nothing else and remain with the sheep night and day."[525] Sephton thus had at least 11 shepherds for his sheep. Altogether he had about 35 servants on his farm. Orpen only had a few shepherds, and most of his sheep ran free in netted camps. The difference between the two farmers in Barkly East was probably the

---

523 Select Committee on Suppression of Stock Thefts, 1923, p. 112

524 Select Committee on Suppression of Stock Thefts, 1923, p. 128.

525 Select Committee on Suppression of Stock Thefts, 1923, p. 128.

extent to which they used jackal-proof fences. Sephton did, however, not want young shepherds: "They are adult natives in most cases, occasionally I have a native under 21, but they are the exception. I generally get a man of years to look after the sheep, because I find that they are more reliable."[526] The practice was perhaps to have an older shepherd working with his sons, but we do not know. On Sephton's farm there were, however, young children, "piccanins", who were paid 7 shillings per month, about half as much as the adults.[527] Considering that shepherding was work for the young, at least some of them most likely worked as shepherds. Orpen paid slightly higher wages, at least to the young shepherds: "The herds get 15s., with the exception of the piccanins, who begin on 10s." Also on Orpen's farm the young shepherds did not work on their own: "Piccanins are not entrusted with flocks."[528] However, this does, not mean that they were not allowed to herd sheep, only that they did not work alone.

In other parts of the Eastern Cape the practice seemed to be somewhat different. Colin Baines, Inspector of Police in the Eastern districts of the Cape Province, stated that in Herschel "the farmers generally engage small boys and pay them 3s. per month". According to him the "rate of pay to native shepherds, [...] ranges from 3s. to 10s. per month".[529] Such low wages as 10s. and less, indicate that a large part of the shepherds were in fact children or young men, at least not adults with families to support. For Queenstown the M. P. C. Willem de Wet, however, remarked that the "herds are not paid as low as 3s. [...]", but rather between 10s. and 15s. per month.[530] Perhaps there were more adults shepherds in Queenstown.

Judging from these accounts, there seems to have been two kinds of farmers: those who did not trust "piccanins" to herd sheep on their own, and those who probably could not afford to distrust them. After all, the wages to young shepherds were considerably lower than to adult ones. Given that many farmers experienced problems in finding labour to the offered wages, and dealt with an uncertain wool market, the use of "piccanin" shepherds was a way to increase profits. However, the wages for adult shepherds and farm labourers had not changed since the early twentieth century, and they had only changed fractionally since the 1860s and 1870s. Considering that the amount of exported wool had tripled since the 1870s, it is obvious that the exploitation of the labour force had increased substantially along with the implementation of new technology. Each shepherd could generate increasingly more profits for farmers. Those farmers who could afford investments into fences could further

[526] Select Committee on Suppression of Stock Thefts, 1923, p. 128.

[527] Select Committee on Suppression of Stock Thefts, 1923, p. 128.

[528] Select Committee on Suppression of Stock Thefts, 1923, p. 111.

[529] Select Committee on Suppression of Stock Thefts, 1923, p. 54.

[530] Select Committee on Suppression of Stock Thefts, 1923, p. 102.

increase profits through hiring fewer shepherds, those who could not afford fences hired more children instead.

Carnarvon – young shepherds and stock thieves

Compared to the turn of the century, farmers in Carnarvon had implemented fairly much fencing and water supply by the 1920s. Still, shepherding was widely practiced, and what is more interesting, many of the shepherds were quite young. It seems as if the farmers in Carnarvon had come to rely on young shepherds to a greater extent than previously. Many of them were accused of stock thefts.

Koos Witbooi worked as a shepherd for Salomon Jacobs on his farm Stilverblyf in 1923. Koos was 15 years old and was hired in March; it does not seem like his father was working on the farm. The farmer Jacobs did not appear to have fenced camps, at least not for the sheep herded by Koos. Jacobs said that "I count my sheep every morning out of the kraal".[531] This was clearly the old fashioned way of farming, where the sheep were kraaled during the night and taken to their grazing pasture by the shepherd in the morning. After less than a month Jacobs noticed that one sheep was missing from the flock herded by Koos. It was never found and Koos could not explain how it had disappeared. In June Jacobs "received a report" of a place on the farm where sheep had been slaughtered. As he went there he found the stomach of a freshly slaughtered sheep. He accused Koos of being the one who slaughtered it, and Koos confessed to stealing that sheep, but also two others. Koos was sentenced to detention in a reformatory until he turned 18 years old.[532]

On Pieter Theron's farm Kaffirskloof there were both sheep and goats running in the same flock. He counted these out in the morning to the shepherd Willem Jan, who was 16 years old. The flock was quite small, only numbering 148.[533] Perhaps because Willem was young he was not entrusted with large flocks. Some three days later the number was, however, incorrect; one sheep and two goats were missing. Willem could not explain how it had happened. On the border of the farm, Theron found a slaughtering place. On the neighbouring farm a 15 year old boy called Barend van Wyk worked as a shepherd. The two young shepherds Willem and Barend had probably killed

---

531 CA 1/CAR 1/1/1/7. Magistrate Carnarvon. Koos Witbooi. June 13, 1923.

532 CA 1/CAR 1/1/1/7. Magistrate's archive, Carnarvon. Koos Witbooi. June 13, 1923.

533 CA 1/CAR 1/1/1/7. Magistrate's archive, Carnarvon. Barend van Wyk and Willem Jan, July 7, 1923.

the sheep, and at the slaughtering place Theron "found the spoors of the two accused & two small barefooted spoors of two youngsters".[534]

While these two boys seem to have been working alone, there were other young shepherds who followed the instructions of their fathers. In August 1923 Gert Abrahams, who was 14 years old, stole 62 sheep of his master Hendrik Sieberhagen on the farm Bitterpoort. Gert said that his father had ordered him to take them. A fencer called Jacobs, saw Gert as he was leaving with the sheep, presumably to give them to his father. The father was on trek and was about to leave the farm when Gert was told to steal the 62 sheep. The Magistrate commented that Gert was in a "tattered & half starved condition & says his father had ordered him to steal the sheep as they had no food to eat at the time".[535]

As boundary fencing was undertaken at Bitterpoort at the time, Gert's father may have wanted to try to remove the sheep from the farm before it was enclosed. His trek offered an opportunity to leave the farm legally with a large flock of sheep, and adding 62 sheep may not have been noticed. After the boundary fence was erected it would be much more difficult to leave the farm with stolen sheep, although boundary fences did not stop thefts to any great extent. Judging by the *Select Committee on Suppression of Stock Thefts* the problem with thefts was not at all stopped by enclosing farms. The heart of the matter was that labourers did not have enough to eat. Colin Baines, Inspector of Police of the Eastern district of the Cape, mentioned that he had seen a magistrate hand out a "small sentence" for theft as the thief was starved. He added: "Some of these boys have a wife and family to support, and are given only a small bit of mealie meal, not enough to keep them going."[536] Under those circumstances stock theft was a means of survival. He further commented that a "boy told me he stole a sheep because he was starved to it. Most of the natives there are badly clothed, and it is a very cold district."[537]

Willem Steenkamp, a coloured boy at the age of 14, who lived together with his uncle on the farm Moller's Vlei in Carnarvon, broke into the house of his master Izak Burger and stole three shillings, rice, coffee, sugar, meal, bread and some other things. Willem's uncle was probably a shepherd as he lived in a hut about three miles from the homestead. Willem may have helped his uncle, but he was registered as having no occupation. He was thus not hired on the farm and was therefore not given a ration. According to the magistrate he had to share his uncle's rations with him. This caused him to break into the master's

[534] CA 1/CAR 1/1/1/7. Magistrate's archive, Carnarvon. Barend van Wyk and Willem Jan, July 7, 1923.

[535] CA 1/CAR 1/1/1/7. Magistrate's archive, Carnarvon. Gert Abrahams, Aug. 10, 1923.

[536] Select Committee on Suppression of Stock Thefts, 1923. Colin Baines, p. 55.

[537] Select Committee on Suppression of Stock Thefts, 1923. Colin Baines, p. 55.

house.[538] A majority of farmers did not ration the families of the labour force unless they worked. In Burger's case it did not lead to losses of sheep, but theft in his house.

An increase in stock thefts, or thefts in general from farmers, could to some extent be seen as resistance to the capitalist development in wool farming. The labourers and especially the shepherds recognized that they would soon be made redundant and therefore stole sheep. In the eastern district the issue of fencing appears to have been central. Those black peasants who were being "fenced out" and not allowed to use their old grazing pastures experienced hardships in the form of limited grazing, which increased stock thefts as they could not support their families. Thefts thus became the easiest way of acquiring meat. As many of the thieves, at least in Carnarvon, were very young, their actions could also be seen as resistance to being exploited in farming. Such an interpretation is in line with Grier's argument of child labourers in colonial Zimbabwe who avoided capitalist farming by running away.[539] Many of those who ran away in Zimbabwe, however, also had to steal to survive. Thefts by children and youths were therefore not so much caused by hostile sentiment towards capitalist interference as by hunger. Their hunger was, however, a result of capitalist interference or expansion in wool farming areas, where the labour force increasingly had become dispossessed of means of production and therefore had fewer possibilities of acquiring food.

As many of the shepherds were young children, it appears that the exploitation of the labourers' families had increased. Farmers in Carnarvon and in other places demanded more labour from those families who lived on the farm instead of hiring adult labour from outside the farm. Stock thefts were thus to some extent both a display of resistance and a way to acquire food. There seems to have been few, if any, attempts at selling the stolen stock. The sheep were slaughtered and eaten, which indicates that the labourers were in fact hungry. In the districts close to reserve areas the stolen sheep were often taken across the border.[540] These sheep may have been used more for accumulation of stock than for immediate relief of hunger, although this is uncertain. In any case, it is useful to distinguish between stock thefts where a sheep was slaughtered on the farm, and where sheep were brought off the farm. In the latter case some money could be made from sales or through accumulation, while the former indicate a state of affairs where labourers stole for immediate survival.

Unlike the children in colonial Zimbabwe who ran away, most of the young shepherds in the Cape stayed on the farms. But there was one exception: the

---

[538] CA 1/CAR 1/1/1/7 Magistrate's archive, Carnarvon. Willem Steenkamp, Aug. 20, 1923. Willem Steenkamp.

[539] Grier, B 2006, pp. 101-05, 113-15.

[540] Drought Commission, 1923 , T. Mellville, Kuruman, p. 177.

apprentices. In Carnarvon, and probably also elsewhere, apprenticeship was a common way for farmers to acquire labour during the early twentieth century. Those eligible for apprenticeship were children under the age of 16 who were destitute, wanderers without home and/or parents or guardians and without visible means of subsistence.[541]

Piet Domkrag became an apprentice on the farm Rietvlei at the age of twelve in May 1922 after a stock theft. During the following seven months he deserted his service four times. Each time he seems to have run to his father, who worked on another farm. On several occasions Piet's father returned him to the farm to serve his apprenticeship. But in January 1923, after the fourth desertion, the farmer at Rietvlei wanted to cancel the apprenticeship contract.[542] Another young boy who found apprenticeship unbearable was Klaas Kaffir, who was apprenticed to the farmer Andries du Toit on the farm De Rust in 1922 when he was ten years old. During the following seven months he ran away three times. The second time he was found guilty of theft and sent back to the farm. The third time the farmer du Toit, however, wanted to end the apprenticeship contract, which was also done. Klaas was instead sent to a reformatory for five years.[543] The desertion of service was serious as it threatened to undermine the entire mode of production in rural areas. Labourers could not desert their service without severe punishment being handed out.

Despite the problems with runaways, farmers benefitted from having apprentices. One example is Hans Jafhta and Jan Boezak, both eleven years old. Jan worked on the farm Joosteswerven as a shepherd, but Hans did not seem to have an occupation. In 1923 they broke into the house of a shepherd on the farm and stole some food and a pocket knife. They were both apprenticed until they turned eighteen. The magistrate, de Vos, explained that in Hans' case apprenticeship was favoured, because "there was an entire lack of either care or control shown on the part of both master and parent. [...]".[544] The parent meant Hans' uncle, Hendrik Pieterse. It did not seem like Hans was apprenticed to the farmer at Joosteswerven, but to another farmer. The magistrate continued to explain that apprenticeship could barely be regarded as punishment since wages were paid "and with proper care and control exercised, the boy practically enters into a new life of respectability [...]", which was better than sending him to a reformatory.[545] The wages were not specified, but a case from Fraserburg in 1937 indicated that a boy aged seven, who was

541 Children's Protection Act, 1913 (No. 25 of 1913). *Statutes of the Union of South Africa, 1911-1961.*

542 CA 1/CAR 1/1/1/7. Magistrates archive, Carnarvon. Piet Domkrag, Jan. 22, 1923.

543 CA 1/CAR 1/1/1/7. Magistrates archive, Carnarvon. Klaas Kaffir, Jan. 23, 1923.

544 CA 1/CAR 1/1/1/7. Magistrates archive Carnarvon. Hans Jafhta, July 16, 1923.

545 CA 1/CAR 1/1/1/7. Magistrates archive Carnarvon. Hans Jafhta, July 16, 1923.

apprenticed for ten years, would not receive wages during the first three years, and thereafter be paid less than others of the same age.[546] Thus, having an apprentice consequently meant very cheap labour. Clearly, the state, through magistrates, could play an important role as labour agents.

Also Jan Boezak was apprenticed. He was probably sent back to Joosteswerven. His father, Klaas Boezak, seems to have lived on the same farm. Some of those who were apprenticed were thus not at all orphans or without relatives, but they were not handed over to their families. Instead, farmers or other persons who were "fit and proper" reaped the benefits of being able to employ young people at low wages. Assuming that Jan Boezak was apprenticed to the farm where his father worked, they were no longer involved in the family labour system, but were individual wage labourers employed directly by the farmer. Consequently, it weakened the position of adult labourers as they had less opportunity to offer the labour of their family to the farmers. Hans Boezak, the father of Jan, was no longer in charge of his son's labour. He would not be able to decide over his son for the apprenticeship period of seven years, until Jan turned eighteen. During that period he could only offer his own labour to the farmer Jacobs.

Jacobs on the farm Joosteswerven already had at least one apprentice called Johannes Madeeling, aged seventeen, who had been apprenticed in 1920 after a stock theft. Madeeling worked as a shepherd. However, in 1924 eleven sheep from his flock were missing and he was found guilty of having stolen one of them. As he was older than sixteen years of age, he could not be apprenticed, but was sent to a reformatory.[547] For the farmers, it was thus better if the stock thefts were conducted by young people as they could be apprenticed. Stock thefts and the apprenticeship system almost seemed to be symbiotic.

Farmers suffered some financial loss when sheep were stolen, but if the thief was young, they would get an apprentice in return, in many cases for as long as eight years. Most sheep in Carnarvon at the time were valued between £1 and £2.[548] The wage to an apprentice did probably not exceed £2 per year, which should be compared to the wage paid to young shepherds, which ranged from £3 to £6 per year or to adults who earned about twice that amount. The wool produced by a merino was probably at the lowest 7 or 8 lbs. per year, and for the better class of merinos as much as 15lbs. was not unusual. The price per lb. of wool in 1920 was 2s. 8d. One sheep could thus generate from 14 shillings. to 16 shillings. up to more than £1.10s. per year. The financial loss from a theft

[546] See Lilja,F 2009.

[547] CA 1/CAR 1/1/1/8. Magistrate's archive Carnarvon. Johannes Madeeling, Aug. 21, 1924. 153/1924.

[548] CA 1/CAR 1/1/1/7 Magistrates archives. Proceedings of court cases. Koos Adams July 9, 1923. Hendrik Smit's sheep valued at 20/- each, but he bought them for £2; Arend & Adam Adams, April 16, 1923. Willem Orange valued missing sheep at 20/-. Thoroughbred rams were more expensive, valued up to £5, see case against Gert Abrahams, Aug. 10, 1923.

was recovered within the same year if an apprentice came on. Over a period of several years, an apprentice was a clearly an asset to a farmer without much cash. The young stock thief was not automatically apprenticed to the farm where he had previously lived, although it obviously occurred. But as a class, farmers benefitted by labourers stealing some sheep and in return being sentenced to apprenticeship. Although the state did not supply farmers with as much labour as they asked for, some of their demands were definitely met through the apprenticeship system.

CHAPTER 10

Droughts, Depression and Wages

Adrijan Reid – the last shepherd on Wellwood

During the 1920s Wellwood was jackal-proof and most of the camps were netted. In 1927 there were nine "main camps", presumably they were all netted. Despite this, there was still a shepherd on the farm, Adrijan Reid, who arrived at Wellwood in 1915. He probably had his family with him; at least he had one son who helped him collecting nenta at one point. During his time on Wellwood he seems to have been a shepherd, although he also performed other work at times. There had been one other shepherd, called Jan, on Wellwood in 1918, but he left before 1923 and was not replaced.[549] Adrijan was thus the only shepherd during most of the 1920s. The place of his work was the mountain camp, which was not jackal-proof until the early 1920s. But also after the mountain was jackal-proof Adrijan stayed on as a shepherd, perhaps because water supplies were not adequate during droughts.

With exception for occasional rains, the Cape was struck by droughts from 1922 to 1928. The jackal-proof camps on Wellwood proved their worth as they enabled Sidney Rubidge to practice rotational grazing. Using camps, however, required a water supply, which proved to be a challenge; even the successful Rubidges could not escape the drought. At the beginning of 1927 the shepherd "Adrijan brought report from Old Mt Netting Camp that well was rapidly giving in [...] & fountain in road Kloof practically dry". The last water supplies on the mountain were thereby about to become exhausted.[550] Following the reports on poor water supply, Sidney Rubidge rearranged the division of camps. He "returned 518 ewes to Woodcliff camp & cut fence [...] to throw old Mtn Camp into one". Apparently he deemed it necessary to have a larger camp; the carrying capacity was not enough. The decision to do so was a setback: "This having to abandon Magnum Camp marks another record in the steady process of back sliding since 1922. The total drying-up of road Kloof fountain was not

549 Rubidge diaries, March 28, May 5, 10, 1918;

550 Rubidge diaries, Jan. 17, 1927.

quite equalled in the 32 months drought of 1914-15, when by being tangled it still supported 18 mules & horses […]."[551] In 1926 and 1927 as many as 24 out of 28 dams in the farm were dry. Sidney Rubidge then made a "vow […] that each camp must have a supply other than being dependent on dams". Several attempts at finding water were conducted during the year, often with no result. Still, the "9 main camps on farm are each provided for in this way, three of the nine camps being duplicated as 12 drinking places provided".[552]

Having a water supply of that kind required investments. During the fiscal year 1925-1926 Sidney Rubidge paid £351 for boreholes for water and during 1927-1928 he spent £298.[553] Such amounts could not have been paid by many of the poorer farmers, who had to get by on natural water where they could find it. The income for the Rubidges during 1927-28 for example was about £1,800, which was not above average for the farm. Participation in the capitalist world-economy and the subsequent capital accumulation during a long period of time was thus a prerequisite for ability to invest in protection against drought. Having secured the water supply, at least relatively well, the sheep could graze by themselves in jackal-proof camps. All the main camps, of which there were nine in 1927, seem to have been provided for with jackal-proof netting and water supplies. This had an impact on Adrijan Reid.

As Adrijan remained on the farm as the only shepherd, he must have done his work properly. Sidney Rubidge was at least not dissatisfied with him. But in February 1927 Sidney "[g]ave Adrijan notice […]" for drunkenness. Apparently Adrijan had lost 39 sheep while being drunk. This did not mean that Adrijan left the farm immediately, already the next day he went to look for the missing sheep and found as many as 30 of them. Finding the sheep did not change the mind of Sidney Rubidge, though. But there was no rush in getting him off the farm. It took almost three weeks before Adrijan left the farm, and he probably worked during that period, which means that the decision to fire him was not firstly out of concern for the sheep.

Adrijan was not the first shepherd or labourer caught drunk on the farm. For example, as mentioned previously, in 1914 the shepherd Janavaries was caught with beer tins in his hut and was sentenced to a fine, which Sidney Rubidge paid. Thereafter Janavaries returned to the farm to work. Neither was Adrijan the first shepherd who lost sheep, quite the opposite, it occurred quite often. One of the worst incidents was in 1895 when a shepherd called Falk lost 255 sheep altogether on four different occasions. Most of them were found, but losing that many sheep must have been regarded as negligent or even a danger to the farm. Still, Falk remained on the farm.[554] On both these occasions the

---

[551] Rubidge diaries, Feb. 3, 1927.

[552] Rubidge diaries, June 29, Aug. 6, 1927.

[553] Rubidge accounts 1925-26, 1927-28

[554] Rubidge diaries, Feb. 10, March 8, July 6, Sept. 21, 1895.

demand for shepherds was greater than in 1927, indicating that negligence or drunkenness was more easily overlooked. The decision to fire Adrijan Reid may therefore have been more an excuse than a decision related to his ability to perform his work. The water supply was about to be improved, which would make shepherds like Adrijan Reid redundant on the farm. A comparison can be made with another incident in 1927 when two other labourers, Jacob and Stephanus Sillie, were found drinking beer. Sidney Rubidge paid their fine of £2. But he did it on condition that "Jacobs works out pay for himself & brother Stephanus whom I no longer require on farm". A few days later Jacob was, however, found drinking again, which caused Sidney Rubidge to fire also him.[555] Being drunk was, thus not in itself a reason for being fired. But if it happened too often it was not profitable for the farmer as it would take a long time to work off the debt.

After having given Adrijan Reid notice to leave, Sidney Rubidge appears to have reconsidered his decision. He wanted Adrijan to stay on the farm, but not as a shepherd. On the day Adrijan left Sidney Rubidge noted that "[h]e now prefers to break up all this sooner than accept my offer (made subsequent to giving him notice) to stay on homestead & be under my direct control".[556] Sidney thus intended to let Adrijan stay on the farm, but in a different position than as a shepherd. He probably meant to transform him into a general labourer. But Adrijan chose not to agree to such an offer. The relative freedom of the shepherd seems to have been valued by him. Being under Sidney's "direct control", he would lose much, if not all, of that freedom. Adrijan Reid probably tried to find a position as a shepherd elsewhere, but we do not know for certain. His decision to leave was, however, facilitated by his ownership of stock. When he left the farm he "got his stock together [...]". In all he had "7 head cattle, 33 sheep (mostly merino) [and] 20 goats". In addition, Sidney and Adrijan "[s]quared off balance of £14 [...] the balance of wool sold in 1925". His ownership of merinos and participation in a corner of capitalist wool production gave him some extra income from the wool, which of course was helpful in his search for a new place to stay. The merinos could be sold to a farmer as a part of his new contract, or he could try to keep them as a means of production for himself and sell the wool. Owning the stock was therefore still the best means to maintain a certain degree of freedom from white farmers who wanted to convert shepherds into general labourers and extend their control over the labour force.

After Adrijan Reid left Wellwood in March 1927 no shepherd was hired to replace him. He was therefore most likely the last shepherd on Wellwood, ending an era of farming which had lasted about 90 years on the farm, since the foundation of it in 1838. But the disappearance of Adrijan did not

---

[555] Rubidge diaries, May 1, 3, 9, 1927.

[556] Rubidge diaries, March 14, 1927.

revolutionize farming on Wellwood. It was just the last stage in a process that had been underway since the early twentieth century, and definitely at least since 1914, when the first camp walker was hired to inspect fences. The disappearance of the last shepherd did, however, signal the completion of the implementation of new farming methods, which did not require shepherds.

Depression and heavy stocking

Like most other parts of the world, the Cape and its wool production was affected by the worldwide depression after the stock market crash in 1929. Wool prices fell, the demand for wool from European and US textile manufacturers was reduced and the economy of South Africa in general was impaired. Poverty and hunger followed and reached also Graaff-Reinet. Sidney Rubidge was outraged when a young girl came to Wellwood in 1932 "pleading for her parents & twin brother who are in poverty along road". He blamed the "arch racialist & republican demon of a National Premier [...]", who provoked "racial hatred" instead of attending to the problems of the country.[557] Sidney Rubidge definitely supported the British Crown, but his comments also indicate that racial divides were deepened during the Depression. Farmers did not, however, side with the labouring class. Sidney Rubidge for example criticised poor blacks who demonstrated at the magistrate's office in Graaff-Reinet and compared with a case of a black labourer who did not want to work on Wellwood as he was "dissatisfied because 14/6 & food & extras too little".[558] Not surprisingly, farmers argued that wages were sufficient.

Some of the difficulties experienced during the Depression years were related to the overall difficulty on world markets. The wool market was no different. In 1930 Sidney Rubidge noted that "London wool sales a further 10% down, therefore our best type wool now about 8' prime merino & capes around 10/-, all far below pre-war [prices]". The wool price was falling during the interwar period, but a low was reached in 1932-1933.[559] That season a record wool clip was shorn in South Africa. On Wellwood a large clip was recorded those years; 128 bales according to the accounts for 1931-1932, but it only generated about £586, which was less than half for an average year.[560] These conditions forced farmers to increase their sheep numbers in order to maintain their profits, or as much of it as possible.

---

557 Rubidge diaries, July 12, 1932.

558 Rubidge diaries, May 23, 1932.

559 Bouch, R 1997, p. 97; Beinart W 2008, p. 23, argues 1931 as the low point.

560 Rubidge accounts 1931-32.

Table 17. South African wool exports 1925 – 1935.

Year	Lbs	£
1925	208,615,868	15,095,446
1929	286,878,450	14,521,088
1930	275,024,421	8,644,490
1931	236,648,924	5,700,673
1932	372,660,575	6,560,576
1933	272,407,718	8,831,366
1934	189,806,651	8,083,665
1935	259,791,037	9,515,832

Source: *Annual Statement on Trade and Shipping*, 1925-1935.

In 1933 Sidney Rubidge calculated that Wellwood could carry 2,253 sheep. Still, in 1932 and 1933 there were more than 2,600 sheep and more than 3,000 small stock altogether. Beinart argues that his decision to increase stock numbers was not a result of financial difficulties during the Depression, but rather caused by implementation of fodder crops such as spineless cactus, improved water supplies and that Sidney Rubidge believed that "heavy stocking was to some degree beneficial".[561] While it is certain that fodder crops and water supplies definitely influenced the decision to overstock, or stock heavily, we should assume that the wool price was at least an additional factor. In 1930 Sidney Rubidge noted that he "[m]ust now realize that things revert here to a dependence on a production of wool clip of 50 bales per annum".[562] The average number of bales produced on Wellwood during the 1920s seems to have been between 50 and 55.[563] The number of bales for previous years has not been established. Although the decrease in the number of bales reported by Sidney Rubidge in 1930 was not great compared to the previous seven years, it is clear that he at least showed a concern over wool sales. As the price dropped considerably the following year, it seems as if the decision to increase sheep numbers partly was a result of a concern for sales.

Furthermore, the profits made on Wellwood were not excessively great. Beinart mentions an average income between £3,000 and £3,500 during the 1920s and 1930s, but does not estimate the expenses.[564] If these are taken into account, the reasons why sheep numbers increased will become clearer.

561 Beinart, W 2008, p. 315-17.

562 Rubidge diaries, Feb. 26, 1930.

563 Rubidge diaries, Nov. 10, 1923 (55 bales); Rubidge accounts 1924-1925 (c. 50 bales); 1927-1928 (56 bales).

564 Beinart, W 2008, p. 309.

Table 18. Rubidge income and expenses (£) 1926 – 1932.

Year	Income	Expenses	Balance
1926-27	5,232	3,863	1,369
1929-30	4,305	3,819	485
1931-32	2,707	2,292	318

Source: Rubidge accounts 1926 – 1932.

Although the Rubidges had considerable assets, it is apparent that the yearly profits were not great during the Depression. And more importantly, they were decreasing during the early 1930s. In view of those figures it is hard to overlook the pure economic factors behind overstocking.

At the same time we should note that the implementation of jackal-proof camps also contributed to the possibility of increasing stock numbers. Or, rather, it lessened the damage to the veld, which made farmers more inclined to push stock numbers closer to, or past the limit. All over the Cape and South Africa sheep numbers increased during these years. It is important to note that far from all, especially those outside the central Cape wool farming districts, were equipped with jackal-proof camps. The increase of sheep was thus a danger to the industry in a long-term perspective as the veld suffered, but few had the luxury of thinking about future problems when the present ones were overwhelming. Still, a part of the explanation of overstocking must be related to the improved farmlands, which facilitated heavy stocking.

Water supplies and land as commodity

Water supplies were always an issue on Wellwood. Drought conditions meant additional pressure on the farm. Sidney Rubidge still allowed grazing for another farmer in 1928 when the farmer on Klipfontein sent 250 sheep to Wellwood.[565] Allowing the Klipfontein sheep to graze on Wellwood was perhaps even more trying since one of the camps containing 200 sheep had been abandoned just a week previously.[566] The Wellwood sheep did not trek off the farm during the droughts, but there were others who did.

In addition to the Depression, yet another drought struck the Cape in 1932-1933. With a few exceptions there had been droughts in the Cape since the early 1920s. The drought of 1932-1933 was, however, one of the worst. In June 1933 Sidney Rubidge was paid a visit by farmers from Carnarvon. They appear to have been trekking due to the drought: "They report that there are now only

565 Rubidge diaries, Feb. 11, 1928.

566 Rubidge diaries, Feb. 3, 1928.

7 farmers left on their farms in Carnarvon Distr – others all having trekked from drought."[567] In 1935 and 1936 there were at least 397 farms in Carnarvon,[568] which means that several hundred farmers from there were trekking with their stock. We do not know where they went, but it is likely that they hired grazing on farms in districts that were not as severely struck by drought until conditions improved enough in Carnarvon for them to return. The party from Carnarvon did not seem to have hired grazing land on Wellwood, but Graaff-Reinet was one place where struggling farmers went to find grazing.

Pieter Meyburgh and David and Willem Erasmus, who all farmed on Garstlands in Cradock, also sought grazing in Graaff-Reinet "in consequence of drought". They placed 1,534 sheep on Cyril Jarrard's farm Fonteinplaas in Graaff-Reinet at a monthly rate of 17s. 6d. per 100 sheep. Jarrard thus received £13 per month for the sheep from Cradock. The sheep were on the farm for at least four months, meaning that Jarrard was paid £52 for the grazing. Renting grazing land was a good option for those who were struck by drought. But trekking the sheep was also detrimental to the sheep. David and Willem Erasmus lost as many as 75 sheep on the trek to Graaff-Reinet. Once on the farm, the sheep were placed in a camp which was netted only on three of the four sides. The sheep thus required supervision. The Cradock farmers hired a man called Gert Mostert, who worked on Fonteinplaas to look after the sheep. The sheep were, however, illegally sold by the farmer, Jarrard, who rented out the grazing land, but the scheme was exposed by a bywoner on the farm, who testified that Jarrard had told him to remark the sheep belonging to the Cradock farmers.[569]

Having sheep stolen by the farmer who rented out land for grazing was probably not common, but it indicates the difficulties and the conflicts caused by drought conditions. Those farmers who were from drought stricken areas became dependent on others, who could offer them grazing for money. Poorer farmers who lived in relatively spared districts could thus make some money off of their fellow farmers and subsequently improve their position. The £52 paid to Jarrard was, for example, the equivalent of the annual wages to one labouring family on Wellwood at the time. If renting out for a whole year, the money would be enough to hire three families or eight youths for labour, given the rate paid on Wellwood. Similarly, about 50 merino sheep could be bought for the money paid to Jarrard. For those farmers who had plenty of land, and few sheep, the droughts could be profitable, and land could be an equally important commodity as sheep and wool were.

---

[567] Rubidge diaries, June 15, 1933.

[568] Agricultural census 1935-36, p 11.

[569] CA 1/GR 2/147 Magistrate Graaff-Reinet. Cyril Lawrence Jarrard. Nov. 18, 1933.

Trekking of sheep over long distances was usually done by train, in 1933 as many as eight million head of sheep. The railway company subsidized such transport; between 1933 and 1936 it paid 50 per cent of the cost of livestock transports. Farmers and the Government shared the remaining half. Railway transport of livestock had been common since 1914 for Cape farmers. This was especially important during droughts.[570]

In order to avoid trekking in times of drought, it was vital to secure water supplies. Some attempts to find underground sources on Wellwood were made in the late 1920s, but little water was found. In order to secure water, Sidney Rubidge, together with John McCabe on Woodcliff, even signed a contract with another neighbour, Arthur Murray on Rockwood, for the right to use his water. Almost 400 yards of piping was laid to lead the water to Wellwood at the cost of £56. The contract entitled Wellwood and Woodcliff "to right of supply of water from Rockwood for a period at the will of Rockwood owner [...]". Murray could thus turn off the water whenever he deemed it necessary. For the "privilege" of using the water, Murray charged £50.[571] The Rubidges thus spent £106 on pumping water from another farm. Although it worked temporarily, it was not a preferable solution to Sidney Rubidge.

The hard economic conditions during the Depression probably prevented a great deal of farm investments on Wellwood. Profits during 1931-1932 were, as we have seen, only a little more than £300. During the mid-1930s profits increased considerably. In 1935 the income on Wellwood was £5,033 and the expenditure 2,485, thus a profit of £2,548. In 1936 the profit was £2,431.[572] This enabled the Rubidges to expand capital investments. As the fencing of the farm was completed, the attention was on water supply. According to the return to the Agricultural census in 1930 there were four windmills on Wellwood.[573] That was, however, not enough.

In 1935 "Old Marais" was hired to find water. He arrived at the farm with a "water boring machine". Sidney Rubidge of course knew from experience that water was not easily found, but his ambition was not only to find water, but to find it where it would be of most use: "the idea being to catch junction of 3 camps [...]".[574] Such a solution reduced costs. Surprisingly enough, within three weeks after he had started drilling Marais found two water sources. One of them, found at 99 feet, gave 272 gallons per hour, but Sidney was disappointed that he could not "test [it] properly for maybe it can be thousands per hour".[575] Three weeks after Marais had started, a new Climax windmill was

570 Beinart, W 2008, pp. 262-64.

571 Rubidge diaries, Oct. 27, 23, 1928.

572 Rubidge diaries, Sept. 2, 1936.

573 Rubidge diaries, Sept. 12, 1930.

574 Rubidge diaries, Sept. 20, 1935.

575 Rubidge diaries, Oct. 2, 1935.

put into place. A Mr. Buckley arrived with the windmill at the farm at 10 AM, and at 6 PM it was in use. About a week later it was time to implement another windmill, an "Aermotor Mill at Sluit Camp [...]".[576] To find two successful underground sources in three weeks was unusual for Wellwood. However, in November Marais continued to drill in the Salt Bush Camp and in December he found two more holes. The cost of boring was £243. The total cost, which must have included the windmills, was considerably higher, though; £723.[577] These investments were probably made possible by an upturn of the wool market, but possibly with some aid from the state.

The Government subsidized drilling for water, especially after 1930.[578] Together with farmers' investments this resulted in a vast increase in mechanical water supplies; between 1911 and 1925-1926 the number of windmills in the Cape increased from 4,671 to 20,821 spread on 35,882 farms.[579] The number of windmills increased to 37,168 in 1936-1937. The same years there were 38,326 farms in the Cape, thus about one windmill per farm.[580] In 1945-1946 there were 49,754 windmills on 40,776 farms in the Cape.[581] This development does not mean that all farms had windmills. As seen, the Rubidges had four windmills in 1930 and introduced at least two more in 1935,[582] indicating that accumulation of capital in the form of windmills was primarily done by the successful farmers. Still, the numbers show that there was a vast expansion of capital during the 1930s and 1940s and that windmills probably became more frequent even in places where they had not been seen before.

Intensified class struggle and intensified farming

During the 1930s, the rural class struggle in South Africa was intensified, according to Morris. Farmers tried to increase production and decrease grazing rights while not compensating by increasing cash wages.[583] Morris does not deal with wool farming in the Cape, but Monica Hunter argued in the 1930s that wages for a married man in the Cape districts of Bedford, Adelaide and Albany had only increased by 2 shillings per month on average during a twenty

576 Rubidge diaries, Oct. 12, 21, 1935.
577 Rubidge diaries, Dec. 9, 1935.
578 Beinart, W 2008, p. 192.
579 Agricultural census 1925-26, pp. 94, 83.
580 Agricultural census 1936-37, pp. 113, 10.
581 Agricultural census 1945-46, pp. 150, 10-11.
582 Rubidge diaries, Sept. 12, 1930.
583 Morris, M 1976, pp. 320-21.

year period. She asserted that an average cash wage for a family of 8.2 members was £10. 3s. per year.[584] The wages on Wellwood were substantially higher than Hunter's estimate. However, the wages were in fact not only kept down during the late 1920s and early 1930s, but reduced, as was the labour force itself.

Table 19. The labour force on Wellwood 1924-1933 (black and coloured). Number and yearly wages (nominal) in £. Cash and rations in value per family and single male.

	Families			Single men	
Year	No.	Cash	Rations	No.	Cash
1924-25	9	20	30.6	3	38.13
1925-26	9	20	30.6	3	32
1926-27	10	20	27.6	2	39
1927-28	9	20	22	3	40
1928-29	9	20	22	2	40
1929-30	9	20	21.10	2	35
1930-31	8	17.10	17.16	2	31.10
1931-32	6	17.10	19.13	2	31.10
1932-33	6	17.10	19.13	2	31.10

Source: Rubidge accounts 1924 - 1933.

The reduction of the labour force on Wellwood during the early 1930s from nine to six families is noticeable. There are few other explanations to it than the effects of the Depression and the lowered income for the Rubidges.

But Sidney Rubidge did not only reduce the number of labourers, he also changed the remuneration. Two things were notable. Firstly, the overall wages for families, both cash and rations, were reduced by 25 per cent between 1924-1925 and 1932-1933. For single males the reduction was about 18 per cent, but they were not given rations at all, meaning that they had to provide food for themselves. Secondly, the part of the wage paid in rations decreased considerably after 1927. In 1924-1925 the rations made up 60 per cent of the total remuneration for families, and in 1932-1933 only about 53 per cent. Both these measures were to some extent a result of the Depression, but not entirely; the rations were reduced already in 1926-1927. The reduction coincided with the hiring of an additional family, but was furthered even when the number of families decreased. This gave some room to increase the wages to single males during the late 1920s, but also their wages were markedly reduced after 1930.

Reducing the wages made an actual difference. Wages to families in 1924-1925 amounted to £450. In 1932-1933 the total was about £223, thus a

584 Hunter, M 1936, pp.516-17.

reduction by £227 per year. The wages to single males were reduced by £57, from £114 to £63. Altogether the wages were reduced by £284. As comparison we can note that the same year about £237 was spent on "dams and furrows", "boreholes and pumping" and "fences" combined.[585]

In addition to the black and coloured families and single males there were also two "youngsters" on the pay roll of Wellwood, at least from 1925. The wages to these were also reduced during the late 1920s from £6 to £3 per year. But in 1932-33 they again earned £6.[586] The wage increase for the "youngsters" was seemingly made possible by the lowered number of families and single males on the farm. These young labourers who were hired on a yearly basis were on their own and not hired through their fathers, which had been done previously. And there were also youths who were hired as day labourers. For example, in 1930 "[t]wo youths, Hendrik and Cornelus began work at 2/- per day".[587] It is not possible to say if the number of youths on Wellwood increased during the 1930s, but hiring youths as day labourers indicates that it was difficult to find adults or considered too costly to hire them. As the Rubidges decreased the number of families and single adult males during this time, it definitely appears that farmers did not only reduce grazing rights and lower wages, they also replaced adult labourers with children and youths. The disruption of the pre-capitalist structure among labourers, which meant that parents lost control over their children's labour, was disliked by farmers as some of the young members of labouring families disappeared from the farms.[588] But it was seemingly also exploited by farmers who could hire youths, without being forced to hire their families. Surely, farmers wanted adults, but lowered income during the 1930s was an incentive to hire younger labourers. However, there were still youngsters who were hired through their fathers. One of the labourers on Wellwood, Piet, and two of his sons were weeding nenta at £2 per bag.[589] Having many children who could help with work was clearly still valuable to a father.

The *Native Farm Labour Committee* surveyed the farming districts, where black farm labourers dominated, during the late 1930s. The Committee estimated that yearly wages to adult males was about £7, and for youths and women about £4. But there were some variations. In some cases a graded wage up to 20 or 30 shillings per month was paid to males, indicating yearly wages of £12 or above. Compared to the early twentieth century, or the 1860s and 1870s, cash wages had not increased much. In the 1860s and 1870s, £10 per

---

[585] Rubidge accounts, 1932-33.

[586] Rubidge accounts 1924-1933.

[587] Rubidge diaries, April 25, 1930.

[588] See Morris, M 1976, pp. 327-28.

[589] Rubidge diaries, Aug. 2, 1930.

year seems to have been the highest cash wage paid and the average was about £6.

When rations were included, the remuneration for labourers in the Cape was considerably higher. The rations constituted slightly less than half of the total remuneration. Married labourers were generally given more mealies and mealie meal than the single ones, "in order that those members of the family who cannot work may be provided for". We should not assume that all farmers gave rations to family members who did not work, though. A "minimum of 21 lb. of grain is allowed for a married man, and 14 lb. for a single one". But these rations were not always enough "to provide for all children who are too small to work, and have to be supplemented by purchases if food cannot be grown".[590] There were also variations in quantity. The "more universal practice is to give one slaughter animal (an old ewe or goat) per month to be killed for the benefit of all hands on the farm, or in other cases an animal is given to each family". Some farmers did not seem to give meat rations at all except for "fallen animals".[591]

The difference in wages to families and single males on Wellwood illustrates how farmers could benefit by paying part of the wage in rations. In 1924-1925 the single males earned 76 per cent of the wage paid to families and in 1932-1933 as much as 86 per cent although their wage was for one person only. The cash wages to single males were intended to reproduce one labourer, that is, to assure that he could stand up for work the next morning. That meant being able to purchase food, which was more expensive to buy than to ration. Without rations to families, farmers would have had to pay considerably higher cash wages. But the difference in wages between single males and families also indicate that much of the reproduction of labour was conducted in the family household. Single males did not have families to take responsibility for the household and were therefore paid higher cash wages. Primarily wives and children were responsible for cultivation of vegetables and mealies around the hut on the farm. This work was unpaid and at the expense of the labouring family.

The farmers were, however, responsible for producing food for rations. A part of the farm thus had to be set aside for cultivation. In 1918 the area under cultivation on Wellwood was 28 morgen (23 hectares) of a total of 6,700 morgen.[592] Nothing is stated in the diary about the produce that year, but we know that 140 sheep and 30 goats were slaughtered for "household purposes" in 1918.[593] Some of these were probably used for rationing. In 1930 there are figures for the cultivation; oats was sown on 7 ½ morgen, mealies sown on 1 ½

590 Native Farm Labour Committee, 1939, p. 41.

591 Native Farm Labour Committee, 1939, p.41.

592 Rubidge diaries, July 22, 1918.

593 Rubidge diaries, Dec. 29, 1918.

morgen. Orchards made up 3 ½ morgen.[594] To that we must add cultivation of lucerne, which was not accounted for in the report to the Agricultural census. Cultivation of mealies, which was the staple food for labourers, thus constituted a very small part of the total cultivated land on Wellwood. The labourers must have produced much of it themselves, but it was also purchased from others. In June 1935 a "Railway bus" brought 26 bags of mealies from H. McCabe at Riverdale.[595] The Railway bus consequently provided a service of food delivery between farms. McCabe was obviously a surplus producer of mealies, which he sold to the Rubidges. The total number of mealie bags (200 lbs.) produced by white farmers in Graaff-Reinet in 1938-1939 was 6,138. Farm labourers only produced 8 bags. For the Cape 1.1 million bags were produced by white farmers, 72,247 bags by farm labourers. But there was a market for sale of mealies. A total of 3 million bags of mealies were recorded 1938-1939, but only 940,000 were retained on farms for consumption. Black peasants in reserve areas, who produced 1.8 million bags of mealies could probably earn some money from these sales.[596]

The total cultivated area for agricultural crops in Graaff-Reinet in 1936-1937 was only 10,357 morgen out of 775,882 morgen. In Carnarvon 3,654 morgen out of 1.6 million morgen was under cultivation; in Beaufort West only 2,643 morgen was cultivated out of 1.9 million morgen. In Hay as little as 565 morgen out of 1.7 million morgen was under cultivation.[597] The wool farming areas were definitely reserved for grazing and not cultivation. Ultimately this meant that farmers were forced to buy some of their produce, some from other areas in the Cape, but also from other provinces. Bouch mentions that in the 1930s farmers in Queenstown were anxious that they would not be able to ration their labourers during drought conditions. At the end of the 1930s they were also forced to buy food for rationing.[598]

During the 1920s and 1930s there was thus a more intensive focus on production of wool and not agricultural crops on farms like Wellwood. The railway, which enabled quicker transports, must be seen as significant for that development. In Graaff-Reinet, transports with the Railway bus started around 1929 or 1930. The bus came at regular intervals and brought large quantities of produce, for example "Govnt Bus brought load cinders 1 P.M. & at 8 PM brought load 70 bales hay from P. J. Pinaar Bethesda [...]". It also took wool from the farm: Murraysburg Railway Bus here & loaded 23 bales wool, 9664 lbs, [...]".[599] The railway was thus an important medium for capitalist

594 Rubidge diaries, Sept. 12, 1930.

595 Rubidge diaries, June 25, 1935.

596 Agricultural census 1938-39, p. 11.

597 Agricultural census 1936-37, p. 10.

598 Bouch, R 1997, p. 104.

599 Rubidge diaries, Sept. 17, 1930; March 30, 1932.

expansion. Farms in the Cape were tied more closely together with the port cities, and from there with capitalist core areas. This was important in relation to both the transport of wool to the market and to transport of fodder and other supplies to the farm. As transports were handled by the railway, and indirectly the state, farmers did not require labourers to perform that time consuming duty. This meant that the labour on the farm could be concentrated on wool production instead of transports, which was an incentive for a smaller labour force.

The Depression and the droughts during the 1920s and 1930s constituted a crisis in Cape wool farming in the sense that wool prices fell, and the land was under severe pressure. This was seen in the reduction of both wages and rations on Wellwood, where profits were low during some of these years. However, it was not the first crisis experienced by wool farmers. As with previous ones it also meant an opportunity to reform the organization of the labour force and production. Lowering the wages was one way of coping with the new situation that had emerged; reducing the number of labourers was another. But such reorganization required a change of production, as fewer labourers would have to produce more. On Wellwood there were prerequisites for lowering the number of labourers. For example, the camp walkers who had replaced the shepherds were few in number, but could supervise several camps. And the introduction of certain machinery enabled a higher production rate per labourer in for example cultivation. In 1930 there were six ploughs, two harrows, three cultivators, two mowers and two forge cutters on Wellwood.[600] These implements required labour, but the mechanization of production freed labour power from cultivation to wool production.

Those farmers, who did not have the same amount of capital equipment, could not be as productive with fewer labourers. Fewer labourers for them instead meant less production. As with the crisis in the 1860s, which according to Dubow stratified those wool farmers who were not equipped for capitalist farming from those who were, the Depression and droughts further enhanced the stratification among farmers. Those who had invested heavily into their farms more easily profited when wool prices rose than those who had not invested.

Wage increase

During the 1940s the wages to labourers appear to have increased. According to the Agricultural census in 1947, farm labourers were paid well over £2 per month in cash, but there was a racial divide: The 8,000 white labourers were

[600] Rubidge diaries, Sept. 12, 1930.

paid about £11 per month, while the black and coloured labourers, of whom there were more than 200,000, were paid about £2 per month in cash and slightly more than £1 in kind.[601] These figures were for the entire Cape, not only the wool districts. However, it is still noteworthy that cash wages for black and coloured labourers were about twice as high as in the 1940s. The ratio between cash wages and rations were also different in the 1940s than in the 1930s. Rations were about 37 per cent of the total for black and coloured labourers. But there was a gender difference; for the males rations were about 35 per cent of the total, for the females they made up about 47 per cent. If we judge by the remunerative system on Wellwood, the lower share of wages being paid in rations to men was related to the single males, who did not get rations.

The rations had thus been reduced throughout the Cape during the 1930s, and cash wages had become the primary form of remuneration. We can see this development on Wellwood during the1940s.

Table 20. Wellwood wages 1943 – 1948. Cash and rations in value (£).

Year	*Cash*	*Rations*	*Total*
1943-44	548	192	740
1944-45	533	192	725
1945-46	587	240	827
1946-47	589	240	829

Source: Rubidge accounts 1943 – 1948.

The rations during these years were between 25 and 30 per cent of the total wages. Compared to the 1920s and 1930s, this was a further reduction of wages.

These were the remuneration to the regular labour force, that is, camp walkers, labourers and domestic servants. Wages to fencers, dam builders, shearers and others were additional. The individual wages cannot be determined, which mean that we do not know the difference in wages between various sorts of labourers and between men and women. We do know, however, that a "boy David" was hired in 1946 at 25 shillings per month.[602] He was seemingly a single male, but his wage was lower than what had been paid previously, about £2 per month, to single males. This indicates that he was young, but we cannot be certain. The expense on wages had, however, clearly increased since the 1920s and 1930s. In 1928-1929 about £180 was paid to the regular labour force. In total £260 was paid in cash wages to all labourers, excluding the white overseer.

601 Agricultural census 1946-47, pp. 90-91.

602 Rubidge diaries, April 25, 1946.

The wage figures must, however, be read with caution. In 1944 Sidney Rubdige answered a questionnaire from the Divisional Council regarding "labour shortages". He specified the remuneration for a man and a wife who had been on the farm for at least 18 months. According to his response, the man earned £1.15s. per month and the wife £1 per month, altogether £33 per year. The rations were valued at £46.3s. per year.[603] The rations were thus worth more than the cash wages to the families where both man and wife worked. However, there may not have been that many families on the farm. There were only five women working on the farm at the time, meaning that there were only five families where both man and wife worked regularly. Other labourers were paid according to other rates, which included less rations.

The remunerative system was definitely becoming more focused on cash wages than rations. But, as we have seen on Wellwood, there was flexibility. Some labourers were paid more in kind than in cash, and others were paid only cash wages. Being able to change remuneration was favourable to farmers, especially when they had little cash. But the Rubidges did not belong to the group of farmers who were forced to pay wages in rations due to lack of cash. Instead, a flexible remunerative system enabled Sidney Rubidge to invest in the farm, in fencing and water supplies.

The Depression was certainly difficult for many wool farmers; the wool price fell and labourers disappeared to the mines. According to the Native Farm Labour Committee, there were farmers in all areas they visited who were unable to attract labour during the interwar period. But the wealthy farmers "were able to offer such conditions of employment as would attract labour".[604] On Wellwood, for example, there was abundance. In 1945-1946 the average number of black and coloured men was 16 or 18 and the women five or six, and in addition there were three white males. And the labour force had even increased since 1917-1918 when the average number of black and coloured labourers was 10 or 12 men and at the most seven women, but four women between July 1917 and February 1918.[605] There were variations during the year, as always. The labour peak in 1945-1946 was September through December in 1945 when there were 27 men and five women, thus 32 in all. There were at least eight shearers on the farm in 1945, but it is uncertain if they were included in the list of employees. They seem to have left in September, but the number of labourers remained the same. There could thus have been 40 people working on the farm in September 1945. Some of the 27 men may have been involved in shearing, but also conducting other work, such as dam building. As much as £360 was spent on wages for dam labourers.[606]

---

603 Rubidge diaries, 1944, "Workmen's earnings".

604 Native Farm Labour Committee, 1939, p. 7.

605 Rubidge diaries, Sept. 2, 1946; July 22, 1918.

606 Rubidge Sept. 2, 1946.

Being able to hire a large labour force was an advantage to the farmer, but it was not an aim in itself. In August 1946 Sidney Rubidge noted that "two weeks ago I had reduced the workmen on farm to about 8, now again find 17 employed".[607] In August 1945, the "farm staff" was constituted by "8 boys",[608] but there were 27 employed a month later. His intention was thus to have about eight male labourers, possibly all of them from families. However, the double amount was required. Most of these were probably required for work with dams.

The larger labour force increased the expense on wages, and could not have been managed without a considerable income.

Table 21. Wellwood income and expenses 1943 – 1947.

Year	Income	Expenses	Balance
1943-44	8,740	5,196	3,544
1944-45	6,872	4,580	2,296
1945-46	8,280	5,663	2,517
1946-47	7,924	5,829	2,094

Source: Rubidge accounts 1943 – 1947.

Compared to the first years of the 1930s, when the annual profit was about £400, the 1940s were good years for farmers like the Rubidges. Profits exceeded £2,000 during these years. As the wool price rose during the last years of the 1940s, we can assume that profits remained on the same level. However, profits were not generated by decreasing expenses. Besides wages to labourers, investments were made each year into dams, fences, windmills, buildings and the veld.

In 1950 there were 13 males and 4 females hired on Wellwood. The males appear to have earned £32 per year and the females £5. However, in addition the males received £49. 8s. worth of food and goods, and the females £5 worth. For the males, rations were thus once again higher than the cash wages. The reason may have been an unusual large amount of cash wages to seasonal and occasional labourer. Cash wages to seasonal labourers amounted to £595 that year, and to occasional labourers £2,265, thus altogether £2,860.[609] At that point, Sidney Rubidge relied more on rations in order to be able to pay the regular labour force.

---

607 Rubidge diaries, Aug. 7, 1946.

608 Rubidge diaries, Aug. 25, 1945.

609 Rubidge diaries, Sept. 5, 1950.

Farmers in the Empire organize

The effects of the Depression and droughts were severe for many farmers. But during the late 1930s and early 1940s prospects were more hopeful for those who managed the crisis. The farmers also became more organized. There had been local farmers' associations since the late nineteenth century, but they were few. After the First World War more were formed, but there was no organization on the national level. Therefore, in 1930, the provincial branches met in Bloemfontein to found the *National Wool Growers' Association* (NWGA). The NWGA would be the voice of the farmers. But the organization also started wool schools to educate farmers in how to farm sheep and how to handle the wool. Furthermore, in order to improve the quality of South African wool it introduced the Springbok brand, which meant a guarantee that the wool held a standard set by the NWGA.[610] Farmers were allowed to use the brand to market their wool if they had a diploma from the NWGA, which could be attained after having been through a wool classing course organized by the NWGA. The Springbok brand was thus a way to accommodate manufacturers and wool brokers, who for a long time had been concerned with the quality of South African wool.

The NWGA thus had an important role as mouthpiece of wool farmers. Visits were made to farms, probably in order to inspect shearing and farming practices in general, but also to secure the support of farmers. In 1935, the president of the NWGA, Moolman, visited Wellwood during shearing time. Sidney Rubidge referred to the organization as a "new firm",[611] indicating that the NWGA was not regarded by farmers as their own organization, but one of many firms in the wool industry. However, due to the importance of the Springbok brand as a mark of quality, it is likely that at least most of the progressive farmers, joined the NWGA relatively early. But there were also other organizations of importance.

In 1929, one year before the NWGA was created, a semi-offical organization, the *Wool Board*, later called the *Wool Council*, was created in South Africa. Its role was to promote the sale of wool on the international market. The Wool Board worked closely with the NWGA to improve the position of wool farmers in relation to wool dealers and textile manufacturers in core areas of capitalist production. One important way of improving the position was to cooperate internationally. In the late 1930s wool farmers in Australia, New Zealand and South Africa decided to work together instead of competing with each other. In 1937 the *International Wool Secretariat* was therefore created. The Secretariat had representatives from the three wool producing dominions. Although the British were not formally represented, the

---

610 British importers of meat also demanded branding from producers, see Hansson, L 2004.

611 Rubidge diaries, Sept. 10, 1935. Sidney Rubidge called it N. W. G.

role of the British textile industry was central, and the head office of the organization was in London. The purpose of the Secretariat was to promote wool from all the three countries.[612] Competition would be eliminated or at least reduced to minimize wool dealers' and manufacturers' exploitation of wool farmers in the dominions. The producers of raw material in the world-economy organized to promote their interests, which was substantially different than the previous colonial relationship where the core largely benefitted from the peripheral, colonial areas.

The creation of the Wool Secretariat did not mean that the producers of raw material had realized their importance to the textile industry in the core of the world-economy. That had always been the case. However, it was an indication that they could act in order to improve their position in the world-economy. Such action required organization on the local level in Farmers Associations and on the national level in the NWGA, which reduced competition nationally in favour of cooperation. Thereafter cooperation on the international level was possible.

The role of the British Empire had been clearly reduced during the first three decades of the twentieth century. The British purchased about 30 per cent of the South African wool in the 1930s compared to more than 90 per cent in the late nineteenth century. But the outbreak of the Second World War resulted in a reinforcement of the ties between South Africa and the British Empire, showing that political power was important in world capitalist relations when pure economic relations did not ensure a supply of wool for Great Britain. In 1939 the British Wool Commission entered an agreement with South Africa to buy all its wool at a fixed price during the war and one year after. The same agreement was done with the other two wool producing dominions Australia and New Zealand. The dominions would share the profits of this scheme, but any losses would be covered by the British.[613] This indicates how much the British valued a steady supply of wool. The wartime did therefore not mean a disruption for South African wool farmers.

After the First World War the international wool market was unsteady. There were large supplies, which affected prices. The wool organizations, and the South African and British governments, wanted to avoid a similar development after the Second World War. During the war large wool reserves accumulated, which would affect the price. The wool produced during the war would be sold according to a predetermined scheme. An organization, the *United Kingdom-Dominion Wool Disposals Ltd*, usually called the Joint Organization or the J.O. was created in 1945 to handle the sale of the reserves. The large stockpiles were disposed of quickly, most of it within a few years. In 1950 the J.O. was subsequently liquidated as it had fulfilled its purpose to

---

[612] Die Wolboer, Oct., 1947.

[613] *Die Wolboer*, July, 1951.

dispose of the wool in a stable manner. The profits from the sales were £200 million. South Africa only received £8 million although the wool from there had made up about one fifth of the total. The British received the largest share, followed by the Australians.[614]

Table 22. Table. South African wool exports 1936 – 1950.

Year	Lbs	£
1936	213,943,614	9,840,566
1937	237,306,990	12,645,349
1938	244,404,095	8,983,495
1939	187,329,957	7,256,301
1940*		
1944	66,514,561	4,574,770
1945	154,071,706	10,693,943
1946	467,404,500	30,487,852
1947	224,817,890	21,787,002
1948	221,529,376	31,724,175
1949	201,478,986	34,979,292
1950	187,158,354	61,105,223

Source: *Annual Statement on Trade and Shipping* 1936-1950. * Not available.

The end of the Second World War undoubtedly meant a recovery for wool farmers, mainly in terms of the price. The disposal of wool through the JO was clearly a favourable alternative for farmers as the price increased to levels unseen previously. The Korea War increased prices drastically in 1950, but the upturn was evident several years before that.

[614] Hanekom, A. J., 1960; *Die Wolboer*, April, 1950.

CHAPTER 11

Generation, Gender and Transformation of Labour Relations

The shepherds – fewer and younger

We have seen that the shepherds were made redundant on Wellwood in the 1920s, which also happened on other farms during the 1930s and 1940s. Between 1911 and 1946 the number of shepherds in the Cape was reduced by about 43 per cent.

Table 23. Sheep and shepherds in the Cape 1911 and 1946.

Year	*Shepherds*	*Sheep*	*Sheep/shepherd*
1911	42,582	17.1 mil	402
1946	24,210	20.7 mil	855

Source: South Africa Census 1911, pp. 564-65, 1208-09; South Africa Census 1946, Vol. V, pp. 20, 152, 106, 118, 194, 204; Agricultural census 1945-46, pp. 102-03, 110.

The reduction in the number of shepherds demonstrates that the efforts of farmers to reduce dependence on shepherding, and the practice of kraaling and trekking, generated results; shepherds were replaced by jackal-proof camps and camp walkers. The increased jackal-proof fencing during the twentieth century, and the hunting for jackals, made them less of a threat to farmers. Most notably, however, the number of sheep per shepherd increased from 402 to 855. As the number of sheep per flock usually did not exceed 700, it means that there was less than one shepherd per flock. The jackal-proof fencing was started on a large scale after the amendment to the Fencing Act in 1922, which included jackal-proof fences. In 1927 there were 3,983 farms (11%) that were fenced with jackal-proof netting in the Cape.[615] Fencing, along with investments into water supply, enabled farmers to manage without shepherds, or at least with substantially fewer shepherds. As seen on Wellwood, there was

[615] Agricultural census 1926-27, p. 25.

only one shepherd, Adrijan Reid, for at least five years until also he left and the Rubidges managed without a shepherd. There were thus farmers who had no shepherds, like the Rubidges after 1927, while others had one who could manage all the flocks.

Whereas the Rubidges, and many others, did not have any shepherds, the national trend was the opposite, at least until 1936. After that the number of shepherds throughout South Africa decreased.

Table 24. Sheep and shepherds in South Africa 1911, 1936, 1946.

Year	Sheep	Shepherds	Sheep/shepherd
1911	30.7 mil	66,758	460
1936	33.3 mil	104,483	319
1946	30.8 mil	58,527	526

Source: South Africa census 1911, pp. 11, 1208-09; South Africa census 1936; South Africa Census 1946, vol v, pp. 2-3, 88-89, 100-01, 138-39, 180-81, 190-91; Agricultural census 1935-36; Agricultural census 1945-46, pp. 102-03, 110.

To some extent the dramatic increase of the number of shepherds between 1911 and 1936 was a result of heavy stocking during the 1930s, but not entirely; the ratio between sheep and shepherds decreased, indicating that the increased number of shepherds must be explained through an analysis of the labour process. Or rather, how the labour process nationwide differed from the one in the Cape. As we do not know the numbers for each province in 1936, it is possible that the number of shepherds in the Cape also increased in a similar way between 1911 and 1936, but it is unlikely. The ratio between sheep and shepherds in the Cape was 855 in 1946, and 443 for the country. It is unlikely that the ratio changed from 319 to 855 in the Cape between 1936 and 1946. However, there could have been an increase of shepherds also in the Cape during the 1920s and 1930s, but not as high as for the rest of the country. We should assume that the increase of shepherds was first and foremost seen outside of the Cape.

It was clear that the Cape was in the lead regarding fencing in general together with the Orange Free State in 1918. The least fenced province was Transvaal, where 14 per cent of the farms were "not fenced" at all and 40 per cent were "wholly fenced". In the Cape about 48 per cent of the farms were "wholly fenced" and 10 per cent were "not fenced" at all.[616] The difference seems quite negligible, but it was primarily how the fences were constructed that made the difference, and in that regard the Cape farmers were at the forefront with jackal-proof fences. The extent of jackal-proof fencing in the Cape was considerably greater than in the rest of the country. In 1927 there

[616] Agricultural census 1918, p. 9.

were 3,983 farms that were fenced with jackal-proof netting in the Cape. In the rest of the country only 279 farms were netted.[617] In 1946 there were 19,110 shepherds in the Transvaal, about the same amount as in the Cape. But there were fewer sheep; only about ten per cent of the total.

However, the number of sheep in the Cape increased considerably more than in the rest of the country between 1911 and 1936. The Cape share in 1911 was about 56 per cent and in 1936 as much as 73 per cent, and the number of sheep increased from 17 to 24 million. It is therefore reasonable to assume that the number of shepherds in the Cape increased in real numbers to some extent during these years, despite jackal-proof fencing and other implements. The increase was partially a result of the Depression and the decision to stock more heavily, but also a gradual increase. In 1924-1925 there were about 20 million sheep in the Cape. There could thus have been an increase in the number of shepherds in the Cape also during the 1920s and 1930s, but not in relation to the sheep.

During the 1940s the shepherding labour force was, however, declining, more so in the Cape than in the other provinces.

Besides an increase in the number of shepherds between 1911 and 1936 and 1946, their age composition changed even more drastically. More than previously shepherding became dominated by the young.

Table 25. Shepherds' ages. 1904 Cape and 1936, 1946 South Africa.

Year	10-19	20-40
1904	37%	25%
1936	91%	4%
1946	87%	6%

Source: Cape of Good Hope census 1904, pp. 360-61; South Africa census 1936, Vol. VII, IX; South Africa census 1946, Vol. V, pp. 2-3, 88-89, 100-01, 138-39, 180-81, 190-91.

The young shepherds had been important already from the start of wool farming, and as seen in 1904, they constituted more than two thirds of the shepherding labour force. If those under 10 years of age are included, the share of young shepherds was about 45 per cent in 1904. For 1936 and 1946 only those aged 10 and older were enumerated, but it is clear that by 1936 almost all the shepherds in South Africa were younger than 20 years old. Such a change was dramatic. To some extent it constitutes a revolutionary phase in South African wool farming and child labour historiography. In no other industry or sector did children and youths play such a central role in production. During the first decades of the twentieth century the children became economic actors to an extent never seen before, or after.

[617] Agricultural census 1926-27, p. 25.

In order to accurately evaluate the role played by children and youths in shepherding we can compare with the share of young people in the general farm labour force. Both in 1904 and in 1936 the age group between 10 and 19 constituted 25 per cent of the labour force and in 1946 about 30 per cent.[618] General farm labour was in some ways heavier and required more physical strength than shepherding did, which may have been an explanation as to why children and youths were not demanded as much as adults. Still, the generational division of labour probably had an impact on who was given what task on a farm, especially as also labouring families regarded shepherding as preferred work for the young boys.

As young shepherds dominated on wool farms, the generational division of labour was exploited to a greater extent than previously during the 1930s and 1940s. However, it also meant that the generational relations among labouring families were disrupted. The generational division of labour was based on education through generations. Fathers and older brothers socialized the younger children through shepherding. The younger children were often the ones who performed the actual work, but fathers had control over them, and the work was shared within the family. As 91 per cent of the shepherds were under 20 years of age in 1936, and 87 per cent were younger that 20 in 1946, it was no longer a work operation shared between father and sons; shepherding was conducted almost exclusively by the sons. The families were still on the farm, but adult males and young boys did not work side by side.

We have seen that the increasing importance of young people in wool farming had an impact in places like Carnarvon, where many of the shepherds involved in stock thefts were very young, and in Barkly East where "picannins" were hired by farmers such as Claude Orpen. In other places of the Cape, such as Graaff-Reinet, there did not appear to be many shepherds at all. However, we should assume that this trend, although perhaps more visible outside of the Cape, and primarily in the Transvaal, was seen also in certain areas of the Cape.

The reasons for the increasing dominance of young people in shepherding appear to be twofold. Firstly, the impact of the mining sector, secondly, the relative cheapness of using children compared to adults.

The mining industry in both Kimberly and the Witwatersrand attracted vast numbers of people who came to look for work. It was primarily the young adult males who were sought after in mining, and they were the ones who disappeared from the farms. According to the Native Farm Labour Committee in 1937, the disappearance of young males from farms was one important reason why farmers had problems attracting labour at the wages they offered.[619] However, many of these migrant mine labourers had families on the farms and

---

[618] Cape of Good Hope Census 1904, pp. 360-61; South Africa Census 1936, Vol. VII, IX; South Africa Census 1946, Vol. V.

[619] Native Farm Labour Committee, 1939, pp. 9-10

returned from time to time as mining contracts lasted for about nine months.[620] Those who remained on farms were thus the youngest and oldest male members of the families, and females of all ages. As shepherding was a male occupation, it appears that the young males were given a greater responsibility for herding sheep when their fathers and older brothers were at the mines. In other words, the resistance among young adult males towards working as shepherds for low wages for white farmers instead of in mining resulted in a reorganization of the labour force along generational lines. As was the case in the early twentieth century, the young adults did not discard shepherding or farm labour per se, only the wages. To some extent the impact of mining seems to have intensified the exploitation of family relations among the labourers; when the older males did not work on farms, but in mining, the young males took their place or were called upon instead.

But having a larger share of young shepherds was also beneficial to farmers. Most notably since it meant they could pay lower wages to a child than to an adult. This must have been an attractive option to those farmers who did not have much capital or cash. However, children could not be expected to be able to handle the same amount of sheep in a flock as adults could. The lowered ratio of sheep per shepherd between 1911 and 1936, from 460 to 319, could thus partially be explained by this fact. The young shepherds therefore probably worked together to a greater extent than they had done before. Simultaneously, the number of camps, an increasing number of which became jackal-proof, also facilitated for children to do the work on their own; herding sheep on a farm that was to a greater or lesser extent enclosed and subdivided was definitely easier than herding on an unfenced farm. While the implementation of fences and windmills for water aimed at making shepherds redundant, they also made it possible to exploit more children in wool farming. The lower wages subsequently improved the possibilities for farmers to increase profits and accumulate capital, which was imperative not least during the Depression, but also before and after.

As half the shepherding labour force disappeared between 1936 and 1946, there were great changes in wool farming. The young members of labouring families became increasingly unemployed. Previously they had a place in production as shepherds, which was their traditional role. But when they were no longer required, they had no place in production. This probably caused many to leave the farms in search of work in mining or in cities. The Native Farm Labour Committee argued that youths left the farms due to the low wages, but also because cash wage labour in mining had enabled them to have a place in society outside of the family. As they could earn cash wages, they could be independent of their fathers.[621] This was of course true, but as long as there

620 Morris, M 1976, p. 332.

621 Native Farm Labour Committee, 1939, pp. 10-11, 20-21.

was employment on farms, they could get cash wages also there. Those wages were lower than elsewhere, however.

Girls and farm labour

While the young men left the farms, the young women stayed. As Wilson mentions, the women became an increasingly important part of the farm labour force during the 1930s and 1940s. It was especially the young girls who became farm labourers. In 1904 the girls made up 2 per cent of the total farm labour force in the Cape, in 1936 they made up 4 per cent. This trend was seen also when viewing the young labour force. In 1904 the girls constituted 4 per cent of the labourers under 20 years of age, in 1936 16 per cent. However, in 1946 the girls made up 14 per cent of the total farm labour force and almost 36 per cent of the labourers under the age of 20.[622] These figures demonstrate that the ratio between young males and females had changed drastically during the first decades of the twentieth century. The young females had become a vital part of the labour force. As Wilson argues, the main reason must have been that the young men disappeared to the mines, which meant that farmers replaced them with women.

The females did, however, seem to have been more involved in agriculture than pastoralism. In 1945 there were only five females hired on Wellwood, and in April 1946 one additional female was hired, compared to seventeen or eighteen males.[623] All the females probably worked in the household. The males thus appear to have been the main labour force in wool farming. The central work operations were camp walking, shepherding where there was still room for it, transport and work with dams, fences and windmills. These were male work operations. Weeding was important on Wellwood, and women were sometimes hired for this, but it was only done occasionally and farmers did not hore large numbers for this purpose. In comparison to agriculture, where women were involved in planting, harvesting and weeding, there were few work operations for them in wool farming.

Still, gendered divisions of labour were not written in stone, only in the soil of the Karroo, which was easily eroding. Farmers who could not find males to herd their sheep could of course not refuse to hire a woman. One example is Leentjie Rooi, who was a "shepherdess" in Carnarvon in the 1920s. She belonged to a very small group of female shepherds. In 1936 there were, for example, only 2,650 black female shepherds in the country compared to more than 100,000 males. But Leentjie Rooi worked as a shepherd on the farm

---

[622] Cape of Good Hope Census 1904, pp. 360-61; South Africa Census 1936, Vol. VII, IX; South Africa Census 1946, Vol. V.

[623] Rubidge diaries, Sept. 2, 1946.

Melkdam. She was 25 years old in 1923 and appears to have worked alone without help from a male, staying at a “”Veepost” with the stock. She earned 5 shillings per month plus rations and clothing.[624] The wage was clearly less than what was paid to adult males, but similar to what was paid to young boys. Hiring women as shepherds was thus equal to hiring young boys and an option for those with little cash.

But women were not important as shepherds. In 1946 only about 500 female shepherds were reported in the Cape. The role of women on farms was mainly reproductive labour, which included cultivation of some crops such as mealies. On Wellwood, the role of females in the labour force had not increased between 1917 and 1946.

Limited grazing rights

As others have pointed out, grazing rights were diminished during the first half of the twentieth century. Let us go through some of the statistics first, and then analyse the process.

According to the Native Farm Labour Committee in 1937, grazing rights for farm labourers were “allowed in a certain percentage of cases, but are very limited”.[625] Grazing rights had always been limited to some extent in wool farming areas, but when capitalist farmers increased their activities the ownership of stock among labourers was further limited. This was most obvious in regards to sheep.

Between 1911 and 1936 the ratio between sheep owned by white and black people did not change drastically. In 1911 white farmers owned 81 per cent of the woolled sheep in the Cape, in 1936 they owned 54 per cent. The share owned by farm labourers was, however, very low in 1936, less than 1 per cent. And between 1925-1926 and 1936-1937 the sheep owned by farm labourers decreased from 97,094 to 58,786.[626] There were some variations throughout the Cape. The Native Farm Labour Committee stated that in the wool districts Cradock, Molteno, Queenstown, Sterkstroom and Tarka white farmers owned 1.7 million sheep. The 28,283 black people, estimated to constitute 5,600 families, together owned 4,744 sheep, thus about 0.8 per family. Apparently, in the “almost exclusively sheep areas the ownership of small stock is discouraged by farmers”.[627] Farmers would thus not hire labourers with stock, at least not if they had the ability to choose. Grazing land was meant for the sheep of the

[624] CA 1/CAR 1/1/1/7. Magistrate Carnarvon. Leentjie Rooi, Feb. 2, 1923.

[625] Native Farm Labour Committee, 1939, p. 39.

[626] South Africa Census 1911, pp. 1208-09; Agricultural census 1925-26, pp. 89-90; Agricultural census 1936-37, p. 57.

[627] Native Farm Labour Committee, 1939, p. 40.

farmer, not those of the labourers. The droughts may have intensified the issue as additional animals meant additional pressure on the veld. Those who could refuse labourers with animals were then probably encouraged to do so.

Ownership of cattle and goats among labourers was somewhat higher than sheep. In the wool farming districts the number of goats was 1.4 and cattle 1.6 per family. Goats and cattle could provide labourers with milk, which farmers would otherwise have to provide. Cattle could also be used as draught animals for ploughing or scraaper work. Labourers thus supplied means of production both for themselves and farmers through ownership of cattle.

In the North-Eastern areas Barkly East, Indwe and Wodehouse ownership of sheep was 3 per family and cattle 1.6. Farm labourers in the coastal districts were in a better position regarding ownership of stock, at least cattle. In Alexandria, Bathurst, East London, Komgha and Peddie the number of cattle was 3.7 per family. These areas were dominated by fruit farming and various other crops, and there were relatively few sheep, in Alexandria for example only about 30,000 and in Bathurst 12,000 belonging to white farmers. The stock belonging to labourers did thus not interfere with the activities of white farmers to the same extent as in wool farming regions. Land which was not used for cultivation could more easily be allowed for grazing for the stock belonging to labourers.

The limited grazing rights were seen on Wellwood early during the twentieth century. In 1913 many of the labourers brought stock to the farm, but they mainly replaced each other, indicating that there was a limit to the number of stock allowed on the farm. Between 1913 and 1923 there was no apparent shift in the number of stock owned by labourers. In 1923 the number of stock owned by labourers was 170, whereof a man called George owned a majority. He had arrived at Wellwood in 1918. He then owned 32 Cape sheep and 3 goats.[628] Five years later George, however, owned "117 of best condition stock on place & 3 head cattle & during period has been sold about 70 sheep for some £60".[629] During the following ten years changes occurred though.

In 1928 and 1930 only two of the labourers on the farm owned stock. In 1928 two labourers owned 44 goats and Cape sheep, while the number of goats owned by labourers in 1930 appears to have been 54.[630] Five years later the number of stock owned by labourers was 35.[631] And in 1937 the labourers owned 39 head of stock.[632] But we do not know what sort of stock. In 1936, however, the number of Angora goats was only 3, and there were no Boer goats. But there were almost 300 cross-bred sheep, of which the labourers may have

628 Rubidge diaries, Feb. 28, 1918.

629 Rubidge diaries, Dec. 5, 1923.

630 Rubidge diaries, March 21, 1930.

631 Rubidge diaries, May, 1935.

632 Beinart, W 2008, p 316.

owned some.[633] As goats had been very common among labourers in the past, it definitely seems as if the Rubidges actively discouraged ownership of them. The labourers still owned cattle though. Four different labourers together owned 12 head of cattle in 1936. The same year Sidney Rubidge himself owned 58 head of cattle,[634] which means that he was not dependent on the labourers for cattle. Altogether, the pattern was quite obvious. The labourers owned fewer and fewer animals of their own. The late 1920s and early 1930s seems to have been the crucial period for the decrease.

The diminishing grazing rights must be seen in relation to the reserve areas. After the 1936 Native Trust and Land Act ownership of land for black people was set at about 14 per cent of the country. It was generally the worst farming land. But ownership of stock among black peasants in reserve areas was much higher than for labourers on white farms. Whereas total ownership of cattle among farm labourers in the Cape was estimated at about 2 per family of 5 members, the number for the Transkei was almost 7. Similarly, ownership of sheep was 0.85 per family for farm labourers, and 10.5 in the Transkei. It thus seemed favourable to be a peasant instead of a farm labourer. However, the ownership was "less evenly distributed in the reserves than on the farms". Certain groups in the reserves, such as chiefs, owned large herds, while others owned very little.[635] Few peasants could therefore make a living in the reserve areas, and were forced into labour on farms, mines or in industries outside the reserves. There had always been stratifications among peasants; for example chiefs and other large owners of stock had been able to live off tribute from others and had been wealthier than the majority. But those who were married had been able to establish a household of their own. The increased capitalist labour relations, which in wool farming meant that labourers could own less and less stock as they did not get grazing rights, coupled with fewer possibilities of owning land, resulted in an increased stratification. Those peasants who owned land that could sustain fairly large herds managed to accumulate capital, but those who owned stock, but no land, or not enough land, could not accumulate capital.

Between 1911 and 1946 the peasantry's share of the population in the Cape decreased from 29 to 12 per cent. Some of the peasants were turned into farm labourers, but far from all. The farm labour force made up about 6 per cent of the population in 1946 compared to 3.5 in 1911. Nevertheless, the proletarianization process was evident during these years. The amount of wool produced by peasants also changed between the 1920s and 1940s. In 1925-1926 black peasants in the reserve areas produced about 11.6 million lbs, which made up 13 per cent of the total wool in the Cape. In 1945-1946 they

[633] Rubidge diaries, July 14, 1936.

[634] Rubidge diaries, May 12, 1936.

[635] Native Farm Labour Committee 1939, p. 43.

produced about 8.7 million lbs., or 7.6 per cent of the total. The peasants' ability to compete in the wool sector definitely diminished during these years, while white farmers improved their position.

Luxemburg claims that capitalism, or the capitalist sector, was dependent on the peasant economy, for example for labour, but that capitalism in the same process consumes other modes of production.[636] Subsequent to her observations in the 1910s, where South Africa was one example, the peasant economy actually became more important in South Africa as capitalist farming increased. The peasant reserves became a place of reproduction of the labour force in the capitalist sector. However, as Guy argues, even production among peasants was based on a capitalist logic. In pre-capitalist production in southern Africa people were the aim of production. Thus, the exchange of cattle for women's labour and subsequently children was the aim. After the capitalist intrusion peasants were still involved in pre-capitalist relations where women's labour was exchanged for cattle or money, but they largely produced commodities.[637] Thereby, even peasants in the reserves were involved in the capitalist economy. Most of them could, however, not sustain themselves on the production in the reserves and were forced into labour in the capitalist sector. The support of the state was central in that regard, as it dispossessed the peasants, which made it possible for farmers to limit the grazing rights. This is well known. But limiting the grazing rights only applied to those animals, which were not useful in accumulating capital.

Donkeys replaced by tractors

Whereas ownership of sheep and goats, and to some extent cattle, was very limited, the farm labourers could own one sort of animal which farmers required: donkeys. Between 1925-1926 and 1936-1937 the number of donkeys owned by both farm labourers and farmers decreased, but during the following ten years, until 1945-46 the number of donkeys owned by farm labourers increased from 22,043 to 32,350, while the donkeys owned by farmers decreased further; from 267,013 to 219,419.[638] This trend was also seen on Wellwood. We have seen that the stock belonging to labourers on the farm decreased during the 1930s, but in 1948 all the 34 donkeys were owned by "workmen".[639] The donkeys were used as draught animals in scraaper work at

---

636 Luxemburg, R 2003, p. 397.

637 Guy, J 2007, pp. 38, 42.

638 Agricultural census 1925-26, p. 88; Agricultural census 1936-37, p. 51; Agricultural census 1945-46, p. 118.

639 Rubidge diaries, June 17, 1948.

dams and furrows, which required constant repairs. Having donkeys on a farm was therefore crucial, which both farmers and labourers benefitted from.

In 1933 a black man called James Jacobs came to Wellwood with 13 donkeys seeking work at dams. He agreed to undertake the work at a dam for £8, which was the equivalent of the yearly wage on many farms at the time. Having donkeys was clearly valuable. The scraapers were owned by the Rubidges, though. Jacobs took them in a scotch cart to the dam after he had arrived at the farm. The shared ownership of the means of production was a solution that suited both farmer and labourer in this case. The farmer did not have to keep donkeys, instead they were provided by the labourer when such work was required. The labourer on the other hand did not have to buy the scraapers, which were presumably quite expensive and difficult to move from one farm to another. And being hired at a farm meant that the labourer, in this case Jacobs, could find grazing for his animals. Jacobs seemed to be more interested in finding grazing than conducting scraaper work. A week after Jacobs was hired the foreman Leon "inspected James' supposed work at top of Kloof, [...] and found the usual thing – donkeys grazing and no work proceeding".[640] The interests of the farmer and labourer were obviously not the same. To Sidney Rubidge the donkeys were only valuable when they worked; to James Jacobs their value would increase the more they could graze. And Jacobs must have continued to graze them more than he was allowed to. About a month later Sidney Rubidge called the police, who came and arrested Jacobs, as there was "scarcely any further work done in the past 16 days [...]".[641] Shared ownership of the means of production was thus problematic if the labourer did not prove willing to follow the agreement.

The dependence on labourers who owned donkeys increased during the 1930s and 1940s. Scraaper work at dams became increasingly important as droughts struck. Sidney Rubidge stated that on Wellwood the labourers were allowed to keep "a pair of Donkeys" along with a cart. However, he also noted that "most of my labourers count a pair as 4 or 6 Donkeys",[642] which means that there were quite a few donkeys on the farm. In 1946 three labourers left Wellwood at the same time, with 40 donkeys altogether. At the time Sidney Rubidge had donkeys of his own, but instead of keeping them, he gave away eight of his best donkeys to one of the labourers "on condition he gets rid of 8 of his worst & so keep a top-work span of only 17".[643] Giving away the donkeys seems to have been Sidney Rubdiges strategy to keep at least one of the labourers with donkeys on the farm. It is likely that the span of 17 good donkeys was worth more to Sidney Rubidge than a span of only nine good

640 Rubidge diaries, May 20, 1933.

641 Rubidge diaries, June 27, 1933.

642 Rubidge diairies, 1944 "Workmen's earnings".

643 Rubidge diaries, May 2, 1946.

ones. He did, however, regard the issue with the lack of donkeys as highly problematic. The solution was a tractor. But, a "tractor today, without accessories, costs £1,000".[644] Besides the tractor, he would also require a white overseer. Investing in a tractor would have to wait.

Two years later a great deal of repair work on dams was conducted on the farm. There had been droughts, which loosened the soil, and when rains came the soil was washed away. This constituted a severe problem. Sidney Rubidge even hired labourers, "Christian & 2 sons with 10 donkeys", specifically for this purpose.[645] Sidney Rubidge had, however, decided to invest in new machinery for scraaper work. In June 1948 the first tractor was bought at Wellwood. It was a D2 tractor purchased at the price of £890. Including a scraaper at £185, the machinery cost well over £1,000. The tractor had "32 H P", which indicates that it more or less equalled the power of the 34 donkeys on the farm.[646] No white foreman seems to have been hired to supervise and drive the machine. Instead three of the farm labourers were instructed on how to service the tractor. The tractor was immediately put to work. Three days after it had been delivered it was used in work on one of the dams, but the labourers may not have been accustomed to working with the tractor; Sidney Rubidge noted that the "[b]oys [were] not progressing satisfactorily with tractor".[647] Tractors had been used in South Africa for quite some time, but there were very few of them until after the Second World War. Labourers did thus not have any experience with this sort of work, which may actually have resulted in less efficiency compared to work with donkeys, which they were accustomed to.

As has been noted by Africa, the introduction of machinery such as tractors in South African agriculture did not lower the demand for manual labour. Quite the contrary, as machinery increased overall production, the demand on manual labour also increased to perform those work operations machines could not perform.[648] This may have been the case on Wellwood, but wool farming, unlike agriculture, mainly depended on tractors for repair work, not production. The tractor, which had 32 horsepower, instead replaced the 34 donkeys, and perhaps also the labourer who owned the donkeys. But although the tractor was more efficient than the donkeys, it was not as reliable. After about two months, while being used in work on a dam, the tractor was "completely out of working order [...]". As rain was expected at the time, the work had to be completed quickly. Instead of waiting for the tractor to be repaired "the old tired mules [...]", not the donkeys, "will have to try &

644 Rubidge diaries, May 5, 1946.

645 Rubidge diaries, April, 5, 8, 1948.

646 Rubidge diaries, June 25, July 16, 1948.

647 Rubidge diaries, July 19, 1948.

648 Africa, R in Wilson et al 1977.

complete the job".[649] It seems as if the donkeys were no longer on the farm, which meant that there was no other option than the mules. The tractor was presumably repaired, but a month later, in November, the mules were again put to repair furrows as there was another "break-down with tractor".[650] Although the tractor was an important improvement of productive forces, it was not necessarily an advantage at all times.

As Sidney Rubidge replaced the donkeys with a tractor on Wellwood, the stock of labourers no longer had any place in production. However, the same year there were 44 goats and 95 Karakul sheep on the farm. Some of these animals most likely belonged to labourers, which means that the practice of grazing rights was not gone. From the farmer's point of view it may even have been beneficial to allow a certain amount of grazing rights as labourers still wanted it. Allowing some goats and bastard sheep also kept cash wages and rations down. However, by the end of the 1940s grazing rights was anything but a vital part of the remunerative system. It was a remnant of the past, but one which related to traditional practices of stock keeping and marriage for men who wanted to secure a homestead of their own in the reserves. But in the 1930s lobola was often paid in cash, not in cattle.[651] The grazing rights were thus important only in a symbolic way.

The camp walkers – new methods, new problems

Although there were many shepherds in the Cape during the 1930s and 1940s they were being replaced by camp walkers or boundary riders as they were also called. It is difficult to know how many camp walkers there were in the Cape. They were not enumerated as a category in the censuses. Presumably, they belonged to the group of farm labourers, meaning that they also did other work than controlling fences. Their absence as a category from the censuses does not mean that they were unimportant. Farmers who had jackal-proof fences were required to inspect their functionality, and unless the farmer or the foreman conducted this, a labourer must have been assigned to do it.

Camp walking was quite different from shepherding, and required different skills. Shepherding was a task based on the generational division of labour, and passed on from father to son, or through the intermediaries of brothers. Camp walking on the other hand was a completely new work operation. While shepherds required skills related to sheep, such as controlling their health, their grazing and water drinking, the camp walkers had to be observant of how technology in the form of fences functioned. It had obviously never been passed

649 Rubidge diaries, Sept. 20, 1948.

650 Rubidge diaries, Nov. 25, 1948.

651 Native Farm Labour Committee, 1939, p. 10.

on from father to son, and there was no education demonstrating how the work was to be done. The first generation of camp walkers, who were pioneers, had to learn while conducting the work, which proved to be difficult at times.

As we have seen, the first camp walker on Wellwood was a man called Jacob who was hired in 1914. He lived in the mountain camp, where he was to walk the fences. As he lived in the camp he was more independent than the farm labourers, who lived near the homestead. In that regard the camp walker was similar to the shepherd. We do not know how Jacob performed his work, or how much he was paid. He did not seem to be on the farm when Hermaans was hired as a camp walker in 1918. We know that Hermaans was paid £36 per year, which was substantially more than what was paid to regular farm labourers and shepherds, who earned around £20 per year. The farmers seem to have valued the work with fences, both because it was important and because it was related to the new technology.

At times there was no labourer specifically hired to be a camp walker on Wellwood. When Sidney Rubidge went on a trip to East Griqualand for almost a month in 1928, he delegated the work to be done during his absence. Out of the "staff of 8" labourers on the farm, one was assigned to "camp walking", while others were instructed to do scraaper repair work and weeding.[652] The one assigned to camp walking was most likely a man called Pyott [?], who was hired in 1927 along with his wife. He stayed on the farm for three years, but did not conduct his work properly. In 1930 he was fired, "after again proving his unbelievable deceptiveness [...]". Sidney Rubidge thereafter sent the rest of the labourers "at looking to fences believed to have been inspected by Pyott [...]".[653] Apparently, the camp walker had been without supervision from Sidney Rubidge, and had not controlled the fences to the extent he was expected to. In comparison to other labourers, who were almost constantly supervised, the camp walker was extremely independent.

The disappointment with Pyott did not make Sidney Rubidge reluctant to using camp walkers. After Pyott left, another camp walker, probably called Dantje, was hired. Dantje was fired in March, and the same day a man called Speelman was hired along with his wife Mina. He became the new camp walker and, for example, reported two ewes dead in the Mountain camp.[654] The camp walkers were thus still mainly in the mountain camp. After five months Sidney fired "camp-walker Speelman, same story as previous one who left in March".[655] There was no reference to what happened to the previous camp walker, but it was evident that the work of camp walkers was not done

652 Rubidge diaries, April 17 to May 12, 1928.

653 Rubidge diaries, Feb. 6, 1930.

654 Rubidge diaries, March 10, 25, 1930.

655 Rubidge diaries, Aug. 7, 1930.

satisfactorily. It is quite possible that they did not know how to do the work, or did not agree with farmers about when fences were in need of repair.

Speelman was replaced by Piet Lett [?], who was already working on the farm. For example, he conducted weeding along with two sons in August before he became a camp walker.[656] Like his predecessors, he did not last long. After only a month "Piet Lett & family left – 3rd worthless camp walker dismissed since March".[657] Sidney Rubidge was apparently not able to find a labourer who could conduct the work the way he wanted it done. We do not know how much he paid these camp walkers who replaced each other after only a few months, but if they were paid at a higher rate than farm labourers, as had been the case in the past, it is strange that Sidney Rubidge could not recruit capable labourers. We should assume that many labourers were willing to work as camp walkers as they would be better paid and be independent from farmers. The supply of camp walkers was therefore not the problem, but the reasons for hiring them. Piet, for example, was not hired because he was experienced as a camp walker, but because he was available on the farm when Speelman was fired. Sidney Rubidge thus had little patience with the camp walkers, and tried a new one as soon as the existing one made mistakes.

Besides controlling fences, the camp walkers reported information on rainfall in camps, water levels in dams and other events in camps. Several also looked for lost sheep and were in charge of trekking sheep to sales. They thus had more or less the same function as a shepherd, but they did not control the condition of the sheep, only the condition of the farm. As they were constantly in the veld, they also had responsibility. And it seems like Sidney Rubidge handed over all responsibility of the condition of the camps to the camp walkers. This resulted in problems during the 1940s.

There had been no jackals on Wellwood since 1920, but in 1946 new ones showed up. Two stud ewes had been killed by a jackal in the old mountain camp. Sidney Rubidge called it "about the biggest blow to me in the last 26 years in the farming line [...]". Apparently, "every mountain camp over-run with jackals [...]". He blamed the camp walkers: The "fences not attended to for at least 20 years in spite of camp-walkers assurances over this period [...]". The return of the jackals was a setback. Sidney even thought that "we are back where we were 26 years ago or in the same state which prevailed for 100 years before, ie that the jackal owned the sheep".[658] The severity of the situation caused him to offer one of his labourers, who had given notice to leave, to continue at the same wage, but as a jackal hunter in the mountain camp and

656 Rubidge diaries, Aug. 2, 1930.

657 Rubidge diaries, Sept. 16, 1930.

658 Rubidge diaries, March 27, 1946.

earn an additional £3.10s. per catch, which he agreed to.[659] It is unclear if any jackals were caught.

Two years later, in 1948, there were still jackals on Wellwood. The camp walker Kleinbooi, who was hired that year, set traps for jackals after one sheep had been caught by a jackal.[660] The traps did, however, not stop the jackals on the farm. In May one lamb was killed and in August the camp walker found a sheep caught by a jackal in the old mountain camp. Sidney thought it was "depressing" and realized he had been wrong in assuming that "after 75 years of herding sheep, the pest had been eliminated". But he was certain that the jackals "were not bred on Wellwood".[661] Kleinbooi, the camp walker, was not directly blamed for the return of the jackal, but after a number of sheep had gone missing, he was no longer wanted on Wellwood; Sidney Rubidge "[d]ismissed camp-walker (loafer) Kleinbooi, after 7 months apparently as big a scoundrel as a previous Gert Rafferty – 18 'unaccounted' for sheep in past 6 weeks".[662] Sidney did thus not believe that the sheep had been caught by jackals, but thought that Kleinbooi had killed the sheep, at least some of them.

After Kleinbooi left there was no sign of any jackal, the sheep numbers in for example the Mill camp were "correct after 3 weeks – unlike when a camp-walker or human jackall [sic] is heavily paid to daily patrol camps".[663] The human jackal or the "two-legged jackal" had been a well-known concept in the Cape.[664] As long as there were jackals on farms threatening sheep, shepherds, farm labourers and others could steal sheep and blame the vermin. But after the jackals had disappeared, this was no longer possible. The return of the jackals to Wellwood caused Sidney to assume that the "human jackal" had accompanied them.

In October further lambs were killed by jackals, and in November two jackals were actually caught. The missing sheep may thus not have been stolen by Kleinbooi, but actually caught by jackals. But Sidney did not acknowledge that he had been wrong in assuming that the camp walker had stolen them. Instead he blamed the camp walkers collectively for their work: "Heaven only knows how many [jackals] have bred & grown up in that area the while my previous 'Camp Walkers' slumbered in the shades".[665] There had been camp walkers on Wellwood since 1914, thus for 34 years, and it seems as if they were all blamed for the return of jackals. As Sidney Rubidge had hired them all, it is strange that he did not blame himself for not finding labourers who could

---

[659] Rubidge diaries, March 21, 1946.

[660] Rubidge diaries, March 23, 1948.

[661] Rubidge diaries, Aug. 17, 1948.

[662] Rubidge diaries, Aug. 30, 1948.

[663] Rubidge diaries, Sept. 16, 1948.

[664] See for example van Sittert, L 2002, p. 98.

[665] Rubidge diaries, Nov. 16, 1948.

conduct the task according to his wishes. The introduction of camp walkers, however, seems to have created new relations between farmer and labourer in regard to control, at least on Wellwood. The demand on wool of better quality from textile manufacturers in Europe and the need to improve the pastures in the Cape were the main reasons for practicing rotational grazing with camp walkers. Both of these factors thus combined to change relations on farms.

Shepherds and farm labourers were usually regarded as lazy, treacherous, thieving and so on by farmers, but when those labourers made mistakes they were often noticed and corrected immediately. Those who were fired were replaced with others regarded as more reliable and hard working. Camp walkers on the other hand were seen as collectively unreliable. And, even though many of them were fired after only a couple of months, their work was barely supervised at all as it seems. The size of the farm, more than 6,000 morgen, and 20 miles of boundary fencing and 36 miles of internal fencing, made it difficult to control the work of camp walkers. The work of shepherds or dam builders was easier to control; the result of their work could be seen immediately. But a small hole in the fence was more difficult to detect and if a jackal entered the farm it would take some time before it was noticed. Sidney Rubidge did not mention that the fences were broken, and as there was constant repair of them, we should assume that they were in fairly good condition. But there were always weak spots even in jackal-proof fences, for example where the veld was uneven. If the fences were not packed with stones the jackal would be able to dig under the fence. If camp walkers did not notice and repair such faults, the jackals would soon take advantage of it.

The jackal-proof fences were supposed to enable the farmer increase his control over the farm through rotational grazing and less dependence on shepherds. But Sidney Rubidge definitely lost some control as he handed over all inspection of fences to camp walkers. Fencing did thus not only make farmers less dependent on the skills of shepherds, it created a new dependence on the skills and reliability of camp walkers. Camp walking required other skills than those that were passed from generation to generation, such as shepherding. At least one of the camp walkers worked together with his son, mostly with collecting sheep, but it is likely that the son also worked with camp walking. The generational division of labour was thus still important as it enabled farmers to gain access to the labour of children, but it was not central to the skills required by labourers. Fathers and sons may have worked together, but with tasks that were new to them both. The skills required for camp walking would have to be learned in other ways than from generation to generation.

CHAPTER 12

Capitalist Expansion and Labour Relations in Cape Wool Farming

Wool farming in the Cape was a part of a process of capital expansion in the capitalist world-economy into new geographical areas and economic sectors. This expansion, and its impact, has been described by Rosa Luxemburg, who argued that capital accumulation cannot continue without constant expansion. Her argument has been used as a point of departure in this analysis of wool farming in the periphery of transnational wool production. The Cape farmers were agents of expansion as they imported sheep from Europe and Australia and hired labourers on their farms in order to produce wool, which was sold to Britain. The purpose of this thesis has been to analyse how labour relations in expanding capitalist wool farming in the Cape changed between c. 1860 and 1950. By doing so, I have been able to show that the prevailing explanations for capitalist development must be revised. Morris and Keegan, for example, have emphasized the role of mining and the state, which was undoubtedly important, but they have largely overlooked the relationship between the Cape and the capitalist world-economy. Wool, unlike other rural sectors, was incorporated into transnational capitalist production from the beginning. Capital therefore expanded into wool farming regions, while it did not expand into other regions at the same rate. Wool was the largest rural commodity and can clearly not be excluded from any explanation of capitalist development in South Africa and the region. By analysing the actual production on wool farms, which was conducted in a peripheral setting of transnational capitalism, this thesis shows the interrelationship between capital accumulation, the environment and labour on a world scale. It was the expansion of capital from core to periphery that enabled farmers to accumulate capital in the periphery, which was the basis for capitalist production. But the transformation of labour relations was affected, and in some cases delayed, by local forces such as the mining industry, labourers' resistance to proletarianization and the impact of the environment. Labour relations were formed by the combination of these forces.

The study of labour relations in Cape wool farming has been conducted through an analysis of the production of the commodity wool, and through the composition of the labour force from a generational and gendered perspective. One farm in particular, Wellwood in Graaff-Reinet, has been used as an example to show how production and labour could be organized, but also the regional level has been analysed. Farm diaries have been the central material for the local level while mainly census material and select committee reports have been used to access the regional level. In order to focus on the production process and to frame the labour relations analytically in their larger context, a transnational perspective has been used. Wool was the largest rural commodity in the Cape and South Africa and was not intended for the domestic market, but for the British textile industry initially, and later also for other parts of the capitalist core, which means that the political economy of the Cape exceeded its geographical borders. A spatial and economic expansion of capital from core to periphery is the crucial context, in which wool farming in the Cape must be regarded.

It has been clear from previous research that grazing rights, cash wages and rations made up the remunerative practices in Cape wool farming during the period analysed, and that the ratio between them changed in favour of more cash wages and less grazing rights. However, the relationship between farmers, labourers and technology, thus the actual production, has not been analysed previously. Unlike for example Bundy, who suggests that shepherding decreased as fencing increased, this thesis shows that shepherding actually increased along with fencing. The role of shepherds only decreased after jackals could be kept out of farms and water supplies were adequate, which mainly happened after the 1920s.

Previous research has shown that male children and youths were often hired as shepherds and that farmers gained access to them through a pre-colonial and pre-capitalist generational division of labour. Male heads of black and coloured families were hired on farms and their sons were given herding duties. But this thesis shows that farmers increasingly exploited the generational division of labour and thereby changed it so that by the 1940s shepherding was almost exclusively an occupation for the young. But by then they were also about to be made redundant as the role of shepherding decreased.

Furthermore, the relationship between farmers, labourers and technology was more complex than what has previously been assumed. The disappearance of shepherds did not mean that production of wool was conducted without labour. Instead it gave rise to a new form of labourer, the camp walker. The camp walkers controlled the fences and were in that regard different from the shepherds, who controlled animals. While it is apparent that fenced camps were meant to make shepherds redundant, and finally also did so, the changed structure created by fencing, which improved the commodity on which to produce wool, also gave rise to new demands on labour. This indicates that capitalist production is a process in constant motion, which does not end when the structure has been changed in order to meet requirements for continued capital accumulation. On the contrary, capitalism *is* recurring structural transformations based on a demand for continued accumulation of capital and its outcome largely decided by the power relations between capital and labour and the impact of the surrounding environment.

An initial measure for capitalist farming in the periphery was the privatization of land. Without a commodified geographical area on which to produce, farmers could not accumulate capital. Hobsbawm argues the same for the Scottish case, which was the first colonization by British capital in order to find suppliers of wool.[666] The spatial expansion of capital thus transforms the land it expands into in order to facilitate accumulation of capital. The subsequent sale of wool from the Cape to Britain furthered the expansion of capital as the sale of wool enabled some farmers to turn money into capital, which was used in production. Fences and windmills were central forms of capital in wool farming. The implementation of these constituted the most crucial technological development in wool farming between 1860 and 1950.

Before fencing, wool farming was conducted on open farms where shepherds took the sheep to grazing during the day and to a sheltered place at night, a system known as trekking and kraaling. This system was detrimental to both the health of the sheep and the wool, and gave the Cape wool a bad reputation and thus a low value on the London wool market. Furthermore, it was detrimental to the land as the long treks over the farm contributed to soil erosion. In the 1870s, about fifty years after commercial wool farming began in the Cape, the land was too heavily exploited. The solution was to create fenced camps, where the sheep could graze on their own during the day and sleep during the night. This enabled farmers to practice rotational grazing, which meant that parts of the veld was given time to recover. Beinart Archer and van Sittert have described this process, but they have largely overlooked its theoretical implications. As profits and accumulation of capital was the aim of capitalist farmers, it is important to note that the incorporation of new areas into capitalist production meant that the land, which was means of production for the farmer, required investments in order to continue the accumulation of capital. Extensive farming on open pastures, where new grazing areas could be incorporated, did not require investments to the same extent, but when the spatial frontier of settlements for capitalist farming no longer could be expanded, the incorporated areas required improvement through new technology and a transformed production.

During the late nineteenth and early twentieth century fencing increased vastly in the Cape. Most of it came from the UK. Cape wool farmers and

---

666 Hobsbawm, E 1980.

English capital were involved in a "wool for wire trade", where the fences constituted another stage in the development and implementation of productive forces. The value of the fences sold to the Cape were only a fraction of what was paid for the wool, in 1890 the UK spent about £2 million on purchases of Cape wool, suggesting that the English made considerable losses from this trade. But the relationship illustrates well the transnational production of wool. The British domestic production of wool decreased steadily during the nineteenth century while production of finished textiles increased. British textile manufacturers relied more on colonial wool, where the Cape was one important supplier. Export of fences, which improved the quality of wool, thus further entrenched the core-periphery relations; it resulted in more and better wool from the colonial areas and made possible an increased production of finished textile products and profits in the core.

Expansion of capital is a spatial and economic process, and according to Luxemburg must continue in order for capital accumulation on a world scale to continue. But from the peripheral perspective, thus the area which it expands into, there is a limit to specific capital expansion. By 1911 fencing started to slow down in some of the largest wool producing districts such as Graaff-Reinet, Cradock, Middelburg and Somerset East. The farms were enclosed for the purpose of increasing capital accumulation. When this was done, fences were repaired and camps subdivided in new ways, but there was not much further spatial expansion in central wool farming districts. Thus, the land had been transformed according to the requirements of capital owners, but the changed structure did not mean that labour relations changed. There were more shepherds in 1911 than any previous census year, and each shepherd was responsible for fewer sheep, which was contrary to expectations. The reason for this was the prevalence of jackals and lack of sufficient water supplies. This meant that capital expansion in the form of jackal-proof fences and windmills continued.

Jackals as vermin followed in the wake of capitalist farming. They became a threat to farmers in the 1880s, as they killed sheep in increasing numbers. Previous research has emphasized the role of jackals as a reason for the continued use of shepherds. But rotational grazing also required water supplies in every camp. This had not been accomplished during the early twentieth century. On Wellwood there were for example six camps during the 1880s and 1890s, but no change in the number of shepherds compared to the 1870s, when the number of camps were few. Jackals did not pose threat on the farm at that time, and could not have been a reason for continued use of shepherds. The water supplies were, however, a problem. There was, for example, only one windmill on the farm until 1905, although there were quite a few dams. And the Rubidges even built new kraals in the 1880s. Old and new methods were thus combined during this time, which must be called a transitional phase.

Capital expansion is thus not a process with a determined outcome. The specific peripheral setting in the Cape, here exemplified by nature in the form of jackals and water supply, was highly influential for how wool farming was organized. Environmental aspects interacted with economic and social ones. While the land itself was a prerequisite for wool farming, and was favourable to wool farming as the sheep thrived, it also caused problems and lowered the profitability when droughts struck and when jackals killed sheep. Intensified capitalist farming and implementation of fences, which changed the land, clearly created new problems, which forced farmers to find new ways to continue to accumulate capital.

The ordinary wire fences could not keep jackals out. Instead, jackal-proof fences, i. e. netting fences were required. These were used in the Cape during the late nineteenth century, but they were rare. Netting fences were not included in the 1912 Fencing Act, which aimed at subsidizing joint purchases of fencing material by farmers. Only in 1922 were they included in the Fencing Act, and they spread after that. The netting fences were imported from the early twentieth century, almost all of it from the UK during the first decades of the twentieth century. The core-periphery relations were thus once again important for the improvement of Cape wool farming. Although much of the land was fenced up in 1911, the expansion of fences continued. Due to the jackals, farmers were forced to fence their farms twice, first with wire, then with netting. While jackals caused problems for farmers, they were clearly profitable for manufacturers of fences.

The netting fences enabled farmers to manage without shepherds. This was seen on Wellwood. Netting fences were implemented there as early as 1895, but primarily after 1912. Water supplies had also been improved during the first decade of the twentieth century. Consequently, in 1914 there were only two shepherds left, which was the number also in 1918. Wellwood was enclosed with netting in 1920 and the same year the last jackal for 26 years was shot on the farm. During most of the 1920s there was only one shepherd on the farm, Adrijan Reid, who left in 1927 instead of being under the "direct control" of Sidney Rubidge as a labourer. After that no shepherd was hired. The same development was also seen elsewhere. Between 1911 and 1946 the number of shepherds in the Cape decreased from 42,582 to 23,624. More importantly, however, each shepherd herded more sheep; in 1946 each shepherd was responsible for 855 sheep compared to 402 in 1911. Netting fences and windmills obviously meant that farming could be conducted without shepherds. Capital expansion in that regard meant that organization of production changed. As a result, the demand on labour in the form of shepherds decreased.

But capital expansion is not a process that allows all to accumulate capital. The shepherds only disappeared on those farms where farmers had implemented jackal-proof fencing and water supplies in each camp. Those farmers who had not invested in these implements were still forced to hire shepherds and had to exploit them harder in order to compete with the farmers who used fences and windmills. The number of shepherds in the country actually increased between 1911 and 1936, which was mainly a result of intensified wool farming outside of the Cape. In 1927 there were 3,983 farms in the Cape that were fenced with jackal-proof fences compared to only 279 in the rest of the country.

Already from the start, farmers exploited pre-colonial and pre-capitalist relations in order to acquire labour. Thus, capitalism takes labour as it finds it.[667] Whole families were hired, and a generational and gendered division of labour was incorporated into capitalist farming. Young males were given shepherding duties; females of all ages were responsible for reproduction through cultivation of for example mealies and through domestic work in the family household. Women were, however, also hired by farmers, both as domestics and as labourers, but the hired labour force on farms such as Wellwood was predominantly male from the 1870s to 1950. While fathers and sons were hired together as shepherds, the sons conducted much of the actual herding. However, those pre-capitalist relations that were useful in accumulating capital were not only exploited, they were increasingly exploited among those farmers who did not change production. In 1904 about 45 per cent of the shepherds were under 20 years old. In 1946 about 87 per cent were younger than 20. Fathers and sons were thus not at all working together as shepherds in the 1940s. The exploitation of the labour force through the generational division of labour thus increased. The reason for this was the disappearance of young adult males to the mines. As the young adults left, farmers called upon younger family members instead to herd the sheep. The children could be paid lower wages than adults, which meant that farmers could hire more shepherds.

The increased use of young shepherds reflects the tendency of increasing numbers of children involved in peripheral capitalist production during the twentieth century, which has occurred at the same time as children of the working classes in core areas have become unemployed.[668] As seen in Cape wool farming, this was not because farmers wanted children per se, they wanted cheap labour, which was found among young family members of male heads of families. But when capital accumulation could be furthered through other means, thus from a changed production, also the young shepherds were discarded. But that does not mean that there was no place for them in production. Some of the shepherds were transformed into farm labourers; the number of young people in that group increased between 1911 and 1946. Even

---

[667] Marx, K 1990, p. 291.

[668] See Olsson, L 1980, p. 9. (Mendelievich)

on Wellwood, where there were no shepherds after 1927, there were at least two youngsters hired during the 1920s and early 1930s and probably later as well. The development and implementation of productive forces did thus not mean that children were redundant in production, as there was a demand for them, and a supply of them.

The decreased number of shepherds meant that there was a quantitative change in labour relations. But there was also a qualitative change, as the shepherds were replaced with camp walkers. Camp walkers were hired from at least 1914 when a man called Jacob was hired on Wellwood to "walk the fences every day". After that camp walkers, or boundary riders as they were also called, were hired continuously on Wellwood. The camp walkers were different than shepherds. While shepherds controlled the health, grazing of sheep, the camp walkers controlled technology in the form of fences. The skills of shepherds, which had been learned through a generational division of labour, were no longer required. Thereby, the labour force partly lost influence over the production process. But also farmers lost control over production. When sheep were herded and kraaled they were counted often and the labour of the shepherd regularly controlled. But when they grazed on their own in camps, the labour of the camp walker was barely supervised. Sidney Rubidge entrusted the camp walkers with controlling the fences and did not do it himself. When jackals once again appeared on the farm in 1946 he blamed the camp walkers for not doing their job properly. As camp walking was a new position, there was confusion over how it should be done. Nonetheless, camp walking was a crucial work operation, which was necessary in order to farm with fenced camps. Capital expansion into new geographical areas and incorporation of pre-capitalist relations thus not only subordinates labour, it changes it as new organization of production creates new demands on labour.

The expansion of capital meant capitalist production of wool, but not necessarily in the sense that labourers were proletarians. Grazing rights were an important part of remuneration long into the twentieth century. The reason was that farmers could not pay much cash wages, and did not want to, but also that labourers wanted animals for *lobola*. These relations changed along with production. Several researchers have noted that grazing rights decreased during the first half of the twentieth century, but not analysed how it happened, which is important as it illustrates how a changed production affects labour. Unlike Morris, who argues that decreasing grazing rights was a way for farmers to exploit the labour force more intensively, this thesis shows that in wool farming this was not the case. On Wellwood the grazing rights were a central feature of remunerations until the 1920s and even later. But from at least 1914 the stock belonging to the labourers was herded in the mountain camp, while the sheep of Rubidges grazed on their own in fenced camps. The introduction of camp walkers, who were paid higher cash wages, also affected grazing rights.

Hermaans, the camp walker who arrived in 1918, was forced to reduce his stock, and the ones he kept were sent to grazing in the "outside veld". As long as farmers relied on shepherds and did not have fenced camps, the animals of labourer and farmers were to a great extent herded together. To have stock of his own in the flock he herded even served as an incentive for the shepherd to take good care of it. But intensified use of the land for wool farming resulted in a separation where the sheep belonging to farmers, i.e. those that produced the commodity of wool for British and other textile manufacturers, were given the best grazing land and the best conditions. Enclosing of land meant the power for the farmer to separate the stock that was not useful in accumulating capital from those that were. During the 1920s and 1930s the stock belonging to labourers were reduced, but with the exception of donkeys that could be used for scraaper work. Those animals that were useful in accumulation of capital were thus still allowed, and the donkeys even increased until they were replaced by tractors in the 1940s.

The issue of grazing rights was related to the limited area of land available to black peasants, especially after the 1913 *Natives Land Act* and the 1936 *Native Trust and Land Act*, which limited their possibilities of finding grazing. This contributed to farmers' possibilities of limiting grazing on farms. As grazing rights diminished, cash and rations became the primary forms of remuneration. Rations decreased during the late 1920s and early 1930s, but may have increased during the 1940s. During the 1920s the cultivated area on Wellwood was reduced. Instead, food was transported to the farm by a railway bus. Droughts during the 1920s may have been a reason for the decrease in cultivation. Instead, the farm was more focused on sheep and production of wool.

Unlike other rural sectors in South Africa, there was not a clear transition from pre-capitalist to capitalist relations regarding production and labour in wool farming. Surely, the grazing rights were a form of tenancy, but labour was a commodity already during the mid-nineteenth century and production was already from the start aimed at the British market. Relations became more capitalist, however, as capital expanded. From this we can conclude that labour relations in peripheral production are not so much evolving from one stage to another, i.e. from pre-capitalist to capitalist, as they are increasingly capitalist along with an expansion of capital.

Farmers in the Cape belonged to a class of peripheral capital owners. They exploited labour on their farms, but were also dependent on selling their wool to manufacturers in Britain and elsewhere. Exploitation of the periphery by the core was consequently only one form of exploitation in transnational wool production. In fact, there was exploitation at every stage in the commodity chain of wool where value was added. Wool washing was the primary example of a process, which added value to the wool before exporting it, but the wool washing industry disappeared from the Cape during the early twentieth century. Other processes of adding value to the wool, such as shearing, sorting and baling the wool properly, could be done on the farm, however. Farmers like the Rubidges invested in shearing sheds and wool presses for proper handling of the wool, which surely contributed to a good reputation as producers of wool of good quality and thereby increased the price on their wool. While improving the commodity of wool was one way for peripheral farmers to enhance their position in relation to capital in the core, another way was to organize. During the 1930s farmers in South Africa, Australia and New Zealand joined forces to improve the position of wool farmers in all the three dominions. The wool farmers were still peripheral in relation to manufacturers in the core, but the relations were not static.

Wool farmers, and farmers in general, were also aided by the state. Through fencing and water subsidies, but also through privatization of land and legislation aimed at dispossessing the black peasantry, the state contributed to capital accumulation by farmers. The state was also instrumental through the construction of railways, and from c. 1930 a railway bus, which serviced the farms by transporting food for labourers, fodder for animals, fencing material etc. The long distance from farm to town, and further on to ports and wool markets in Britain and other core areas, was thereby shortened. Railways and the state provided a solid structure for capitalist relations throughout the rural areas. The importance of the railway for the capitalist expansion in South Africa has been largely neglected by historians, and it is a subject worthy of further research.

The international division of labour within the wool commodity chain was initially an imperial division of labour. Almost all the wool from the colonies was sent to the British textile industry. However, the position of the British was diminished during the twentieth century as the core of capitalist textile production increased. Textile manufacturers in countries like Germany, the US and Japan started to challenge British interests and purchased increasing amounts of South African wool. Capitalism based on transnational production was then more important for wool farmers than imperial relations. During the Second World War the British managed to purchase all the South African wool, though, which was more due to political rather than economic power.

Capitalism in peripheral areas thus differs from capitalism in core areas. We can say that the expansion of capital was quicker than the expansion of capitalism as a structure or that capital expansion precedes capitalist expansion. Without capital, there can be no capitalist production. Still, expansion and accumulation of capital did not lead to cash wage labour, as if that was the goal of history, at least of capitalism. For farmers it was much more profitable to rely on rations and grazing rights. In fact, the reliance on other forms of remuneration than cash enabled many farmers to invest in their farms. In general there was flexibility in the remunerative system. To some extent it favoured labourers, who could be paid in cattle if they wanted to, but most of all it seems to have favoured farmers, who could change remuneration when this was required, for example during the Depression when profits were low or other expenses higher. But labourers were clearly in a process of proletarianization, just as farmers were in the opposite, but connected, process of accumulation and capitalization. More precisely then, capitalist production in those peripheral areas that produced wool was different from capitalist production in those areas where the wool was turned into finished commodities. Production in the periphery did not generate as much profits as production in the core. We identified at least eleven stages of production in the wool commodity chain: shepherding (later camp walking), shearing, sorting, baling, transport from farm to ports, transport to overseas markets, transport to factories, washing, spinning, weaving and production of finished textile products. These are important to consider since the accumulation of capital through the commodity chain is based on the finished product. Finished products contain the most labour, and thereby the most value. Preceding steps in the chain contribute with less value, and labourers in those stages receive very little of the overall profits.

But it is crucial to regard the labour relations and remunerative practices in both periphery and core as results of historic processes based on capital accumulation on a world scale and impact of local forces, not as static categories. Labour relations in Cape wool farming changed constantly and gradually as capitalist relations of production were established in response to demands on wool quality, competition over labour from mining and threats from nature in the form of jackals and droughts. Initially, families were incorporated into capitalist production. Enclosing of land ultimately reduced the demand for shepherds, but created a demand for camp walkers. At the same time farmers withdrew access to land in the form of grazing rights for labourers and family relations were more intensively exploited among those farmers who lacked capital. We can thus conclude that expansion of capital means that pre-capitalist relations are both intensified and discarded at the same time, as there are only two ways of profiting and accumulating capital in farming; either to change production and labour through use of technology or to exploit land and labour more intensively. Thus, capital expansion changes the structure for capital accumulation, in which labour relations are formed. Power relations between capital and labour, and the impact of the environment, subsequently decide how they are formed in the specific, peripheral setting.

Sources and Literature

Sources

Unpublished sources

Wellwood farm, Graaff-Reinet
Rubidge diaries, 1874 to 1950.

Rubidge accounts, 1875 – 1879, 1885 – 1886, 1907, 1924 – 1933, 1943 – 1948.

Cory Library, Grahamstown (CL)
Old Extracts from Old Wellwood. MS 6189.

Van Niekerk diaries, Bedford. PR 3418.

Halse farm diaries. Sterkstroom. MS 17507, MS 17508.

National Library, Cape Town (NL)
Charles Rubidge Collection, MSB 406.

Western Cape Provincial Archives and Records Service, Cape Town (CA)
Magistrate Carnarvon. Proceedings of Court Cases 1/CAR 1/1/1/2; 1/CAR 1/1/1/7; 1/CAR 1/1/1/8.

Magistrate Graaff-Reinet. Proceedings of Court Cases 1/GR 2/95 Part I; 1/GR 2/132 Part II; 1/GR 2/103 Part I; 1/GR 2/147.

Published sources

Censuses and statistics

Cape of Good Hope. *Census of the Colony of the Cape of Good Hope, 1865*. G. 20-1866.

Cape of Good Hope. *Colony of the Cape of Good Hope Census, 1875*. G. 42-1876.

Cape of Good Hope. *Census of the Colony of the Cape of Good Hope, 1891*. G. 6-1892.

Cape of Good Hope. *Census of the Colony of the Cape of Good Hope, 1904*. G. 19-1905.

Union of South Africa. *Census of the Union of South Africa 1911. Report and Annexures*. U.G. 32-1912.

Union of South Africa. *Sixth Census of the Population of the Union of South Africa, 1936*.
Vol. I. Population. Sex and Geographical Distribution of the Population. U.G. 21-1938.
Vol. IX Natives (Bantu) and other Non-European Races. U.G. 12-1942.

Union of South Africa. *Population Census 1946. Vol. I, Geographical Distribution of the Population of the Union of South Africa*. U.G. 51-1949;*Vol. V, Occupation and Industries of the European, Asiatic, Coloured and Native Population*. U.G. 41-1954.

Union of South Africa, *Report on Agricultural and Pastoral Production*:
Agricultural census 1918, U.G. 53-1919.

Agricultural census 1924-25. No. 8.

Agricultural census 1925-26, No. 9. U.G. 24-1928.

Agricultural census 1926-27, No. 10. U.G. 37-1928.

Agricultural census 1929-30, No. 13. U.G. 12-1932.

Agricultural census 1935-36. No. 16.

Agricultural census 1936-37, No. 17. U.G. 18-1939.

Agricultural census 1938-39, No. 19. U.G. 27-1941.

Agricultural census 1945-46, No. 20. U.G. 77-1948.

Agricultural census 1946-47, No. 21. U.G. 57-1949

Cape of Good Hope. *Statistical Register of the Colony of the Cape of Good Hope*. 1886, 1890, 1895, 1896, 1900, 1905, 1909.

Union of South Africa. Department of Customs and Excise, *Annual Statement on Trade and Shipping*. 1910, 1912, 1914, 1916, 1918, 1920, 1923, 1925, 1927, 1930, 1932, 1934, 1935, 1937, 1939, 1941, 1945, 1947-48-49, 1950.

Select Committees and Commissions

Cape of Good Hope. *Proceedings of, and Evidence taken by, the Commission on Native Affairs*. Grahamstown 1865.

Cape of Good Hope. *Report of the Select Committee on Fences Bill 1872*. A. 18-1872.

Cape of Good Hope. *Report of the Select Committee appointed to consider and report on the Supply of the Labour Market, 1879*. A. 26-1879.

Cape of Good Hope. *Report of the Select Committee on Fencing or Enclosing of Lands 1889*. A. 10-1889.

Cape of Good Hope. *Report of the Select Committee on the Labour Question 1890*. A. 12-1890.

Cape of Good Hope. *Report of the Select Committee on Farm Labour Supply, 1907*. C. 2-1907.

Cape of Good Hope. *Department of Native Affairs. Blue Book on Native Affairs 1909*. G. 28-1910.

Union of South Africa. *Report of the Natives Land Commission. Volume II. 1916*. U. G. 22-1916.

Union of South Africa. *Final Report of the Drought Investigation Commission 1923*. U. G. 49-1923.

Union of South Africa. *First and Second Reports of the Select Committee on the Suppression of Stock Thefts 1923*. S. C. 4-1923.

Union of South Africa, Province of the Cape of Good Hope. *First and Second Reports of the Vermin Extermination Commission 1924*. C. P. 3-1924.

Grosskopf, J. F. W., *Rural Impoverishment and Rural Exodus*. Report of the Carnegie Commission, Part I. Stellenbosch 1932.

Union of South Africa. *Native Farm Labour Committee 1937 – 1939*. Pretoria 1939. G.P. – S.9523 – 1940 – 400.

Union of South Africa. *Statutes of the Union of South Africa, 1911 – 1961*. Children's Protection Act 1913.

Journals

Agricultural Journal of the Cape of Good Hope. 1905, Vol. XXVII; 1910, Vol XXXVII.

Journal of the Department of Agriculture. 1920, vol I; 1925.

Farmers' Weekly. 1917, 1927 1937, 1947.

Die Wolboer. 1947, 1950, 1951.

Books

Mallinson, Charles. *Sheep and Wool in South Africa and Their Relation to Industrial Development*. Industries Bulletin Series No. 23. Pretoria, 1919.

Mallinson, Charles. *The Merino in South Africa*. Sydney 1915.

McKee, W. M. *South African Sheep and Wool.* Cape Town 1913.

Noble, John, *A Descriptive Handbook of the Cape Colony. Its Condition and Resources*, Cape Town 1875.

Photographs

Wellwood, Graaff-Reinet. CA AG. 9448 (with permission).
Shepherd's hut. CA Jeffrey's Collection J1651 (with permission).
Sheep shearing. CA Jeffrey's Collection J1342 (with permission).

Literature

Archer, Sean, "Technology and Ecology in the Karroo. A Century of Windmills, Wire and Changing Farming Practice", *Journal of Southern African Studies*, 26:4, 2000, pp. 675-696.

Beinart, William, *The Rise of Conservation in South Africa. Settlers, Livestock, and the Environment 1770 – 1950*, Oxford 2008 (2003).

Beinart, William, "Academic Amnesia and the Poverty of Polemics", *Journal of African History*, 46:1, 2005, pp. 127-134.

Beinart, William, *Twentieth-Century South Africa*, Oxford 2001 (1994)

Beinart, William, "Transkeian Migrant Workers and Youth Labour on the Natal Sugar Estates 1918 – 1948", *Journal of African History*, 32:1, 1991. pp. 41-63.

Beinart, William, Delius, Peter and Trapido, Stanley, (eds.) *Putting a Plough to the Ground. Accumulation and Dispossession in Rural South Africa 1850 – 1930*, Braamfontein 1986.

Bouch, Richard, "Eastern Cape Wool Farmers. Production and Control in Cathcart", in Alan Jeeves and Jonathan Crush (eds.) *White Farms, Black Labour. The State and Agrarian Change in Southern Africa, 1910 – 50*, Pietermaritzburg 1997.

Bundy, Colin, "Vagabond Hollanders and Runaway Englishmen", in William Beinart, Peter Delius and Stanley Trapido (eds.) *Putting a Plough to the Ground. Accumulation and Dispossession in Rural South Africa 1850 – 1930*, Braamfontein 1986.

Bundy, Colin, *The Rise and Fall of the South African Peasantry*, London 1979.

Collett, Joan, *A Time to Plant. Biography of James Lynford Collett, Settler*, Cape Town 1990.

Crais, Clifton C, *White Supremacy and Black Resistance in Pre-Industrial South Africa. The Making of the Colonial Order in the Eastern Cape, 1770 – 1865*, Cambridge 1992.

Chirwa, Wiseman Chijere, "Child and Youth Labour on the Nyasaland Plantations, 1890 – 1953", *Journal of Southern African Studies*, 19:4, 1993. pp. 662-680.

De Jongh, Michael, "No Fixed Abode. The Poorest of the Poor and Elusive Identities in Rural South Africa", *Journal of Southern African Studies*, 28:2, 2002, pp. 441-460.

Denoon, Donald, *Settler Capitalism. The Dynamics of Dependent Development in the Southern Hemisphere*, Oxford 1983.

Dubow, Saul, *Land, Labour and Merchant Capital in the Pre-Industrial Rural Economy of the Cape. The Experience of the Graaff-Reinet District (1852 – 72)*, Centre for African Studies, University of Cape Town 1982.

Engels, Friedrich, *The Condition of the Working Class in England*, London 2009 (1845).

Engren, Jimmy, *Railroading and Labor Migration. Class and Ethnicity in Expanding Capitalism in Northern Minnesota, the 1880s to the mid 1920s*, Växjö 2007.

Garson, N. G., "South Africa and World War I", in Norman Hilmer and Philip Wigley (eds.), *The First British Commonwealth. Essays in Honour of Nicholas Mansergh*, London 1980.

Giliomee, Hermann, *The Afrikaners. Biography of a People*, London 2011 (2003).

Grier, Beverly Carolease,. *Invisible Hands. Child Labor and the State in Colonial Zimbabwe*, Portsmouth, NH 2006.

Grier, Beverly Carolease, "Invisible Hands. The Political Economy of Child Labor in Colonial Zimbabwe, 1890 – 1930," *Journal of Southern African Studies*, 20:1, 1994.

Guy, Jeff, "'No Eyes, No Interest, No Frame of Reference'. Rosa Luxemburg, Southern African Historiography, and Pre-Capitalist Modes of Production", in Patrick Bond, Horman Chitonge & Arndt Hopfman (eds.) *The Accumulation of Capital in Southern Africa: Rosa Luxemburg's Contemporary Relevance*, Rosa Luxemburg Foundation, Johannesburg & Centre for Civil Society, University of KwaZulu-Natal. 2007.

Guy, Jeff, "Analysing Pre-Capitalist Societies in Southern Africa", *Journal of Southern African Studies*, 14:1, 1987, pp. 18-37.

Hanekom, A. J., *The Wool Industry in South Africa*. South African Wool Board. Johannesburg 1960.

Hansson, Lars, *Slakt i takt. Klassformering vid de bondekooperativa slakteriindustierna i Skåne 1908 – 1946*, Växjö 2004.

Harvey, David, *Spaces of Global Capitalism. Towards a Theory of Uneven Geographical Development*, London 2006.

Hobsbawm, Eric J., *The Age of Empire, 1875 – 1914*, London 1994 (1987).

Hobsbawm, Eric, J., "Scottish Reformers of the Eighteenth Century and Capitalist Agriculture", in E. J. Hobsbawm et al (eds.), *Peasants in History. Essays in Honour of Daniel Thorner*, Calcutta 1980.

Hobsbawm, Eric J., *The Age of Capital, 1848 – 1875*, London 1975.

Hobsbawm, Eric J., "From Social History to the History of Society", *Daedalus*, 100:1, 1971, pp. 20-45.

Hopkins, Terence and Wallerstein, Immanuel, "Commodity chains. Construct and research", Gary Gereffi, and Miguel Korzeniewicz (eds.) *Commodity Chains and Global Capitalism*, Westport 1994.

Hopkins, Terence and Wallerstein, Immanuel, *World-Systems Analysis. Theory and Methodology*, Beverly Hills 1982.

Houghton, D. Hobart and Dagut, Jenifer, *Source Material on the South African Economy: 1860 – 1970. Volume 1, 1860 – 1899*, London 1972.

Hunter, Monica, *Reaction to Conquest. Effects of Contact with Europeans on the Pondo of South Africa*, London 1936.

Jenkins, D. T. and Ponting, K. G., *The British Wool Textile Industry 1770 – 1914*, London 1982.

Keegan, Timothy J., *Colonial South Africa and the Origins of the Racial Order*, London 1996.

Keegan, Timothy J., *Rural Transformations in Industrializing South Africa. The Southern Highveld to 1914*, Basingstoke 1987.

Kirk, Tony, "The Cape Economy and the Expropriation of the Kat River Settlement, 1846 – 53", in Shula Marks and Anthony Atmore (eds.) *Economy and Society in Pre-Industrial South Africa*, London 1980.

Levine, Susan, "Mapping Children's Work in South African History", in Hugh D. Hindman (ed.) *The World of Child Labor. An Historical and Regional Survey*, New York 2009.

Lilja, Fredrik, "Child and Youth Labour in Eastern Cape agriculture. Wool Farming and Changing Labour Relations, c. 1900-1960", *Barn*, No. 3-4, 2009, pp. 53-71.

Lindegren, Jan, *Varat, staten och diket. Tre historieteoretiska uppsatser*, Uppsala 1988.

Luxemburg, Rosa, *The Accumulation of Capital*, Cornwall 2003 (1913).

Mabin, Alan, *The Making of Colonial Capitalism. Intensification and Expansion in the Economic Geography of the Cape Colony*, Unpublished PhD thesis, Simon Fraser University 1984.

Magubane, Bernard, "The Evolution of the Class Structure in Africa", in Peter Gutkind and Immanuel Wallerstein (eds.) *Political Economy of Contemporary Africa*, Second Edition. Beverly Hills 1985.

Marx, Karl, *Capital. A Critique of Political Economy. Volume I*, London 1990 (1976, 1867).

McMichael, Philip, *Settlers and the Agrarian Question. Foundations of Capitalism in Australia.* Cambridge 1984.

Morris, Mike, "The Development of Capitalism in South African Agriculture. Class Struggle in the Countryside", *Economy and Society*, 5:3, 1976, pp. 292-343.

Morris, Mike, "Social History and the Transition to Capitalism in the South African Countryside", *Review of African Political Economy*, No. 41, 1988, pp. 60-72.

Olsson, Lars, "Landlords, Land Companies, Farmers, and Migrant Workers in Global Agrarian Capitalism Until the First World War", *Przeglad Polonijny*, 31:1, 2005, pp. 67-86.

Olsson, Lars, *Då barn var lönsamma. Om arbetsdelning, barnarbete och teknologiska förändringar i några svenska industrier under 1800 – och början av 1900 – talet*, (*When Children were Profitable. On Division of Labour, Child Labour and Technological Change within some Swedish Industries during the 19th and the beginning of the 20th Century)*, Stockholm 1980.

Rahikainen, Marjatta, *Centuries of Child Labor. European Experiences from the Seventeenth to the Twentieth Century*, Aldershot 2004.

Ross, Robert, *A Concise History of South Africa*, Cambridge 1999.

Ross, Robert, "The Origins of Capitalist Agriculture in the Cape Colony. A Survey", in William Beinart, Peter Delius and Stanley Trapido (eds.) *Putting a Plough to the Ground. Accumulation and Dispossession in Rural South Africa 1850 – 1930*, Braamfontein 1986.

Smith, Kenneth Wyndham, *From Frontier to Midlands. A History of the Graaff-Reinet District, 1786 – 1910*, Grahamstown 1976.

Van der Linden, Marcel, *Workers of the World. Essays Towards a Global Labor History*, Leiden 2008.

Van der Linden, Marcel, "The 'Globalization' of Labor and Working-Class History and its Consequences", *International Labor and Working-Class History*, No 65, 2004, pp. 136-156.

Van Onselen, Charles, *The Seed is Mine. The Life of Kas Maine. A South African Sharecropper 1894 – 1985*, Cape Town 1997 (1996).

Van Sittert, Lance, "Reply" to "Academic Amnesia and the Poverty of Polemics", *Journal of Southern African History*, 46:1, 2005, pp. 135-137.

Van Sittert, Lance, "The Nature of Power. Cape Environmental History, the History of Ideas and Neoliberal Historiography", *Journal of African History*, 45:2, 2004, pp. 305-313.

Van Sittert, Lance, "Holding the Line. The Rural Enclosure Movement in the Cape Colony, c. 1865 – 1910", *Journal of African History*, 43:1, 2002, pp. 95-118.

Wallerstein, Immanuel, *The Capitalist World-Economy. Essays.* Cambridge 1979.

Wilson, Francis, Kooy, Alide and Hendrie, Delia (eds.) *Farm Labour in South Africa*, Cape Town 1977.

Wilson, Francis, "Farming, 1866 to 1966", in Monica Wilson and Leonard Thompson (eds.) *The Oxford History of South Africa, 1870 – 1966*, (vol. II), Oxford 1971.

Internet references

Cooper's dip: www.dacorumheritage.org.uk/coopers.htm (2012-11-26).

List of tables and maps

Tables

Maps

Acta Universitatis Upsaliensis
STUDIA HISTORICA UPSALIENSIA

Department of History, University of Uppsala,
Thunbergsvägen 3A, SE-751 26 Uppsala, Sweden

1. *Gustaf Jonasson:* Karl XII och hans rådgivare. Den utrikespolitiska maktkampen i Sverige 1697–1702. 1960.
2. *Sven Lundkvist:* Gustav Vasa och Europa. Svensk handels- och utrikespolitik 1534–1557. 1960.
3. *Tage Linder:* Biskop Olof Wallquists politiska verksamhet till och med riksdagen 1789. 1960.
4. *Carl Göran Andræ:* Kyrka och frälse i Sverige under äldre medeltid. 1960.
5. *Bengt Henningsson:* Geijer som historiker. 1961.
6. *Nils Runeby:* Monarchia mixta. Maktfördelningsdebatt i Sverige under den tidigare stormaktstiden. 1962.
7. *Åke Hermansson:* Karl IX och ständerna. Tronfrågan och författningsutvecklingen 1598–1611. 1962.
8. Hundra års historisk diskussion. Historiska föreningen i Upsala 1862–1962. 1962.
9. *Sten Carlsson:* Byråkrati och borgarstånd under frihetstiden. 1963.
10. *Gunnar Christie Wasberg:* Forsvarstanke og suverenitetsprinsipp. Kretsen om Aftenposten i den unionspolitiske debatt 1890–mars 1905. 1963.
11. *Kurt Ågren:* Adelns bönder och kronans. Skatter och besvär i Uppland 1650–1680. 1964.
12. *Michael Nordberg:* Les ducs et la royauté. Etudes sur la rivalité des ducs d'Orléans et de Bourgogne 1392–1407. 1964.
13. *Stig Hadenius:* Fosterländsk unionspolitik. Majoritetspartiet, regeringen och unionsfrågan 1888–1899. 1964.
14. *Stellan Dahlgren:* Karl X Gustav och reduktionen. 1964.
15. *Rolf Torstendahl:* Källkritik och vetenskapssyn i svensk historisk forskning 1820–1920. 1964.
16. *Stefan Björklund:* Oppositionen vid 1823 års riksdag. Jordbrukskris och borgerlig liberalism. 1964.
17. *Håkan Berggren & Göran B. Nilsson:* Liberal socialpolitik 1853–1884. Två studier. 1965.
18. *Torsten Burgman:* Svensk opinion och diplomati under rysk-japanska kriget 1904–1905. 1965.
19. *Erik Wärenstam:* Sveriges Nationella Ungdomsförbund och högern 1928–1934. 1965.
20. *Torgny Nevéus:* Ett betryggande försvar. Värnplikten och arméorganisationen i svensk politik 1880–1885. 1965.
21. *Staffan Runestam:* Förstakammarhögern och rösträttsfrågan 1900–1907. 1966.
22. *Stig Ekman:* Slutstriden om representationsreformen. 1966.
23. *Gunnar Herrström:* 1927 års skolreform. En Studie i svensk skolpolitik 1918–1927. 1966.
24. *Sune Åkerman:* Skattereformen 1810. Ett experiment med progressiv inkomstskatt. 1967.
25. *Göran B. Nilsson:* Självstyrelsens problematik. Undersökningar i svensk landstingshistoria 1839–1928. 1967.
26. *Klaus-Richard Böhme:* Bremisch-verdische Staatsfinanzen 1645–1676. Die schwedische Krone als deutsche Landesherrin. 1967.
27. *Gustaf Jonasson:* Karl XII:s polska politik 1702–1703. 1968.
28. *Hans Landberg:* Statsfinans och kungamakt. Karl X Gustav inför polska kriget. 1969.
29. *Rolf Torstendahl:* Mellan nykonservatism och liberalism. Idébrytningar inom högern och bondepartierna 1918–1934. 1969.
30. *Nils Runeby:* Den nya världen och den gamla. Amerikabild och emigrationsuppfattning i Sverige 1820–1860. 1969.
31. *Fred Nilsson:* Emigrationen från Stockholm till Nordamerika 1880–1893. En studie i urban utvandring. 1970.
32. *Curt Johanson:* Lantarbetarna i Uppland 1918–1930. En studie i facklig taktik och organisation. 1970.
33. *Arndt Öberg:* De yngre mössorna och deras utländska bundsförvanter 1765–1769. Med särskild hänsyn till de kommersiella och politiska förbindelserna med Storbritannien, Danmark och Preussen. 1970.
34. *Torgny Börjeson:* Metall 20 – Fackföreningen och människan. 1971.
35. *Harald Runblom:* Svenska företag i Latinamerika. Etableringsmönster och förhandlingstaktik 1900–1940. 1971.
36. *Hans Landberg, Lars Ekholm, Roland Nordlund & Sven A. Nilsson:* Det kontinentala krigets ekonomi. Studier i krigsfinansiering under svensk stormaktstid. 1971.
37. *Sture Lindmark:* Swedish America 1914–1932. Studies in Ethnicity with Emphasis on Illinois and Minnesota. 1971.
38. *Ulf Beijbom:* Swedes in Chicago. A Demographic and Social Study of the 1846–1880 Immigration. 1971.
39. *Staffan Smedberg:* Frälsebonderörelser i Halland och Skåne 1772–76. 1972.
40. *Björn Rondahl:* Emigration, folkomflyttning och säsongarbete i ett sågverksdistrikt i södra Hälsingland 1865–1910. Söderala kommun med särskild hänsyn till Ljusne industrisamhälle. 1972.
41. *Ann-Sofie Kälvemark:* Reaktionen mot utvandringen. Emigrationsfrågan i svensk debatt och politik 1901–1904. 1972.
42. *Lars-Göran Tedebrand:* Västernorrland och Nordamerika 1875–1913. Utvandring och återinvandring. 1972.
43. *Ann-Marie Petersson:* Nyköping under frihetstiden. Borgare och byråkrater i den lokala politiken. 1972.
44. *Göran Andolf:* Historien på gymnasiet. Undervisning och läroböcker 1820–1965. 1972.
45. *Jan Sundin:* Främmande studenter vid Uppsala universitet före andra väldskriget. En studie i studentmigration. 1973.
46. *Christer Öhman:* Nyköping och hertigdömet 1568–1622. 1973. (Ej i bokhandeln)

47. *Sune Åkerman, Ingrid Eriksson, David Gaunt, Anders Norberg, John Rogers & Kurt Ågren:* Aristocrats, Farmers and Proletarians. Essays in Swedish Demographic History. 1973.
48. *Uno Westerlund:* Borgarsamhällets upplösning och självstyrelsens utveckling i Nyköping 1810–1880. 1973. (Ej i bokhandeln)
49. *Sven Hedenskog:* Folkrörelserna i Nyköping 1880–1915. Uppkomst, social struktur och politisk aktivitet. 1973. (Ej i bokhandeln)
50. *Berit Brattne:* Bröderna Larsson. En studie i svensk emigrantagentverksamhet under 1880-talet. 1973.
51. *Anders Kullberg:* Johan Gabriel Stenbock och reduktionen. Godspolitik och ekonomiförvaltning 1675–1705. 1973.
52. *Gunilla Ingmar:* Monopol på nyheter. Ekonomiska och politiska aspekter på svenska och internationella nyhetsbyråers verksamhet. 1870–1919. 1973.
53. *Sven Lundkvist:* Politik, nykterhet och reformer. En studie i folkrörelsernas politiska verksamhet 1900– 1920. 1974.
54. *Kari Tarkiainen:* "Vår gamble Arffiende Ryssen". Synen på Ryssland i Sverige 1595–1621 och andra studier kring den svenska Rysslandsbilden från tidigare stormaktstid. 1974.
55. *Bo Öhngren:* Folk i rörelse. Samhällsutveckling, flyttningsmönster och folkrörelser i Eskilstuna 1870–1900. 1974.
56. *Lars Ekholm:* Svensk krigsfinansiering 1630–1631. 1974.
57. *Roland Nordlund:* Krig på avveckling. Sverige och tyska kriget 1633. 1974.
58. *Clara Nevéus:* Trälarna i landskapslagarnas samhälle. Danmark och Sverige. 1974.
59. *Bertil Johansson:* Social differentiering och kommunalpolitik. Enköping 1863–1919. 1974.
60. *Jan Lindroth:* Idrottens väg till folkrörelse. Studier i svensk idrottsrörelse till 1915. 1974.
61. *Richard B. Lucas:* Charles August Lindbergh, Sr. A Case Study of Congressional Insurgency, 1906–1912. 1974.
62. *Hans Norman:* Från Bergslagen till Nordamerika. Studier i migrationsmönster, social rörlighet och demografisk struktur med utgångspunkt från Örebro län 1851–1915. 1974.
63. *David Gaunt:* Utbildning till statens tjänst. En kollektivbiografi av stormaktstidens hovrättsauskultanter. 1975.
64. *Eibert Ernby:* Adeln och bondejorden. En studie rörande skattefrälset i Oppunda härad under 1600-talet. 1975.
65. *Bo Kronborg & Thomas Nilsson:* Stadsflyttare. Industrialisering, migration och social mobilitet med utgångspunkt från Halmstad, 1870–1910. 1975.
66. *Rolf Torstendahl:* Teknologins nytta. Motiveringar för det svenska tekniska utbildningsväsendets framväxt framförda av riksdagsmän och utbildningsadministratörer 1810–1870. 1975.
67. *Allan Ranehök:* Centralmakt och domsmakt. Studier kring den högsta rättskipningen i kung Magnus Erikssons länder 1319–1355. 1975.
68. *James Cavallie:* Från fred till krig. De finansiella problemen kring krigsutbrottet år 1700. 1975.
69. *Ingrid Åberg:* Förening och politik. Folkrörelsernas politiska aktivitet i Gävle under 1880-talet. 1975.
70. *Margareta Revera:* Gods och gård 1650–1680. Magnus Gabriel De la Gardies godsbildning och godsdrift i Västergötland. 1975.
71. *Aleksander Loit:* Kampen om feodalräntan. Reduktionen och domänpolitiken i Estland 1655–1710. 1975.
72. *Torgny Lindgren:* Banko- och riksgäldsrevisionerna 1782–1807. "De redliga män, som bevakade ständers rätt". 1975.
73. *Rolf Torstendahl:* Dispersion of Engineers in a Transitional Society. Swedish Technicians 1860–1940. 1975.
74. From Sweden to America. A History of Migration. Red. Harald Runblom & Hans Norman. 1976.
75. *Svante Jakobsson:* Från fädernejorden till förfäders land. Estlandssvenskt bondfolks rymningar till Stockholm 1811–1834; motiv, frekvens, personliga konsekvenser. 1976.
76. *Lars Åkerblom:* Sir Samuel Hoare och Etiopienkonflikten 1935. 1976.
77. *Gustaf Jonasson:* Per Edvin Sköld 1946–1951. 1976.
78. *Sören Winge:* Die Wirtschaftliche Aufbau-Vereinigung (WAV) 1945–53. Entwicklung und Politik einer „undoktrinären" politischen Partei in der Bundesrepublik in der ersten Nachkriegszeit. 1976.
79. *Klaus Misgeld:* Die „Internationale Gruppe demokratischer Sozialisten" in Stockholm 1942–1945. Zur sozialistischen Friedensdiskussion während des Zweiten Weltkrieges. 1976.
80. *Roland Karlman:* Evidencing Historical Classifications in British and American Historiography 1930–1970. 1976.
81. *Berndt Fredriksson:* Försvarets finansiering. Svensk krigsekonomi under skånska kriget 1675–79. 1976.
82. *Karl Englund:* Arbetarförsäkringsfrågan i svensk politik 1884–1901. 1976.
83. *Nils Runeby:* Teknikerna, vetenskapen och kulturen. Ingenjörsundervisning och ingenjörsorganisationer i 1870-talets Sverige. 1976.
84. *Erland F. Josephson:* SKP och Komintern 1921–1924. Motsättningarna inom Sveriges Kommunistiska Parti och dess relationer till den Kommunistiska Internationalen. 1976.
85. *Sven Lundkvist:* Folkrörelserna i det svenska samhället 1850–1920. 1977.
86. *Bo Öhngren:* GEOKOD. En kodlista för den administrativa indelningen i Sverige 1862–1951. 1977.
87. *Mike L. Samson:* Population Mobility in the Netherlands 1880–1910. A Case Study of Wisch in the Achterhoek. 1977.
88. *Ugbana Okpu:* Ethnic Minority Problems in Nigerian Politics: 1960–1965. 1977.
89. *Gunnar Carlsson:* Enköping under frihetstiden. Social struktur och lokal politik. 1977.
90. *Sten Carlsson:* Fröknar, mamseller, jungfrur och pigor. Ogifta kvinnor i det svenska ståndssamhället. 1977.
91. *Rolf Pålbrant:* Arbetarrörelsen och idrotten 1919–1939. 1977.
92. *Viveca Halldin Norberg:* Swedes in Haile Selassie's Ethiopia 1924–1952. A Study in Early Development Co-operation. 1977.
93. *Holger Wester:* Innovationer i befolkningsrörligheten. En studie av spridningsförlopp i befolkningsrörligheten utgående från Petalax socken i Österbotten. 1977.
94. *Jan Larsson:* Diplomati och industriellt genombrott. Svenska exportsträvanden på Kina 1906–1916. 1977.
95. *Rolf Nygren:* Disciplin, kritikrätt och rättssäkerhet. Studier kring militieombudsmannaämbetets (MO) doktrin- och tillkomsthistoria 1901–1915. 1977.

96. *Kenneth Awebro:* Gustav III:s räfst med ämbetsmännen 1772–1799 – aktionerna mot landshövdingarna och Göta hovrätt. 1977.

97. *Eric De Geer:* Migration och influensfält. Studier av emigration och intern migration i Finland och Sverige 1816–1972. 1977.

98. *Sigbrit Plaenge Jacobson:* 1766-års allmänna fiskestadga. Dess uppkomst och innebörd med hänsyn till Bottenhavsfiskets rättsfrågor. 1978.

99. *Ingvar Flink:* Strejkbryteriet och arbetets frihet. En studie av svensk arbetsmarknad fram till 1938. 1978.

100. *Ingrid Eriksson & John Rogers:* Rural Labor and Population Change. Social and Demographic Developments in East-Central Sweden during the Nineteenth Century. 1978.

101. *Kerstin Moberg:* Från tjänstehjon till hembiträde. En kvinnlig låglönegrupp i den fackliga kampen 1903–1946. 1978.

102. *Mezri Bdira:* Relations internationales et sousdéveloppement. La Tunisie 1857–1864. 1978.

103. *Ingrid Hammarström, Väinö Helgesson, Barbro Hedvall, Christer Knuthammar & Bodil Wallin:* Ideologi och socialpolitik i 1800-talets Sverige. Fyra studier. 1978.

104. *Gunnar Sundberg:* Partipolitik och regionala intressen 1755–1766. Studier kring det bottniska handelstvångets hävande. 1978.

105. *Kekke Stadin:* Småstäder, småborgare och stora samhällsförändringar. Borgarnas sociala struktur i Arboga, Enköping och Västervik under perioden efter 1680. 1979.

106. *Åke Lindström:* Bruksarbetarfackföreningar. Metalls avdelningar vid bruken i östra Västmanlands län före 1911. 1979.

107. *Mats Rolén:* Skogsbygd i omvandling. Studier kring befolkningsutveckling, omflyttning och social rörlighet i Revsunds tingslag 1820–1977. 1979.

108. *János Perényi:* Revolutionsuppfattningens anatomi. 1848 års revolutioner i svensk debatt. 1979.

109. *Kent Sivesand:* Skifte och befolkning. Skiftenas inverkan på byar och befolkning i Mälarregionen. 1979.

110. *Thomas Lindkvist:* Landborna i Norden under äldre medeltid. 1979.

111. *Björn M. Edsman:* Lawyers in Gold Coast Politics c. 1900–1945. From Mensah Sarbah to J.B. Danquah. 1979.

112. *Svante Jakobsson:* Osilia–Maritima 1227–1346. Studier kring tillkomsten av svenska bosättningar i Balticum, i synnerhet inom biskopsstiftet Ösel-Wiek. 1980.

113. *Jan Stattin:* Hushållningssällskapen och agrarsamhällets förändring – utveckling och verksamhet under 1800-talets första hälft. 1980.

114. *Bertil Lundvik:* Solidaritet och partitaktik. Den svenska arbetarrörelsen och spanska inbördeskriget 1936–1939. 1980.

115. *Ann-Sofie Kälvemark:* More children of better quality? Aspects on Swedish population policy in the 1930's. 1980.

116. *Anders Norberg:* Sågarnas ö. Alnö och industrialiseringen 1860–1910. 1980.

117. *Jan Lindegren:* Utskrivning och utsugning. Produktion och reproduktion i Bygdeå 1620–1640. 1980.

118. *Gustaf Jonasson:* I väntan på uppbrott? Bondeförbundet/Centerpartiet i regeringskoalitionens slutskede 1956–1957. 1981.

119. *Erland Jansson:* India, Pakistan or Pakhtunistan? The Nationalist Movements in the North-West Frontier Province, 1937–47. 1981.

120. *Ulla-Britt Lithell:* Breast-feeding and Reproduction. Studies in marital fertility and infant mortality in 19th century Finland and Sweden. 1981.

121. *Svenbjörn Kilander:* Censur och propaganda. Svensk informationspolitik under 1900-talets första decennier. 1981.

122. *Håkan Holmberg:* Folkmakt, folkfront, folkdemokrati. De svenska kommunisterna och demokratifrågan 1943–1977. 1982.

123. *Britt-Marie Lundbäck:* En industri kommer till stan. Hudiksvall och trävaruindustrin 1855–1880. 1982.

124. *Torkel Jansson:* Samhällsförändring och sammanslutningsformer. Det frivilliga föreningsväsendets uppkomst och spridning i Husby-Rekarne från omkring 1850 till 1930. 1982.

125. *Per Jansson:* Kalmar under 1600-talet. Omland, handel och krediter. 1982.

126. *Svante Jakobsson:* Fattighushjonets värld i 1800-talets Stockholm. 1982.

127. *Runo Nilsson:* Rallareliv. Arbete, familjemönster och levnadsförhållanden för järnvägsarbetare på banbyggena i Jämtland–Härjedalen 1912–1928. 1982.

128. *J. Alvar Schilén:* Det västallierade bombkriget mot de tyska storstäderna under andra världskriget och civilbefolkningens reaktioner i de drabbade städerna. 1983.

129. *Bodil Nävdal-Larsen:* Erik XIV, Ivan Groznyj og Katarina Jagellonica. 1983.

130. *Birgitta Olai:* Storskiftet i Ekebyborna. Svensk jordbruksutveckling avspeglad i en östgötasocken. 1983.

131. *Ann Hörsell:* Borgare, smeder och änkor. Ekonomi och befolkning i Eskilstuna gamla stad och Fristad 1750–1850. 1983.

132. *Ragnar Björk:* Den historiska argumenteringen. Konstruktion, narration och kolligation – förklaringsresonemang hos Nils Ahnlund och Erik Lönnroth. 1983.

133. *Björn Asker:* Officerarna och det svenska samhället 1650–1700. 1983.

134. *Erik Tiberg;* Zur Vorgeschichte des Livländischen Krieges. Die Beziehungen zwischen Moskau und Litauen 1549–1562. 1984.

135. *Bertel Tingström:* Sveriges plåtmynt 1644–1776. En undersökning av plåtmyntens roll som betalningsmedel. 1984.

136. *Curt Ekholm:* Balt- och tyskutlämningen 1945–1946. Omständigheter kring interneringen i läger i Sverige och utlämningen till Sovjetunionen av f d tyska krigsdeltagare. Del 1: Ankomsten och interneringen. 1984. Andra upplagan 1995.

137. *Curt Ekholm:* Balt- och tyskutlämningen 1945–1946. Omständigheter kring interneringen i läger i Sverige och utlämningen till Sovjetunionen av f d tyska krigsdeltagare. Del 2: Utlämningen och efterspelet. 1984. Andra upplagan 1995.

138. *Sven H. Carlson:* Trade and dependency. Studies in the expansion of Europe. 1984.

139. *Torkel Jansson:* Adertonhundratalets associationer. Forskning och problem kring ett sprängfullt tomrum eller sammanslutningsprinciper och föreningsformer mellan två samhällsformationer, c:a 1800–1870. 1985.

140. *Bernt Douhan:* Arbete, kapital och migration. Valloninvandringen till Sverige under 1600-talet. 1985.

141. *Göran Rydeberg:* Skatteköpen i Örebro län 1701–1809. 1985.

142. *Habib Ben Abdallah:* De l'iqta' étatique à l'iqta' militaire. Transition économique et changements sociaux à Baghdad, 247–447 de l'Hégire/861–1055 ap. J. 1986.
143. *Margot Höjfors Hong:* Ölänningar över haven. Utvandringen från Öland 1840–1930 – bakgrund, förlopp, effekter. 1986.
144. *Carl Johan Gardell:* Handelskompani och bondearistokrati. En studie i den sociala strukturen på Gotland omkring 1620. 1986.
145. *Birgitta Olai:* "... till vinnande af ett redigt Storskifte ...". En komparativ studie av storskiftet i fem härader. 1987.
146. *Torkel Jansson:* Agrarsamhällets förändring och landskommunal organisation. En konturteckning av 1800-talets Norden. 1987.
147. *Anders Florén:* Disciplinering och konflikt. Den sociala organiseringen av arbetet: Jäders bruk 1640–1750. 1987.
148. *Tekeste Negash:* Italian Colonialism in Eritrea 1882–1941: Policies, Praxis and Impact. 1988.
149. *Lotta Gröning:* Vägen till makten. SAP:s organisation och dess betydelse för den politiska verksamheten 1900–1933. 1988.
150. *Ove Pettersson:* Byråkratisering eller avbyråkratisering. Administrativ och samhällsorganisatorisk strukturomvandling inom svenskt vägväsende 1885–1985. 1988.
151. *Knut Ohlsson:* Grosshandlare, bönder, småfolk. Trönös skogsnäringar från och med det industriella genombrottet. 1988.
152. *Eva Österberg & Dag Lindström:* Crime and Social Control in Medieval and Early Modern Swedish Towns. 1988.
153. *Marie C. Nelson:* Bitter Bread. The Famine in Norrbotten 1867–1868. 1988.
154. *Gísli Ágúst Gunnlaugsson:* Family and Household in Iceland 1801–1930. Studies in the relationship between demographic and socioeconomic development, social legislation and family and household structures. 1988.
155. *Elsa Lunander:* Borgaren blir företagare. Studier kring ekonomiska, sociala och politiska förhållanden i förändring, Örebro under 1800-talet. 1988.
156. *Ulla-Britt Lithell:* Kvinnoarbete och barntillsyn i 1700- och 1800-talets Österbotten. 1988.
157. *Annette Thörnquist:* Lönearbete eller egen jord? Den svenska lantarbetarrörelsen och jordfrågan 1908–1936. 1989.
158. *Stefán F. Hjartarson:* Kampen om fackföreningsrörelsen. Ideologi och politisk aktivitet på Island 1920–1938. 1989.
159. *György Nováky:* Handelskompanier och kompanihandel. Svenska Afrikakompaniet 1649–1663. En studie i feodal handel. 1990.
160. *Margareta Åman:* Spanska sjukan. Den svenska epidemin 1918–1920 och dess internationella bakgrund. 1990.
161. *Sven A. Nilsson:* De stora krigens tid. Om Sverige som militärstat och bondesamhälle. 1990.
162. *Birgitta Larsson:* Conversion to Greater Freedom? Women, Church and Social Change in North-western Tanzania under Colonial Rule. 1991.
163. *Dag Lindström:* Skrå, stad och stat. Stockholm, Malmö och Bergen ca 1350–1622. 1991.
164. *Svenbjörn Kilander:* Den nya staten och den gamla. En studie i ideologisk förändring. 1991.
165. *Christer Öhman:* Den historiska romanen och sanningen. Historiesyn, värdestruktur och empiri i Georg Starbäcks historiska författarskap. 1991.
166. *Maria Ågren:* Jord och gäld. Social skiktning och rättslig konflikt i södra Dalarna ca 1650–1850. 1992.
167. *Stina Nicklasson:* Högerns kvinnor. Problem och resurs för Allmänna valmansförbundet perioden 1900–1936/1937. 1992.
168. *Lars Petterson:* Frihet, jämlikhet, egendom och Bentham. Utvecklingslinjer i svensk folkundervisning mellan feodalism och kapitalism, 1809–1860. 1992.
169. *Alberto Tiscornia:* Statens, godsens eller böndernas socknar? Den sockenkommunala självstyrelsens utveckling i Västerfärnebo, Stora Malm och Jäder 1800–1880. 1992.
170. *Iréne Artæus:* Kvinnorna som blev över. Ensamstående stadskvinnor under 1800-talets första hälft – fallet Västerås. 1992.
171. *Anders Fröjmark:* Mirakler och helgonkult. Linköpings biskopsdöme under senmedeltiden. 1992.
172. *Hernán Horna:* Transport Modernization and Entrepreneurship in Nineteenth Century Colombia. Cisneros & Friends. 1992.
173. *Janne Backlund:* Rusthållarna i Fellingsbro 1684–1748. Indelningsverket och den sociala differentieringen av det svenska agrarsamhället. 1993.
174. *Agneta Breisch:* Frid och fredlöshet. Sociala band och utanförskap på Island under äldre medeltid. 1994.
175. *Åsa Karlsson:* Den jämlike undersåten. Karl XII:s förmögenhetsbeskattning 1713. 1994.
176. *Elisabeth Elgán:* Genus och politik. En jämförelse mellan svensk och fransk abort- och preventivmedelspolitik från sekelskiftet till andra världskriget. 1994.
177. *Lennart Thorslund:* Humanism mot rationalism. Mora 1890–1970: Om två förhållningssätt och deras betydelse i småstadens planeringshistoria. 1995.
178. *Paul A. Levine:* From Indifference to Activism. Swedish Diplomacy and the Holocaust; 1938–1944. 1996. (2nd revised and enlarged edition, with a new postscript by the author. 1998.)
179. *Bengt Nilsson:* Kvinnor i statens tjänst – från biträden till tjänstemän. En aktörsinriktad undersökning av kvinnliga statstjänstemäns organisering, strategier och kamp under 1900-talets första hälft. 1996.
180. *Tsegaye Tegenu:* The Evolution of Ethiopian Absolutism. The Genesis and the Making of the Fiscal Military State, 1696–1913. 1996.
181. *Sören Klingnéus:* Bönder blir vapensmeder. Protoindustriell tillverkning i Närke under 1600- och 1700-talen. 1997.
182. *Dag Blanck:* Becoming Swedish-American. The Construction of an Ethnic Identity in the Augustana Synod, 1860–1917. 1997.
183. *Helene Carlbäck-Isotalo:* Att byta erkännande mot handel. Svensk-ryska förhandlingar 1921–1924. 1997.
184. *Martin Melkersson:* Staten, ordningen och friheten. En studie av den styrande elitens syn på statens roll mellan stormaktstiden och 1800-talet. 1997.
185. *Henrik Ågren:* Tidigmodern tid. Den sociala tidens roll i fyra lokalsamhällen 1650–1730. 1998.
186. *Peter Reinholdsson:* Uppror eller resningar? Samhällsorganisation och konflikt i senmedeltidens Sverige. 1998.
187. *Gudrun Andersson:* Tingets kvinnor och män. Genus som norm och strategi under 1600- och 1700-tal. 1998.

188. *Leos Müller:* The Merchant Houses of Stockholm, c. 1640–1800, A Comparative Study of Early-Modern Entrepreneurial Behaviour. 1998.
189. *Ylva Hasselberg:* Den sociala ekonomin. Familjen Clason och Furudals bruk 1804–1856. 1998.
190. *Marie Lennersand:* Rättvisans och allmogens beskyddare. Den absoluta staten, kommissionerna och tjänstemännen, ca 1680–1730. 1999.
191. *Örjan Simonson.* Den lokala scenen. Torstuna härad som lokalsamhälle under 1600-talet. 1999.
192. *Cecilia Trenter:* Granskningens retorik och historisk vetenskap. Kognitiv identitet i recensioner i dansk historisk tidsskrift, norsk historisk tidsskrift och svensk historisk tidskrift 1965–1990. 1999.
193. *Stefan Johansson:* En omskriven historia. Svensk historisk roman och novell före 1867. 2000.
194. *Martin Linde:* Statsmakt och bondemotstånd. Allmoge och överhet under stora nordiska kriget. 2000.
195. *Lars Båtefalk:* Staten, samhället och superiet. Samhällsorganisatoriska principer och organisatorisk praktik kring dryckenskapsproblemet och nykterhetssträvandena i stat, borgerlig offentlighet och associationsväsende ca 1700–1900. 2000.
196. *Lena Milton:* Folkhemmets barnmorskor. Den svenska barnmorskekårens professionalisering under mellan- och efterkrigstid. 2001.
197. *Maj-Britt Nergård:* Mellan krona och marknad. Utländska och svenska entreprenörer inom svensk järnhantering från ca 1580 till 1700. 2001.
198. *Silke Neunsinger:* Die Arbeit der Frauen – die Krise der Männer. Die Erwerbstätigkeit verheirateter Frauen in Deutschland und Schweden 1919–1939. 2001.
199. *Lars Geschwind:* Stökiga studenter. Social kontroll och identifikation vid universiteten i Uppsala, Dorpat och Åbo under 1600-talet. 2001.
200. *Samuel Edquist:* Nyktra svenskar. Godtemplarrörelsen och den nationella identiteten 1879–1918. 2001.
201. *Torbjörn Eng:* Det svenska väldet. Ett konglomerat av uttrycksformer och begrepp från Vasa till Bernadotte. 2002.
202. *Peter Ericsson:* Stora nordiska kriget förklarat. Karl XII och det ideologiska tilltalet. 2001.
203. *Rosemarie Fiebranz:* Jord, linne eller träkol? Genusordning och hushållsstrategier, Bjuråker 1750–1850. 2002.
204. *Håkan Gunneriusson:* Det historiska fältet. Svensk historievetenskap från 1920-tal till 1957. 2002.
205. *Karin Hassan Jansson:* Kvinnofrid. Synen på våldtäkt och konstruktionen av kön i Sverige 1600–1800. 2002.
206. *Johan Sjöberg:* Makt och vanmakt i fadersväldet. Studentpolitik i Uppsala 1770–1850. 2002.
207. *Hanna Hodacs:* Converging World Views. The European Expansion and Early-Nineteenth-Century Anglo-Swedish Contacts. 2003.
208. *Louise Berglund:* Guds stat och maktens villkor. Politiska ideal i Vadstena kloster, ca 1370–1470. 2003.
209. *Kristina Tegler Jerselius:* Den stora häxdansen. Vidskepelse, väckelse och vetande i Gagnef 1858. 2003.
210. *David Ludvigsson:* The Historian-Filmmaker's Dilemma. Historical Documentaries in Sweden in the Era of Häger and Villius. 2003.
211. *Börje Henningsson:* Det röda Dalarna. Socialdemokrater, anarkosyndikalister och kommunister inom Dalarnas Arbetarrörelse 1906–1937. 2004.
212. *Sofia Ling:* Kärringmedicin och vetenskap. Läkare och kvacksalverianklagade i Sverige omkring 1770–1870. 2004.
213. *Leos Müller:* Consuls, Corsairs, and Commerce. The Swedish Consular Service and Long-distance Shipping, 1720–1815. 2004.
214. *Märit Gunneriusson Karlström:* Konsten att bli och förbli folklig. Svenska kyrkans och IOGT:s strategier och omvandling i kampen på offentlighetens arena 1880–1945. 2004.
215. *Carl Henrik Carlsson:* Medborgarskap och diskriminering. Östjudar och andra invandrare i Sverige 1860–1920. 2004.
216. *Henrik Edgren:* Publicitet för medborgsmannavett. Det nationellt svenska i Stockholmstidningar 1810–1831. 2005.
217. *Göran Norrby:* Adel i förvandling. Adliga strategier och identiteter i 1800-talets borgerliga samhälle. 2005.
218. *Tomislav Dulić:* Utopias of Nation. Local Mass Killing in Bosnia and Herzegovina, 1941–42. 2005.
219. *Mats Hemström:* Marschen mot makten. Västra arméns revolt och väg till Stockholm 1809. 2005.
220. *Esbjörn Larsson:* Från adlig uppfostran till borgerlig utbildning. Kungl. Krigsakademien mellan åren 1792 och 1866. 2005.
221. *Janne Holmén:* Den politiska läroboken. Bilden av USA och Sovjetunionen i norska, svenska och finländska läroböcker under Kalla kriget. 2006.
222. *Joakim Malmström:* Herrskapen och den lokala politiken. Eds socken, ca 1650–1900. 2006.
223. *Patrik Winton:* Frihetstidens politiska praktik. Nätverk och offentlighet 1746–1766. 2006.
224. *Anna Hansen:* Ordnade hushåll. Genus och kontroll i Jämtland under 1600-talet. 2006.
225. *Johanna Widenberg:* Fäderneslandets antikviteter. Etnoterritoriella historiebruk och integrationssträvanden i den svenska statsmaktens antikvariska verksamhet ca 1600–1720. 2006.
226. *Erik Axelsson*: Historien i politiken. Historieanvändning i norsk och svensk EU-debatt 1990–1994. 2006.
227. *Anders Sundin*: 1809. Statskuppen och regeringsformens tillkomst som tolkningsprocess. 2006.
228. *Stefan Lundblad:* Hedersam handelsman eller verksam företagare. Den ekonomiska kulturens omvandling och de ledande ekonomiska aktörerna i Gävle 1765–1869. 2007.
229. *Sara Hansson*: I den goda vårdens namn. Sinnesslövård i 1950-talets Sverige. 2007.
230. *Fredrik Thisner*: Militärstatens arvegods. Officerstjänstens socialproduktiva funktion i Sverige och Danmark ca 1720–1800. 2007.
231. *Laura Palosuo*: Yellow Stars and Trouser Inspections. Jewish Testimonies from Hungary, 1920–1945. 2008.
232. *Johannes Westberg*: Förskolepedagogikens framväxt. Pedagogisk förändring och dess förutsättningar, ca 1835–1945. 2008.
233. *Karin Kvist Geverts*: Ett främmande element i nationen. Svensk flyktingpolitik och de judiska flyktingarna 1938–1944. 2008.
234. *Hanna Enefalk*: En patriotisk drömvärld. Musik, nationalism och genus under det långa 1800-talet. 2008.
235. *Jonas Lindström*: Distribution and Differences. Stratification and the System of Reproduction in a Swedish Peasant Community 1620–1820. 2008.
236. *Jonas Larsson Kraus*: Att odla ett samhälle. Råby räddningsinstitut och 1840-talets sociala ingenjörskonst. 2009.

237. *Jan Mispelaere*: Guldmynt eller äpple. Straffrättsligt ansvar för barn och ungdomar i Sverige och Nederländerna 1590–1800. 2009.
238. *Bo G Hall*: Perspektiv på Patron. Bruksägaren och statsministern Christian Lundeberg (1842–1911). 2010.
239. *Stina Bohman*: Omsorg om livet. Spädbarnsdödlighetens förändring i Ådalen under 1800-talet. 2010.
240. *Andreas Åkerlund*: Mellan akademi och kulturpolitik. Lektorat i svenska språket vid tyska universitet 1906–1945. 2010.
241. *Anne Berg*: Kampen om befolkningen. Den svenska nationsformeringens utveckling och sociopolitiska förutsättningar ca 1780–1860. 2011.
242. *Per Sandin*: Ett kungahus i tiden. Den bernadotteska dynastins möte med medborgarsamhället c:a 1810–1860. 2011.
243. *Sven Olofsson*: Till ömsesidig nytta. Entreprenörer, framgång och sociala relationer i centrala Jämtland ca. 1810–1850. 2011.
244. *David Ludvigsson (red.)*: Historiker i vardag och fest. Historiska föreningen i Uppsala 1862–2012. 2012.
245. *Lars Garpenhag*: Kriminaldårar. Sinnessjuka brottslingar och straffrihet i Sverige, ca 1850–1930. 2012.
246. *Christopher Pihl*: Arbete. Skillnadsskapande och försörjning i 1500-talets Sverige. 2012.
247. *Fredrik Lilja:* The Golden Fleece of the Cape. Capitalist expansion and labour relations in the periphery of transnational wool production, c. 1860–1950. 2013.